Michigan

Trip Trivia

compiled by

Michael Heim

T.O.N.E. Publishing
Travel Organization Network Exchange, Inc.
Wabasha, Minnesota
2004

For more information, contact:
T.O.N.E. Publishing
Travel Organization Network Exchange, Inc.
67 County Road 76
Wabasha, MN 55981

Note: the information included has been compiled for the purpose to merely entertain and inform travelers of information along their travel routes. It is not intended and should not be construed to be a definitive or comprehensive compilation. All information contained in this publication has been compiled from various sources including, but not limited to, general reference materials including travel guides and books, internet websites, brochures and pamphlets, and newspapers; as well as via information obtained from Destination Marketing organizations such as Convention and Visitor Bureaus, Chambers of Commerce, Tourism Associations, etc.; In addition to information provided by numerous individuals like professional tour directors, motor coach drivers, and general people interested in a specific destination. For this reason, every attempt has been made to secure factual information and the reediting of all information provided to comply with copyright laws. Therefore, if any information is inadvertently misused, please contact the publishing company.

The author and publishing company specifically disclaim any responsibility for any liability, loss, or risk, personal or otherwise, which is incurred as a consequence, directly or indirectly, of the use and application of any of the contents of this book.

Cover and graphic design by Toby Mikle at tmcreations.com
Special thanks to Val Courter, of Grinnell, Iowa, for assistance with editing.

Printed in the United States
ISBN 0-97443-582-1

Special Thanks
to my lifetime travel buddies

This book is dedicated to my long time traveling companions - my wonderful wife Cindy, and our beautiful children, Robbie and Sara. Without their patience, encouragement and wonderful company, this book would not have been possible, or nearly as much fun.

I offer a heartfelt "thank you," and I look forward to our continued travels...wherever they may take us.

Turn Your Next Trip into an Entertaining Adventure!

Exploring America's Highway: Michigan Trip Trivia is much more than a travel guide - it turns trips into fun, educational and interesting ventures. Unlike any other book or product on the market, Exploring America's Highways enables you to quickly and easily find information to enhance your trip, turning going from "Point A to Point B" into an entertaining adventure.

Wherever you're going in Michigan, you can find your route. Then follow along to learn fascinating historical facts, local landmarks, prominent people, geographical insights, industry, inventions, as well as plain old fun trivia.

The cities and towns are arranged conveniently in your route order. You don't have to waste time looking back and forth throughout the book; we've laid it all out for you!

With travel details for many interstates and highways, easy-to-follow maps, and point-by-point descriptions, you trip will become as much fun as the destination!

What you'll find along your route:

Place Names	• Fascinating backgrounds of the names of cities and towns
Historical Significance	• Overview of significant local events throughout history
Local Landmarks	• Noteworthy points of interest from man-made to natural, unusual or just plain interesting.
Prominent People	• "Hometown" people who've gone on to achieve fame or importance in some way.
Geological	• Explanations of why we see what we see.
Industry	• What towns and areas produce what, how things are made, who makes them ... and why.
Inventions	• Interesting anecdotes of where things are created.

We all know every town has a story, and every road crosses paths with history. Now, Michigan is yours to explore. With Exploring America's Highway: Michigan Trip Trivia you will find the journey as enjoyable as the destination!

Happy Traveling!

Michael Heim

Michael Heim

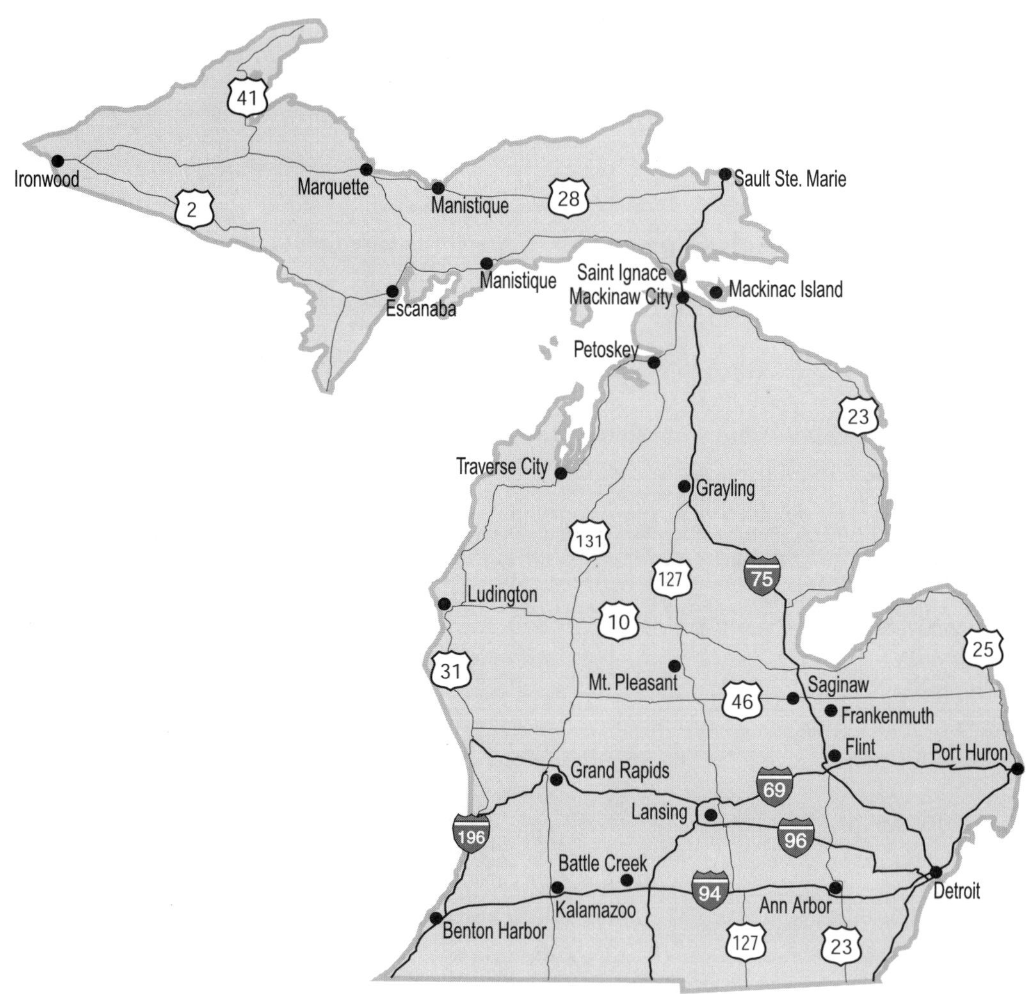

41
Ironwood
2
Marquette
Manistique
28
Sault Ste. Marie
Manistique
Escanaba
Saint Ignace
Mackinaw City
Mackinac Island
Petoskey
23
Traverse City
Grayling
131
127
75
Ludington
10
25
31
Mt. Pleasant
46
Saginaw
Frankenmuth
Flint
Port Huron
Grand Rapids
69
Lansing
196
96
Battle Creek
94
Detroit
Kalamazoo
Ann Arbor
Benton Harbor
127
23

Table of Contents

INTERSTATE
96

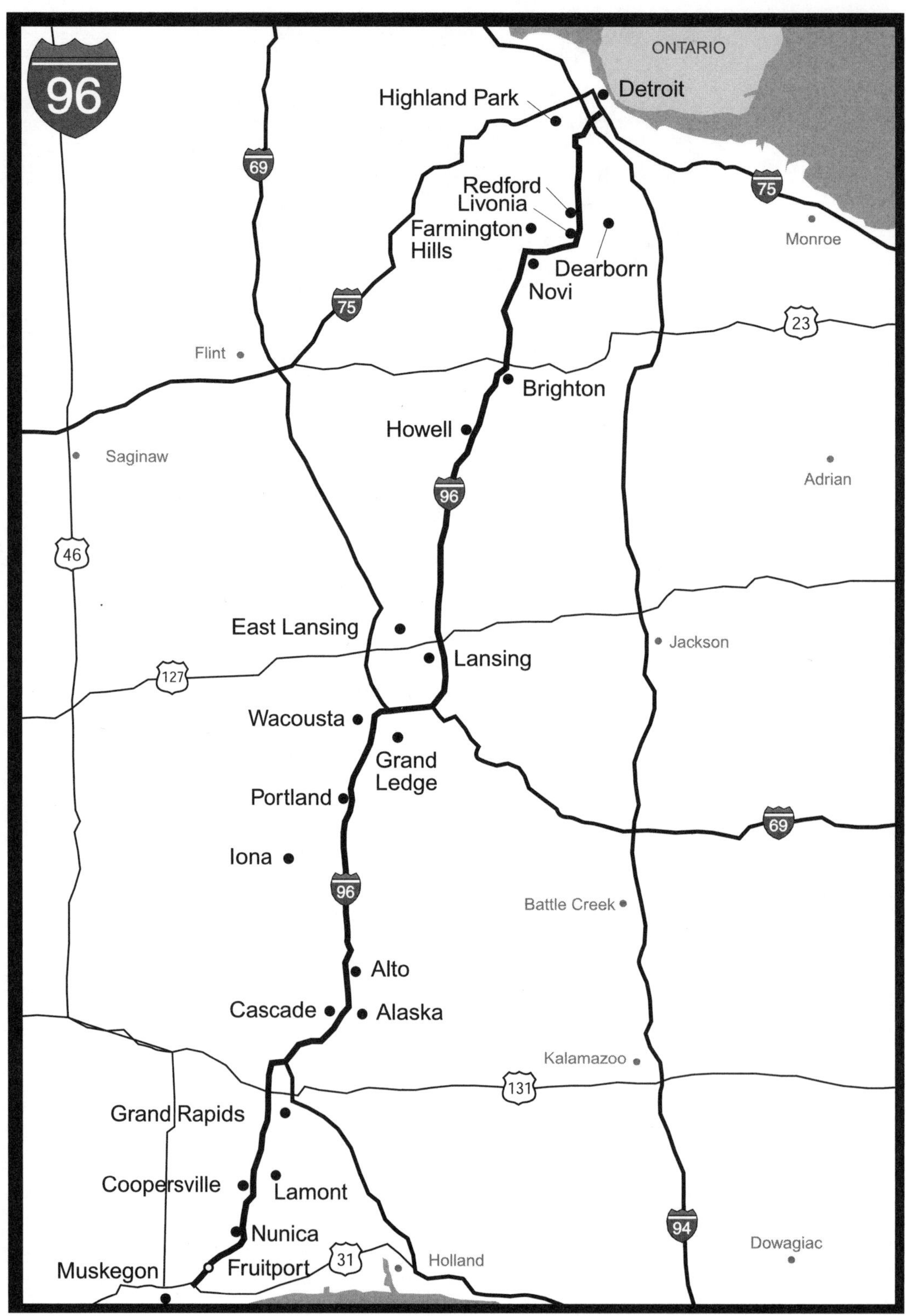
96
ONTARIO
Detroit
Highland Park
69
75
Redford
Livonia
Farmington
Hills
Dearborn
Novi
Monroe
75
23
Flint
Brighton
Howell
Saginaw
Adrian
96
46
East Lansing
Lansing
Jackson
127
Wacousta
Grand
Ledge
Portland
Iona
69
96
Battle Creek
Alto
Cascade
Alaska
Kalamazoo
131
Grand Rapids
Coopersville
Lamont
Nunica
94
Dowagiac
Muskegon
Fruitport
31
Holland

Detroit

Place Name

Detroit was founded in 1701, making it the oldest city in the Midwest. French explorer Antoine de la Mothe Cadillac was the one who named the place "Ville d'Etroit", City of the Strait.

Its name came naturally from the 27-mile-long Detroit River, part of the U.S./Canadian border. (Detroit is the only place where Canada lies south of the United States.) The Detroit River connects Lake Erie with the St. Clair.

Historical Significance

Because of its strategic location, many battles and skirmishes were fought for this piece of land. It was under French control until 1760. At that time the British took occupation and built Fort Lernoult, which became their western headquarters. Technically, Detroit became part of the United States with the end of the Revolutionary War in 1783. But the U.S. didn't take control until 1796.

Auto Industry

Detroit was incorporated as a city in 1815 and just a few years later the first steam vessel was launched on the Great Lakes. The resulting shipbuilding and commerce made the area prosper.

Detroit also became known for the brewing of beer and building of stoves. But what changed the city forever was Henry Ford and his Model T. The auto industry grew so rapidly that Detroit needed to find more workers. The city had doubled in population every decade from 1830 to 1860. It continued to grow with the auto industry and people came from across the world to live and work here.

Detroit consists of just 138 square miles out of the more than 2,000 square miles of the metro area. Detroit's first city planners laid out the city like the spokes of a wheel. Ironically, it was the wheel, as attached to automobiles, that would really make Detroit the great manufacturing city that it is.

The auto industry also became a symbol of America's manufacturing power. And the way cars were manufactured by assembly line changed the way other products were made and greatly changed people's lives.

> John and Thomas Clegg built the first self-propelled vehicle driven in Michigan. It was powered by steam.

* * * *

The first gas-powered horseless carriage appeared in Detroit in 1896, designed and driven by Charles King.

The automobile would change the economy of Detroit — and it would also change its appearance. Cozy, tree-lined streets would be widened to broad avenues to allow for cars — and the place was not as quiet as it had been. The many elegant mansions became boarding houses for workers and the city exploded in size and in attitude. Thanks to Ford, Olds,

Durant, Dodge, Chevrolet, Buick and others, Detroit was now Motor Town, USA!

* * * *

Of all the auto barons, it's probably Henry Ford who makes the best story. He was born on July 30, 1863 in the Detroit area, the oldest of six children. His grandparents were Irish immigrants, who had come to America during the potato famine in 1847. The Fords were a farming family and Henry was expected to take over the family business. But he instead created a new family business. He was intelligent and curious and he couldn't miss what was happening around him. He also liked to experiment. Wanting to prove how powerful steam was, he plugged up the spout of a tea kettle and turned the water on to boil. The kettle blew up! His parents did encourage him with his tinkering. His mother even gave him darning needles and corset stays that he made into tools for repairing watches.

The turning point for young Henry came when he was thirteen. He and his father were riding along in their wagon when they encountered a steam engine. It was traveling down the road on its own power. Henry couldn't restrain himself. He jumped from the wagon and bombarded the driver with questions about this incredible machine. After that, farming was out of the question. Henry Ford was going to be an engineer. From that day on he could envision a self-propelled vehicle and the dream wouldn't go away. By the age of 15, Ford was finished with school. He built a threshing machine at sixteen, but stayed home on the family farm. Finally, when he turned seventeen, his father gave Henry his blessing and the young man was off to Detroit. He worked for $1.10 a day at the Michigan Car Company. He didn't last long there, because he could make repairs in thirty minutes that took older employees five hours to do. In his spare time he read about gas engines and experimented.

By 1891 Ford was married to his wife Clara and began work for Detroit Edison Illuminating Company. His Ford Quadricyle was ready for a test spin in 1896. It scared the heck out of the horses and many people didn't like it, but it ran. While working at Detroit Edison, Ford met Thomas Edison. He was introduced to the famed inventor as "the young fellow who's made a gas car." Edison thought Ford was on the right track and his words of encouragement inspired the younger man to work even harder. By 1899 Ford had made a car that ran well enough to be covered in the Detroit Journals. Its inventor was described as a "mechanical engineer". (Soon he was forced to choose between his "paying" job and his invention.) Detroit Edison liked Ford so much that they offered him the position of General Superintendent. But he would have to choose. Could he devote himself to the company or did he want to pursue his hobby of making automobiles? Ford had known the answer to that for years. With the help of ten investors and his own patents, experience and engine, Ford Motor Company was incorporated on June 16, 1903.

> Henry Ford's development of the assembly line to mass-produce automobiles changed manufacturing forever.

The famed Model T was the ninth made by Ford. From its introduction in 1908, Ford dominated sales with the Tin Lizzie for eighteen years. The Model T wasn't fancy, but it served its purpose. It was hard working and sturdy and it sold! Henry Ford had stated that his purpose in life was to "build a motor car for the great multitude...constructed of the best materials, by the best men to be hired, after the simplest of designs that modern engineering can devise...so low in price that no man making a good salary will be unable to own one and enjoy with his family the blessing of hours of pleasure in God's great open spaces." Henry Ford's dream had come true.

Industry

Back in the 1920s Joseph Vlasic started a milk route in Detroit. Being a master promoter he knew how to target his customers with the right product and as a result developed the state's largest wholesale milk company. In 1937 a small pickle plant asked him to distribute what would in turn become their famous "Pampered pickle".

The Vlasic company says that the idea for a Stork for their advertising character came about in the late 1960s when they launched their first television advertising campaign.

Most storks are known for delivering bouncing bundles of joy. This stork delivers crunchy pickles!

Common folklore of the time held that pregnant women craved pickles, so Vlasic marketed themselves as "the pickle pregnant women crave . . . after all, who's a better pickle expert?"

This made the product unique and memorable. Later, during the '70s, when women were entering the workforce in force, the Vlasic stork's commercials had the theme: "With the birth rate down, I deliver Vlasic pickles instead."

Invention

Pharmacist James Vernor tried to create a new beverage in 1862, when he was called to serve his country in the Civil War. Four years later upon his return he noticed the beverage he stored in an oak case had acquired a delicious gingery flavor. Ginger Ale became the first soda pop in the United States.

* * * *

Arnold Willot revolutionized the cosmetology industry with the development of the cold permanent wave.

> The original Boston cooler was made by pouring Vernor's Ginger Ale over vanilla ice cream.

* * * *

The first paper milk carton was patented by toy factory owner, John Van Wormer of Toledo, Ohio. His patent was later acquired by the American Paper Bottle Company. Several years were spent perfecting the Pure-Pak container and the machinery which formed, filled and sealed it. The first six machines were built between 1929 and 1934.

The Ex-Cell-O Corporation in Detroit was approached by the American Paper Bottle Company in 1934. The Detroit-based company, which specialised in supplying machinery to the growing automobile and airplane industries, started by building machines for the American Paper Bottle Company and eventually acquired the rights to manufacture and distribute the Pure-Pak system.

Upon taking over the first thing Ex-Cell-O set out to do was to make a tab on the side of the gable which would make pouring possible. This opening device was primitive by today's standards and it was not until the mid-1950s that today's spout was introduced.

Geological

Besides the automobile industry, there are a couple of other unique forms of commerce in Detroit. One of the least known is 1,200-feet underground. It covers over 1,400 acres and has fifty miles of roads. A huge sea once covered this region of Michigan. When it evaporated more than 400 million years ago, salt deposits formed, but were buried by glacial activity. This bed of salt spread over 170,000 square miles and lies beneath Michigan, Ontario, Ohio, Pennsylvania, New York and West Virginia. Indian tribes used salt springs from the time they first arrived here. The state's first salt well was sunk in Central Michigan in 1841 by Douglas Houghton. This led to further borings and the beginning of the Dow Chemical Company. Oil and gas fields were discovered in central Michigan.

> It is said that the salt beneath Detroit alone could last up to seventy million years.

The first salt mining in Detroit started in 1896. The investors sunk an 1,100-foot shaft, but they went broke. Flooding and natural gas killed six men in this first attempt, but there have been no additional deaths in the mines. Detroit Salt Company took over and operated the shaft until 1907 when the rights were acquired by International Salt Mine Company. They ran the mines until 1963. The first uses of the salt were for homemade ice cream and cattle licks. Later the salt would be used for industry and ice and snow control on Michigan's roads. Getting the salt out proved difficult. In the early days, mules would be lowered by rope into the caves. They would work there until they died. Vehicles, such as jeeps and trucks, had to be taken apart and rebuilt piece by piece in the shop areas below the surface. Some dump truck tires were too large for the shaft. They would have to be compressed and bound before they would fit.

Mammoth trucks with seven-foot-tall wheels and forty-ton beds carry the salt rocks to a crusher. There the salt is reduced to chunks the size of a football. Thousands of feet of conveyor belts then carry the salt to a variety of crushers and sorters. The salt is separated into many sizes. When International Salt closed in 1963, they said they could no longer compete because of rising costs and cheaper Canadian salt.

Musical Trivia

The "Motown Sound" was created from 1959 to 1972. The company started with an $800 loan from the savings club of the Bertha and Barry Gordy Sr. family. Originally called Tamla Records, the company's first national release was "Money (That's What I Want)," in August 1959. The founder, choosing a name that reflected the Motor City, coined the word "Motown" for the company that was incorporated as the Motown Record Corporation on April 14, 1960. That same year it produced its first gold record, "Shop Around." In 1968 the company, which had grown from a family-oriented business to an international enterprise, moved its business operations to 2457 Woodward. Motown provided an opportunity for Detroit's inner-city youth to reach their full potential and become super stars.

> By the end of its first decade,Motown was the largest independent manufacturer of single 45 rpm records in the world.

Among Motown's record labels were Tamla, Motown, Gordy, Soul, VIP, Rare Earth, Black Forum, Workshop, Jazz, Divinity and others. In 1972

Motown moved its headquarters to Los Angeles, California. The company expanded its television productions and entered the motion picture industry. Lady Sings the Blues, Motown's first feature-length film, received five Academy Award Nominations. By 1975, Motown Industries was the largest black-owned corporation in the world. In 1980 the Motown Historical Museum was established at Hitsville U.S.A. to commemorate the Motown Sound and to memorialize Motown's distinctive heritage and its global impact.

(Historical marker located on West Grand River)

* * * *

Smokey Robinson is one of Motown's greatest musical resources. While in high school Robinson formed his first band, the Miracles. Ed Sullivan launched their debut appearance on his show by announcing, "from Detroit, Michigan, Smokey and the Little Smokeys!" Robinson would compose more than 4,000 songs during his career including their first million- selling single "Shop Around" and "You Really Got a Hold On Me."

Smokey named his son "Berry William Borope" in honor of Berry Gordy and his Miracle singing partners, Bobby, Ronnie and Pete.

* * * *

Marvin Gaye (whose surname was Gay, without the 'e') was the son of a Washington, D.C. Minister. His career started as a session drummer for Motown playing on all the early hits recorded by Smokey Robinson and the Miracles. Gaye, who married Berry Gordon's sister, Anna, recorded his first hit in 1962, "Stubborn Kind of Fellow." During the next ten years Gaye would produce 20 hits including "What's Going On?", "Let's Get It On," and his Grammy-award winning single "Sexual Healing."

Note: Marvin had bunions on his feet that made he hobble when he walked. Smokey Robinson nicknamed him 'Dad' because he looked like an old man.

* * * *

Smokey Robinson first meet Aretha Franklin when he was only six years old. Franklin was three at the time. They grew up in the same Detroit neighborhood. Learning to play piano from listening to records, she developed her four-octave voice. Dropping out of high school, Franklin devoted herself to the gospel circuit, latering specializing in rhythm and blues. The "Queen of Soul" defined soul music in the 1960s with such hits as "Respect," "Natural Woman," and "Chain of Pools." Aretha was the first female to be inducted into the Rock and Roll Hall of Fame honored for her 21 gold records and 15 Grammy awards.

Note: Aretha Franklin suggested that Detroiter Wilson Pickett change the name of Sir Mack Rice's hit, "Mustang Mama," to "Mustang Sally," which later became a big hit.

* * * *

Recording superstar Diana Ross was born in Detroit. Ross grew up in Detroit's Brewster Housing Projects and graduated from Cass Technical High School. Diana and two of her friends, who called themselves the Primettes, were rechristianed by Motown Records as the Supremes.

In January 1965, Music Business Magazine named The Supremes the #1 Female Soul

Artist. The Supremes were the best selling group behind the Beattles. Their first number one single was "Where Did Our Love Go?" in 1964.

Note: Barbara Martin was the fourth member of the Supremes. Martin left the group after their first single flopped in 1961.

On November 8, 1969, Diana Ross announced that she was leaving The Supremes in order to pursue her solo career. Ross recorded a number of hit songs including "Endless Love."Diana Ross was elected to the Rock and Roll Hall of Fame as a member of the Supremes in 1988.

* * * *

According to musical publicity legend, the Jackson Five were discovered by Diana Ross. However, in reality the musical family was introduced to Motown by Bobby Taylor. Ross was supposedly used for her marquee value. In any event, the five young brothers sang and danced their way into Motown with their first hit single "I Want You Back, released in 1968.

* * * *

The Commodores picked their name by opening a dictionary and selecting randomly from the page. The Commodores could have been become *The Commodes* if their selection was slightly higher on the page.

* * * *

"The Twist" was written and recorded in Detroit by Hank Ballard in 1958, before Chubby Checker played it as a cover tune.

Local Landmark

The most visible symbol of Detroit is the Renaissance Center, which dominates the skyline. Six office towers and a 73-story Marriott Hotel are found in this city within a city. Located on the Detroit River, the complex includes stores, restaurants and other services. General Motors purchased the building in 1997 and has made it its world headquarters.

Note: in 1983 two "human flies" scaled the outside of the 73-story hotel in 6 1/2 hours using special gripping devices.

The Detroit River forms the international border and Detroit is the only point where Canada lies directly south of the United States.

* * * *

The Detroit-Windsor tunnel was the world's first underwater vehical tunnel opened to traffic to a foreign country. Nearly a mile long (2,200 feet) the roadway lies fifty feet below the Detroit river.

* * * *

The Detroit Institute of Arts is ranked fifth in the nation among major fine art museums. It was first opened in 1885 and its collections cover the full history of art, from prehistoric to the 20th century. Among its most significant treasures are Van Gogh's "Self-Portrait" and Rodin's "The Thinker".

* * * *

Detroit has the largest African-American museum of history in the nation.

* * * *

The historic Eastern Market is home to the largest flower-bedding market in the world. This sprawling market, consists of open air sheds and adjacent food retail and wholesale businesses, is one of the largest public markets in the country.

Reverend Martin Luther King speech "I Have a Dream" debut in Detroit two months before his famous Washington, D.C. presentation in 1963.

Sport Trivia

Detroit is a fun place and it loves its sports. In the winter, it's the Detroit Red Wings hockey team and the Pistons for basketball.

The Red Wings won their first Stanley Cup in 1936, followed up with a back-to-back win in 1937. Forty two years later (1997) the Red Wings captured another world title, with a repeat in 1998. In 2002 the Red Wings win their fifth Stanley Cup, their third in six years.

Canadian-born Gordie Howe played 25 of his 32 seasons with the Red Wings. The Hall of Famer, nicknamed "Blinkie" because of a accident that left him with an uncontrollable twitch in his eye, was the league's top scorer four years and a five time winner of the Hart Trophy which is awarded to the league's most outstanding player.

The Pistons won their second consecutive NBA world championship in 1987.

One of the NBA's best small guards was Isiah Thomas. He played 13 NBA seasons with the Detroit Pistons (1981-1994), 12 of which he was named an NBA All-Star, and was MVP of the 1984 and 1986 All-Star Games. He ranks as Detroit's all-time leading scorer (18,822, 19.2 ppg, 34th best in NBA history) and assist-holder (9,061).

* * * *

In summer the Detroit Tigers take the field in their brand new baseball stadium, Comerica Park (built in 2000)

The Tigers won their first World Series in 1935. A second won in 1945 followed by their third in 1968. The team's fourth World Series was won in 1984.

Detroit Tiger Ty Cobb played twenty-two years for the Tigers before retiring in 1929 with more-than-twenty-five-major-league records including: highest lifetime averages (.367), most hits (4,191), and most steals of home (35).

Ty Cobb was the first player selected for the Baseball Hall of Fame in Cooperstown, New York.

Tiger first baseman, Henry "Hank" Greenberg was the first Jewish player ever inducted into the Baseball Hall of Fame. Other players in the Hall of Fame include;

First basemen	Dan Brouthers and Bucky Harris
Infielder	Charlie Gehringer
Catcher	Mickey Cochrane
Outfielders	Sam Crawford, Goose Goslin and Earl Averill

* * * *

> The Lions won their first National League Championship in 1935.

The Detroit Lions football team play their home games in the Pontiac Silverdome from 1975 until 2002 when they moved into their new stadium, Ford Field playing the Pittsburg Steelers.

Legendary running back Barry Sanders rushed for 15,269 yards during his illustrious 10-year career and set numerous rushing benchmarks with the Lions. Sanders joins an elite company as the 13th member of the Detroit Lions franchise to be elected into the Pro Football Hall of Fame.

Some of the other Lions inducted into the Hall of Fame include;

Quarterbacks	Earl "Dutch" Clark and Bobby Layne
Halfbacks	Bill Dudley and Doak Walker
Fullback	John Henry Johnson
Defensive backs	Jack Christiansen, Dick "Night Train" Lane and Yale Larry
Linebackers	Joe Schmidt and Alex Wojciechowicz

* * * *

Hall of Fame head coach George Allen was born in Detroit. Allen has the distinction of never having a losing season in 12 years as a head coach in the NFL. Taking over the Los Angeles Rams in 1966, Allen turned around the perennial losing team. He performed his same magic with the Washington Redskins, who had just one winning season in the 15 years prior to his arrival.

* * * *

Figure skater Tara Lapinski moved to Bloomfield Hills at the age of 13 to train at the Detroit Skating Club. Lapinski won a gold medal at the Nagano, Japan Winter Olympics in 1998.

Prominent People

Of course, a city the size of Detroit has given a lot of famous people to the world. The list includes: singer Bob Seger, Della Reese (who also stars on "Touched by an Angel"), rocker Ted Nugent, Bebe and CeCe Winans of gospel fame, and Johnny Desmond, who was once with the Glenn Miller Band. From stage and screen, there's George Peppard, Jason Robards, Robert Wagner, Ellen Burstyn, and Julie Harris. Comediennes Gilda Radner and Lily Tomlin hailed from here. Other famous sons include Ed McMahon and Casey Kasem.

* * * *

Actress Piper Laurie, the sex symbol who appeared with Ronald Reagan and Tony Curtis in numerous films. Born in Detroit, Rosetta Jacobs is the daughter of a Polish immigrant and his Russian-American wife.

When she switched to more serious roles she received a couple Oscar nominations.One for her supporting Oscar nomination for her role of Margaret White, the eccentric religious zealot mother of a shy young psychic girl named Carrie. And another for her role as Mrs. Norman in "Children of a Lesser God."

* * * *

Former auto worker, turned comedian, Dick Martin was born in Detroit. He wrote radio comedy before forming a night club act with car-salesman Dan Rowan. Together they gained fame on the NBC TV show, "Rowan and Martin's Laugh-In."

* * * *

Actor Tom Selleck,was born in Detroit. Selleck was planning to go into architecture. But when he arrived [to sign up for courses] Architecture was filled up. Acting was right next to it. So he signed up for acting instead. His first TV appearance was as a college senior on "The Dating Game" in 1967. Soon after, Tom appeared in commericials for products such as Pepsi-Cola.

Selleck starred in 6 failed TV pilots before hitting ratings gold with "Magnum, P.I." Seleck also appeared in "Her Alibi" and "Three Men and a Baby."

Joined the Detroit Tigers in 1992 for spring training. He actually took an at-bat (as a pinch hitter) in a game against the Cincinnati Reds, facing Reds' pitcher Bobby Ayala. Selleck ended up striking out after fouling away half a dozen pitches.

> Steven Spielberg wanted Tom Selleck to play Indiana Jones in Raiders of the Lost Ark (1981), but Tom was still under contract for the "Magnum, P.I."

* * * *

Alice Cooper, the son of a minister, was born Vincent Damon Furnier, in Detroit. He moved to Phoenix, AZ at a young age. At 17, he joined a rock band called Alice Cooper, named after a woman who was persecuted for being a witch in Miedeval Europe. The band got their first big break playing in Los Angeles at the Wiskey-a-GoGo when Frank Zappa discovered them one night and signed them to an album deal in 1969.

They were later signed by Warner Bros. and came out with their first major album, "Love It to Death" in 1971.

The band broke up in 1975 and a court dispute broke out over who would be able to coninue using the Alice Cooper name, the band or the man who played Alice. Vincent ended the dispute by having his name legally changed to Alice Cooper, so the band rocked on as the Billion Dollar Babies.

* * * *

Salvatore "Sonny" Bono was born in Detroit. As a backup singer for the Ronettes, Sony met his future wife Cher. They became overnight sensations after the release of their hit single, "I've Got You, Babe," which led to a Las Vegas act and enormous success on their own television variety show.

Singer-entertainer who left show business and found himself in politics. He became mayor of Palm Springs, California, and was eventually elected to the U.S. House of Representatives as Congressman from the State of California, a position he held until his death.

* * * *

Award-winning director Francis Ford Coppola was born in Detroit. He directed "The Godfather," which became one of the highest-grossing movies in history and brought him an Oscar for writing the screenplay with Mario Puzo. Coppola's other films include "Apocalypse Now" and "Peggy Sue Got Married."

Note: Coppola helped to make a star of his nephew, Nicolas Cage.

* * * *

Although Detroit native Harry Morgan has enjoyed a fifty-year career in films and television, he is probably best known for as the lovable Col. Sherman T. Potter, in the television series "M*A*S*H", for which he won an Emmy in 1980. Morgan was also known for role as Detective Friday's sidekick, officer Bill Gannon, on TV's Dragnet in the 1960s.

* * * *

U.S. attorney general John Mitchell was born in Detroit. He was the first U.S. attorney general in history to serve a (19 month) prison sentence for his role in the Watergate conspiracy, break-in, and attempted cover-up during President Richard Nixon's term.

* * * *

"That Girl," Marlo Thomas was born in Detroit. The daughter of Danny Thomas, was married to talk-show host Phil Donahue in 1980.

* * * *

Brothers Harry and Albert Gumm were born in Detroit. Both of them became songwriters and eventually changing their surnames to Von Tilzer, their mother's maiden name. Harry joined the circus as a teenager before starting his songwriting with some musical memories such as "I Want a Girl Just Like the Girl that Married Dear Old Dad," "In the Sweet Bye-and-Bye." Albert wrote the ever popular, "Take Me Out to the Ball Game."

* * * *

"Popeye the Sailor Man" was composed by Detroit native, Sam Lerner.

Detroit native, James McGinnis changed his name to James Bailey and became a partner in the Great Show on Earth, the Barnum & Bailey Circus.

* * * *

TV's Happy Days Leather Tuscadero was portrayed by Detroit native, Suzi Quatro.

* * * *

Bill Haley composed the hit singles, "Shake, Rattle and Roll" and "Rock around the Clock."

* * * *

The famous character, Trixie Norton of the television's "The Honeymooners" was originated by Detroit born actress Joyce Randolph.

* * * *

Ordinary People was written by Detroit-born author Judith Ann Guest in 1976. Published by Viking Peguin, Inc. in 1976, Guest's novels, *Ordinary People* (1976), marked an important milestone in that she sent the manuscript to Viking unsolicited. Viking generally doesn't look at unsolicited texts, however, a secretary read it and liked it enough to pass it on to the appropriate management. Within a few months, Viking notified Guest that they would be publishing her book, which was the first time in twenty-six years that the company published an unsolicited manuscript.

Guest won the Janet Heidinger Kafka Prize from the University of Rochester for *Ordinary People*. Several years later, the book became a motion picture directed by Robert Redford. The film won the 1980 Academy Award for Best Picture.

* * * *

Hollywood screenwrite Jack Epps, Jr. comes from Detroit. Epps works include such movies as "Top Gun," "The Secret of My Success," "Turner & Hooch," "Dick Tracy," and "The Flinestones in Viva Rock Vegas."

General Trivia

The crime fighting adventure series, "The Green Hornet" debut in 1936 on WWJ in Detroit with the "Flight of the Bumblebee" as its theme song.

Al Hodge was the original Green Hornet on radio before World War II, and returned to the program after he had served as a lieutenant in the Navy.

* * * *

Based on consumer consumption, Detroit was known as the potato chip capital of the world.

During the 1940s and '50s competition among potato chip manufacturers in Detroit was huge. Better Made Potato Chips founded by Peter Cipriano and Cross Moceri, competed with New Era Potato chips and others such as Superior Chips for market share.

By the early 1950s New Era had four plants in the Midwest and outselling the competition three-to-one. Frito-Lay bought out New Era eventually closing the company in 1981.

Detroit radio station WXYZ was the first public broadcast of "The Lone Ranger" radio program in 1933. Ten years later it was carried on over four-hundred stations nationwide.

* * * *

The first Kiwanis club was organized in Detroit, Michigan in 1914. Started by Allen Browne and some business associates in 1914. The name "Kiwanis" was coined from an expression in an American Indian language of the Detroit area, "Nunc Kee-wanis," which means, "we

trade" or "we share our talents." The first clubs were organized to promote the exchange of business among the members. However, even before the Detroit club received its state charter, the members were distributing Christmas baskets to the poor. A lively debate ensued between those who supported community service as the Kiwanis mission and those who supported the exchange of business. By 1919, the service advocates won the debate.

Henry Ford began mass producing automobiles here on a moving assembly line in 1913. Two years later Ford built a million Model Ts. Within ten years over nine thousand were assembled daily.

Industry

On June 6, 1925, the Chrysler Corporation was founded here after a reorganization of the Maxwell and Chalmers automotive companies by Walter P. Chrysler.

The first cars to bear the Chrysler name were manufactured in the Maxwell plant which was built here in 1909 and which is now the center of the corporation's worldwide administrative and engineering headquarters.

Chrysler had its origin in some 130 auto companies founded as early as 1894 and today is one of the few survivors in an industry that has included approximately 1,500 companies.

By 1930 Chrysler had become the world's third largest producer of automobiles; during World War II its production of war materials helped make Detroit the world's "Arsenal of Democracy."

(Historical marker located on Oakland Avenue)

Place Name

The town was named for General Henry Dearborn, American commander in the War of 1812.

Historical Significance

Dearborn's history is built on the industrial innovation of Henry Ford. Ford's world headquarters towers over the city.

Local Landmark

The Henry Ford Estate, a National Historic Landmark on the campus of the University of Michigan-Dearborn, is the former home of automaker Henry Ford and his wife Clara.

Here Henry and Clara Bryant Ford lived from 1915 until their deaths in 1947 and 1950.

The eminent American auto magnate and inventor named Fair Lane after the road on which his father, William Ford, was born in County Cork, Ireland.

The fifty-six room mansion made of marblehead limestone and concrete was completed in 1915. Inventor Thomas A. Edison, a frequent guest here, laid the cornerstone in 1914 for the powerhouse which supplied power for the entire estate.

Ford's popularization of the automobile propelled America into an era of accelerated urbanization. Yet the home of this man of controversy and varied interests reflects a love of nature and the countryside.

(Historical marker located on Evergreen Road)

* * * *

Henry Ford built the Dearborn Inn in 1931 to accommodate overnight travelers arriving at the Ford Airport. Located opposite the inn on Oakwood Boulevard, the airport opened in 1924. The 179-room inn was designed by Albert Kahn.

The Dearborn Inn was the world's first airport hotel.

The Georgian-style structure features a crystal-chandeliered ballroom and high ceilings. Its rooms are decorated with reproductions of furniture and fabrics of the eighteenth and nineteenth centuries. The guest quarters along Pilots Row originally were used by the airline's crews. The inn and adjacent colonial homes reflect Henry Ford's fondness for American history.

In 1937 the Dearborn Inn's accommodations were expanded with replicas of historically famous homes. Constructed on this twenty-three acre wooded complex, the additions included the Barbara Fritchie House, the Patrick Henry House, the Oliver Wolcott House, the Edgar Allen Poe House, and the Walt Whitman House.

The homes are furnished with brass candlesticks on the mantles, English shaving mirrors, brass or pencil four-poster beds, traditional lighting fixtures and Dutch doors.

In 1933 the dormitory building was added to house the inn's employees. It served this purpose until 1961. The 54-unit Motor House was completed in 1960.

(Historical marker located on Oakwood Blvd)

* * * *

Henry Ford began construction of this complex on the banks of the River Rouge in April, 1917. Here the Ford Motor Company built World War I submarine chasers known as "Eagle" boats.

By the mid-1920s this plant was the largest manufacturing center in the world. The transfer of the assembly line from nearby Highland Park to Dearborn in 1927 fulfilled Ford's vision of an industrial complex which encompassed all aspects of automotive production.

The first automobile to be completely assembled here, the Model A, was introduced in December, 1927.

The Ford Trade School operated at this location for twenty years until 1946.

During World War II, massive amounts of material for air, amphibious, and land transport were produced. Beginning with raw materials, the Ford Rouge plant makes component parts and assembles vehicles.

(Historical marker located on Shaeffer Road)

* * * *

Henry Ford and Thomas Edison became great friends — a friendship built on mutual admiration and respect.

> It took the genius of two men (Ford and Edison) to create what is one of the most exceptional museum complexes on the planet — the Henry Ford Museum and Greenfield Village.

Edison laid the cornerstone for the 254-acre park in 1928 and it was dedicated just a year later. The Museum's exhibits cover a broad range of subjects: communications, industry, culture, agriculture, transportation, and, needless to say, the automobile. The story of American manufacturing over three centuries is told here. One of the largest exhibits depicts "The Automobile in American Life." It explains how cars have changed our lifestyles. Six presidential limousines are on display — including the one in which President Kennedy was assassinated. Another unique item is the rocking chair President Lincoln was sitting in when he was murdered by John Wilkes Booth.

Greenfield Village is a "town" of eighty famous historic structures, including Ford's own home. There's the Wright Brothers bicycle shop where they built their first plane. There's an Illinois courthouse where Abraham Lincoln practiced law. There's the home of Noah Webster and buildings where visitors can see blacksmiths, glass blowers, printers, potters and other crafts. Transportation is also featured, with steam trains, carriages, a paddlewheel steamboat and a 1913-era carousel. All can be ridden by guests. Most notable here is the Menlo Park, New Jersey laboratory of Thomas Edison. It was in this building where many of his most popular inventions came to life — things like the light bulb, phonograph, mimeograph and telephone transmitter.

* * * *

At the Ford Airport, built by Henry Ford in 1924, world and national history was made, ushering in a new era of flight embracing the all-metal airliner, radio control devices, air mail, scheduled flights, and the airline services that the generation of the 1930s came to expect.

For the first time in the world: A hotel, the Dearborn Inn, was designed and built for the air traveler; A guided flight of a commercial airliner was made by radio. For the first time in the U.S.A.: An all-metal, multi-engine, commercial air-liner was built; A regularly scheduled passenger airline in continuous domestic service was inaugurated; An airline terminal for passenger use was constructed.

The airport's closing in 1933 ended Ford's experimental work in aviation.

(Historical marker located on Oakwood Blvd)

Prominent People

Born in Illinois, William B. Stout came to Michigan as an automotive designer in 1914. During World War I he turned to aviation.

In 1922 he produced America's first all-metal plane, a navy torpedo plane. The same year he organized the Stout Metal Airplane Company. In the next two years he built America's first successful commercial metal planes.

The company occupied the new airplane factory at the Ford Airport in 1924 and became a division of the Ford Motor Co. in 1925. While he was the division's consulting engineer the Ford tri-motor was developed.

In 1926 he founded the Stout Air Services, this countries first regularly scheduled passenger airline. Later, in his Dearborn workshop, Stout designed the "Sky Car," a combination airplane and automobile; the "Rail Plane," a gas-driven railroad car; a collapsible "House Trailer," and the "Scarab Car," a spacious, rear-motor auto.

(Historical marker located on Oakwood Blvd)

Dearborn hosts the largest Arabic population outside the Middle East.

General Trivia

Dearborn native Keven St. Onge, set a Guinness Book world record by throwing a standard playing card 185 feet, one inch.

Prominent People

Known as "The Great Impostor." Barry Bremen, a 34-year-old insurance salesman, had begun what would become a decade-long series of impromptu stunts.

He has made a hobby of popping up unexpectedly at major events around the country. First by wearing a Kansas City Kings uniform and getting onto the floor during pre-game warmups for the '79 NBA All-Star game in the Pontiac (Mich.) Silverdome.

Bremen would play three practice rounds of the U.S. Open with such luminaries as Jack Nicklaus, Fred Couples and Curtis Strange.

Remarkably, his counterfeit appearance took place at the Kingdome under the nose of a half-dozen Secret Service agents while he shagged fly balls. Ironically they and their bloodhounds were busily sniffing all over grounds as advance of former President Gerald Ford, a ticketholder that night.

In 1985, he suddenly arose from a front-row seat in Pasadena, and accepted (from a confused Peter Graves) an Emmy award for "Hill Street Blues" actress Betty Thomas.

Because of his exploits, Bremen has appeared with Jay Leno as a guest on the Tonight Show.

Place Name

This town's name was derived from Rouge Ford, having been a favorite crossing place over the River Rouge by the Native Americans on their trips to Detroit to receive presents from British officers.

Prominent People

Reford born actor, Richard Kiel, at seven foot, two inches tall, is best known for playing

Jaws, a giant and seemingly unstoppable assassin with steel teeth who battled James Bond in "The Spy Who Loved Me" and "Moonraker." He also appeared in such films as "The Longest Yard," and on TV including "The Riflemen," "I Spy," and "Barbary Coast."

Originally Kiel was the choice to play the character of the Incredible Hulk in the television series. After 2 days of filming, it was decided that he was not "bulky" enough for the role. He was paid for the two movies of the week and replaced by Lou Ferigno. Kiel was happy this happened because he only had sight in one eye and the full contact lens were bothering him.

* * * *

Actor George C Scott grew up in Redford. His mother died when he was eight years old and raised by his father, who was an executive at Buick. Scott graduated from Redford High School. In 1945 George joined the Marines and spent four years with them, no doubt an inspiration for portraying General Patton years later. When Scott left the Marines he then enlisted in journalism at the University of Missouri, but it was while performing in a play there that the acting bug bit him.

The only products that George C. Scott ever endorsed in a TV commercial shown in the USA were the Renault Alliance Sedan and Encore Coupe (later the Alliance Coupe), built in the USA. by American Motors.

Scott was the first actor ever to refuse an Academy Award (1970—for Patton). He was followed by Marlon Brando, who also turned down the award for Godfather, The (1972).

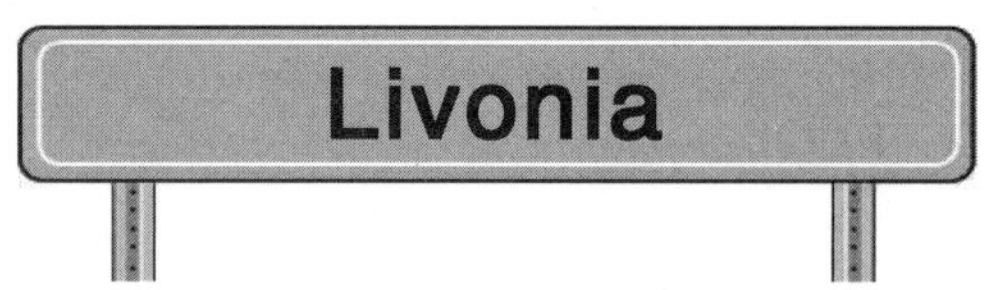

Place Name

Located in Wayne County, this community was named for many early settlers who came here from Livonia, New York. This name originated as a province in western Russia.

Prominent People

It all began in 1976 when Jim Purol played the drums nonstop for 320 hours. The next year he played the drums underwater. Then in 1979, he crawled 25 miles with tire treads attached on his hands and knees.

Livonia is home to multiple record-breaker, Jim Purol.

During the Great American Smokeout Day, he stuffed dozens of lit cigarettes in his mouth. His record to date is 151 smoking cigarettes. He followed this up by briefly smoking 41 cigars and 40 pipes.

Believe it or not, Jim Purol showed how wide he could open his mouth on the Ripley's Believe It or Not TV show, by filling it with 18 hot dogs!

On Guinness World Records, Jim Purol attempted another world record by expanding his mouth to stuff about 151 drinking straws into his mouth.

Purol wants to drive a car from New York to Los Angeles backward. Once there, he wants to sit in each and every of the 104,464 seats in the Rose Bowl in Pasadena.

* * * *

The Leggs panty hose company liked Mrs. Alta Becker's endorsement of their product that they asked the Livonia native to read her "Our legs fit your legs" praise of their product for a radio commercial.

Industry

From a small office in Livonia, Michigan, Seedlings have shipped reasonably priced braille books to over 40,000 blind school children located throughout every state in the US, plus in every province of Canada, and to several other countries! The company name comes from the idea that placing a book in a child's hands is like planting a seed. And with the proper nourishment (like good books to read!), we can help our children grow and flourish!

Seedlings started by Debra Bonde in 1984 as a nonprofit organization so that donations could be obtained to subsidize the cost of book production. Braille books are very expensive to produce, but with the help of grants and donations, Seedlings is able to make braille books available at a much-reduced cost (at an average of approximately $10 per book!)

* * * *

Roush Industries is one of the nation's most versatile, progressive and fastest-growing full-service engineering company. Roush Industries is a leading innovator in areas as diverse as aviation and medicine, but its primary focus is on the automotive sector.

General Trivia

Owner Jack Roush has also built the famous racing team fielding as many as seven cars in some races. The NASCAR effort features top drivers Mark Martin and Jeff Burton, while Roush also fields multiple entries in the Busch Grand National Series and the Winston Craftsman Truck Series.

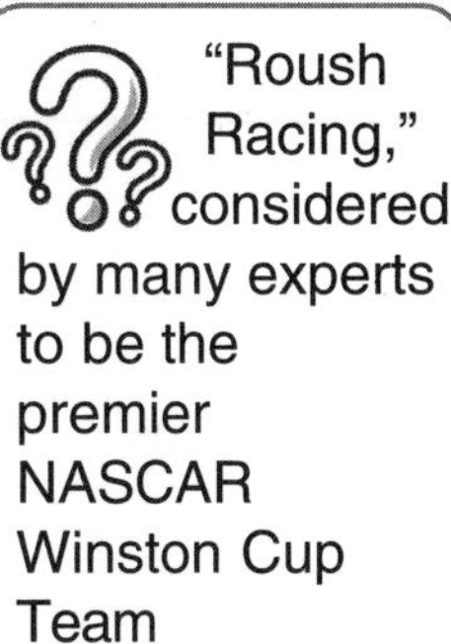

"Roush Racing," considered by many experts to be the premier NASCAR Winston Cup Team

Place Name

A meeting of the settlers was held to select an official name for the community. The downtown area was known unofficially as "Podunk", and the north end of town at Main and Mill was known as "Joppa".

At the meeting, the name "Peking" was proposed in honor of the Chinese city, since there was much interest in China in this country at the time.

When the dust settled, the first choice was "LeRoy", but if that name has already been used. The the second choice was "Plymouth", which was proposed for its historical ties to Plymouth, Massachusetts, the area from which some of the local settlers had come.

Prominent People

Actress Pam Dawber, comes from Farmington Hills. ABC cast Pam as the female lead in the TV sitcom "Mork and Mindy," co-starring with Robin Williams.

Place Name

Dr. J.C. Emery's wife suggested the name for the town when it was settled in 1832. Some believe the name was derived from its designation as Stagecoach Stop #6 or No. VI, while others thought it was derived from a Latin word meaning new, implying that here they were to have a fresh new start in life.

Brighton

Place Name

Brighton's original name was Ore Creek because of the mineral deposits found in the nearby stream.

The town was founded by Maynard Maltby in 1832. Like many Michigan towns, most of the first settlers here came from the east. They renamed the town Brighton after their hometown in New York.

Historical Significance

The U.S. Surveyor General declared the soil here to be unfit for farming back in 1815. However, that would have been surprising news to the Chippewa and Potawatomi Indians, who had farmed it for years. The Native Americans were eventually proved correct. The region is an important one for raising livestock and grain.

Place Name

The town began in 1834 when George and James Sage, John Pinckney and David Austin became the first settlers here. They called the place Livingston Centre, because it was in the middle of Livingston County. The name was changed to Howell in honor of Thomas Howell of Canandaigua, New York. He was a friend of Flavius Crane, who platted the town in 1835.

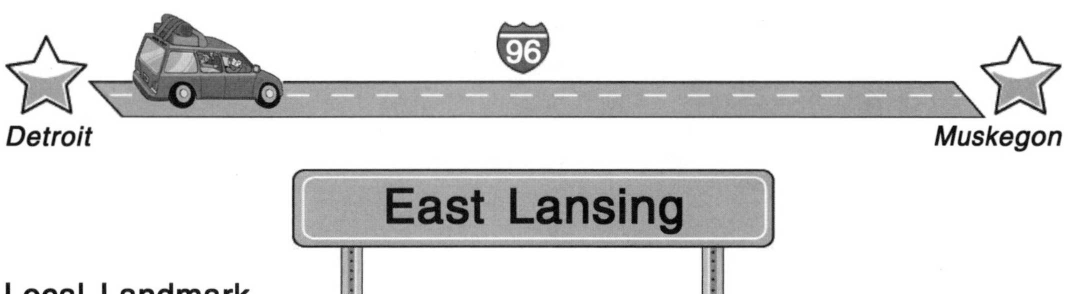

Local Landmark

East Lansing may be physically close to Lansing, but the cities are far apart in terms of life style and ambience.

The driving force here is Michigan State University, which makes for a more residential, less business- oriented, community.

The University started life in 1855 as Michigan Agricultural College — hence its nickname of "Moo U". It is noted both as the first agricultural college and first pioneer land-grant university.

The school and town grew together. At the time, villages which housed schools were designed around the needs of the teacher and student. William James Beal, the college's world famous botanist, became the village planner, along with mathematician Rolla C. Carpenter. They platted a residential tract just north of the campus, which became known as "Collegeville". As the nineteenth century gave way to the twentieth, expansion boomed. Collegeville and other nearby neighborhoods were chartered in 1907 as East Lansing.

Today that wonderful college gothic look of the Michigan State University campus still is found in these homes which date to the first quarter of the 1900s.

Enrollment at MSU is 20,000-plus students, who study and live on a campus of 5,000 acres. Its landscape features 7,000 different species and varieties of vines, trees and shrubs. A standout among the many gardens is the Beal Botanical Garden, established in 1873.

Historical Significance

Lansing is the capital of Michigan. How it achieved that honor makes for a very interesting story among the state's historians.

Detroit was the original capital when the state entered the union. However, its mandate as the capital expired in 1847. Legislators at the time feared that Detroit's location on the state's border made it vulnerable to invasion. They wanted to move the capital to a new site.

Lansing then consisted of a log cabin and a sawmill, but it was still offered as a possibility — mainly in jest. However, no other option sounded any more exciting. With a great deal of laughter, Lansing won the vote. It became the seat of government for Michigan in 1847.

Becoming the capital gave the settlement the boost it needed to grow into an actual town.The city was further helped along when R.E. Olds started building his "merry Oldsmobiles" here in the early 1900s. Production of cars and gasoline engines are still a vital part of Lansing's diversified economy.

Lansing receives its name from the town of Lansing, New York, which was named after a Revolutionary War hero named John Lansing.

Local Landmark

The State Capitol Building required six years of construction and is considered a Victorian masterpiece. It was dedicated in 1879 and resembles the United States Capitol with its high dome and extending wings.

The state renovated the interior of the building in 1992 at a cost of $45 million.

* * * *

Michigan's history is extensively covered in the Michigan Historical Museum, with four floors and twenty-five permanent galleries of exhibits. The building also contains the state's archives and library.

* * * *

The R. E. Olds Transportation Museum features antique cars, aircraft, bicycles and carriages, which date from 1833 to today.

A little-known fact is that it was Olds, not Henry Ford, who created the first mass-produced car in the world. From 1901 to 1907, The Runabout sold more models than all other cars combined.

Prominent People

Malcolm Little came to Lansing with his family as a small child where he saw his house burned down. Two years later his father was murdered here. While police ruled both accidents, but the Little's were certain that members of the Black Legion were responsible.

While Malcolm graduated from junior high at the top of his class, one of his favorite teacher's told him his dream of becoming a lawyer was "no realistic goal for a nigger," Malcolm lost interest in school. He dropped out, spending some time in Boston, Massachusetts working various odd jobs before moving to Harlem, New York. There he was coordinating various narcotics, prostitution and gambling rings.Eventually Malcolm and his buddy, Malcolm "Shorty" Jarvis, moved back to Boston. Eventually he was arrested and convicted on burglary charges. Malcolm was sentenced to 10 years in prison. (He was paroled after serving seven years.)

Recalling his days in school, he used the time to further his education. It was during this period of self-enlightenment that Malcolm's brother Reginald would visit and discuss his recent conversion to the Muslim religion. Reginald belonged to the religious organization the Nation of Islam (NOI).

By the time he was paroled in 1952, Malcolm was a devoted follower with the new surname "X." (He considered "Little" a slave name and chose the "X" to signify his lost tribal name.)

> Earvin "Magic" Johnson star of the Los Angeles Lakers grew up in Lansing, attending Everette High School.

* * * *

Lansing born actor Timothy Busfield appeared in the 1987 TV series "Thirtysomething." He replaced Tom Hulce on the original Broadway run of Aaron Sorkin's "A Few Good Men." Later working with Aaron as a director on "Sports Night" and as Danny on "The West Wing."

Place Name

Edmund Lamson settled this town in 1848. Its name was inspired by the high ledges of rock along the Grand River which flows through town.

Place Name

Wacousta was named for the Indian maiden who, in the Conspiracy of Pontiac in 1763, had warned Major Henry Gladwin of the intended surprise attack on the fort at Detroit. Thwarting the plot saved many lives.

Place Name

Portland sits at the mouth of Looking Glass River where it flows into the Grand River. The area is dominated by the rivers and explains where the city got its name back in 1838. The town was a major lumber port at the time and made an excellent place to load boats.

Place Name

This area was settled by a party of sixty-three people from Herkimer County, New York. Under the leadership of Samuel Dexter, they settled in the area (and county) named for an ancient Greek province.

Place Name

The town's name was given by Lucy Skidmore McVean, wife of the first postmaster, in reference to the highest point of land between Grand Rapids and Detroit.

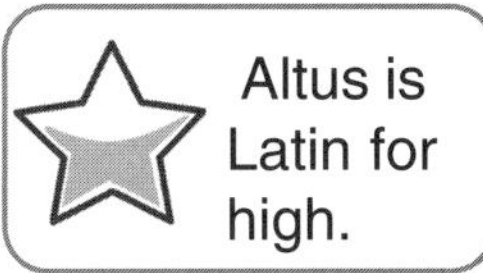

Altus is Latin for high.

Place Name

This town's name was influenced by the American purchase of the state of Alaska from Russia in 1867.

Place Name

D.S.T. Weller purchased the land he platted for the village in 1845. He gave the town the name Cascade in reference to "the fine fall of water" he hoped would lead to the development of water-powered mills.

Place Name

The Grand River, whose rapids inspired the city's name, has always been at the heart of the city's growth.

Historical Significance

The first European immigrants arrived here in 1820, when Chief Noonday was the leader of the Ottawa Indians. A trading post was opened by Louis Campau six years later. Campau was a far-sighted businessman and made an excellent real estate deal in 1831. He bought what became the city's main business district for $90.00.

As is the story of many Michigan communities, Grand Rapids started as a trading post for furs, then quickly grew with the lumber boom. Not all of the men in the lumber industry were as scrupulous in their business dealings as they should have been. There was a practice known as "hogging", where small mill owners would steal logs floating down the Grand River and cut them into lumber.The logs, however, had been cut and were owned by larger sawmills to the south. Fights erupted and the lumber companies, trying to protect their property, would have men actually ride the wet, rolling logs down the river. They were called river drivers.

Industry

Grand Rapids was blessed with having the resources of water, transportation and timber at its doorstep. It became a major producer of fine furniture and remains so today. Steelcase and Herman Miller, two of the country's largest manufacturers of office furniture, are based here.

The city has had its economic ups and downs, like all other communities, but it is ranked today as one of the fastest growing cities in the country. A major expansion and renovation of the city's airport is just one example of how Grand Rapids is responding to its growth. Major companies based here include the Amway Corporation and Meijer Corporation. They have led the city's redevelopment and also donated exciting recreational and cultural facilites, used by both residents and visitors.

* * * *

Melville Bissel invented a sweeper which scooped up the dust from the dusty packing straw he used in his china shop which had aggravated his allergic headaches. Bissell received the nation's first carpet sweeper patent which was the start of the Bissell Carpet Sweeper Company.

* * * *

Kent County is Michigan's largest apple-producing county. It is also a major producer of peaches, celery, carrots, onions, corn, wheat and Christmas trees.

* * * *

Zondervan is one of the top Christian publishers in the world. The world's largest Bible publisher, Zondervan holds the exclusive North American publishing rights to the New International Version of the Bible with over 150 million copies distributed worldwide.

Local Landmark

Grand Rapids' downtown area features sculptures prising quality for a city of this size. One of the century's most noted modern sculptors, Alexander Calder, created La Grand Vitesse. Bright red and weighing over forty tons, its design honors the rapids for which the city is named.

A very popular piece is the five-level Fish Ladder Sculpture. It is made of concrete. The ladder aides spawning salmon in jumping over a six-foot dam to their spawning grounds. Fall is the best time to see the salmon.

* * * *

Gerald R. Ford presidential library sits on the bank of the Grand River. It contains a replica of the Oval Office, a holographic tour of the White House, burglary tools used in the break-in at the Watergate Hotel, which led to Ford's becoming president, as well as many other displays.

The most famous native son of Grand Rapids is, of course, the 38th president, Gerald R. Ford.

* * * *

The Van Andel Museum Center is the newest cultural facility in Grand Rapids. The gift of the Van Andel family, it is considered by some to be the best of the city's museums. The Grand Rapids of old has been reconstructed and features a working 1928-era Spillman carousel and an authentic 1890s street car. Guests entering the museum are welcomed by a 76-foot long whale skeleton, which hangs from the ceiling. The collection at the Van Andel is vast and varied.

* * * *

Fred Meijer, who created a grocery and discount store chain, gave the city his own special

The Sculpture Park features world's largest bronze sculpture of the Leonardo da Vinci's American Horse.

gift in 1995 — the Frederik Meijer Gardens. The complex covers one hundred twenty-five acres and includes Michigan's largest tropical conservatory. The 15,000-square-foot structure is made of glass and contains plants from five continents. Designed to be enjoyed year 'round, there is also an indoor desert garden, a 14-foot waterfall, and waterways that wind past orchids and Egyptian papyrus. A world-class sculpture park is also on the grounds, with more than seventy bronzes by the world's best sculptors. There are also themed gardens, wetlands, boardwalks, nature trails and many seasonal events.

* * * *

Like all cities of this size, Grand Rapids has areas of homes that were built so that the wealthy industrialists could show off their wealth. Most notable is the Heritage Hill Historic District, with more than 1,300 homes reflecting at least sixty styles of architecture. Two homes which stand out here are the Voigt House and the Meyer May House. The Voight House is a three-story Victorian home from the late 19th century and is one of the few homes open to the public. It still has many of the family's original furnishings, including pieces that show off the quality of furniture making in Grand Rapids. Frank Lloyd Wright designed the Meyer May House, which was built in 1908. It is considered by many as the most authentically restored and most beautiful of Wright's prairie-style houses. The restoration was underwritten by Steelcase.

* * * *

One of Michigan's most important archaeological sites is The Norton Mound Group. The site is meticuloulsly preserved and helps to define the northern extension of the Hopewell culture. The Hopewells are thought to have originated in Illinois during the period of 500 B.C. and 300 B.C. They then spread to Ohio. From there, the influence of the Hopewell culture extended east to New York, south to Louisiana and southern Florida, and west to Kansas and Missouri. The northern extension includes sites in Minnesota, Wisconsin and Michigan, probably going back to the time of Christ. Over thirty burial mounds were once in the Norton Mound Group.

W. L. Coffinberry was the first to excavate the site in 1874, finding seventeen mounds with sizes varying from thirty feet in diameter and 1-1/2 feet in height to one hundred feet in diameter and fifteen feet in height. With the expansion of Grand Rapids, many of the mounds were destroyed. Today there are only eleven left which retain their original form.

Grand Rapids native, Jack Lousma piloted the 1973 Skylab II mission.

Prominent People

Jack Lousma and commander Alan Bean, along with Owen Garriott spend 59 1/2 days in flight, orbiting the earth 858 times, traveling 24.4 million miles. Lousma and Garriott set a record six-hour, 31-minute space walk.

* * * *

Senator Arthur Vandenberg, played an important role in the creation of the United Nations in the 1940s.

* * * *

Research by internationally known bactriologist Pearl Kendrick of Grand Rapids, led to the first whooping cough vaccine.

* * * *

Cartoonist Dick Calkins, the first artist to work on the comic strip "Buck Rogers in the 25th Century" was from Grand Rapids.

* * * *

Local artist, Frederick Stuart Church, known for his decorative work with a sense of fun and humor, especially of anthropomorphic animals, provided the illustrations for author Joel Chandler Harris southern folk classic, "Uncle Remus, His Songs and His Sayings."

* * * *

Author Chris Van Allsburg grew up in Grand Rapids. His story Jumanji starring Robin Williams and Bonnie Hunt became a hit at box offices around the country. Another one of his books, "The Polar Express" won national recognition and quickly became a Christmas classic.

* * * *

Ray Teal, aka Sheriff Roy Coffee in the television series, Bonanza was born in Grand Rapids. Teal made notable TV guest appearances on such shows as "Lassie," "I Dream of Jeannie," "The Lone Ranger" and many others.

* * * *

Actor Dick York, of the 1960s TV series "Bewitched" died in Grand Rapids.

* * * *

Grand Rapids-born actor Richard Shoberg played Tom Cudahy on "All My Children." Tom also made guest appearances on "Law and Order."

Grand Rapids native Kurt Mamre Luedtke, a former reporter turned Hollywood screenwriter wrote the screenplays for "Absence of Malice," "Random Hearts," along with "Out of Africa" starring Robert Redford and Meryl Streep which won him an Oscar.

* * * *

Elizabeth Wilson from Grand Rapids, received the 1972 Tony Award as Best Featured Actress in a Play for her performance in "Sticks and Bones" by David Rabe. Wilson also portrayed Roz Keith in the movie "Nine to Five."

General Trivia

Grand Rapids is the birthplace of the United States airline industry. On July 31, 1926, Miss Grand Rapids took off for Detroit from Cassard Field, the original Grand Rapids Airport. The inaugural flight of Stout Air Services was the first regularly scheduled passenger flight in the United States.

* * * *

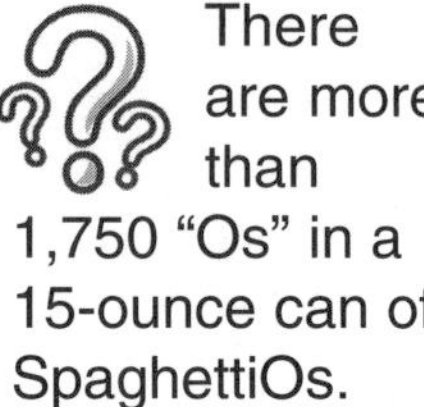

There are more than 1,750 "Os" in a 15-ounce can of SpaghettiOs.

If placed them side by side, the O's could create a chain at least 30 feet long.

The Franco-American company has proclaimed Grand Rapids as one of the "SpaghettiOs Capitols of the World" because their per-capita consumption of the tomato and cheese sauce pasta.

Place Name

The town was called Steele's Landing when it was settled by Harry and Zine Steele. The name was changed when Lamont Chubb from Grand Rapids, offered a road scraper in exchange for naming the town after him.

Note: Road draggers, scrapers, and levelers were used to build, grade, and maintain rural dirt and gravel roads.

Place Name

Coopersville is one of many Michigan towns that was settled by transplanted New Yorkers. It is named for its founder, Benjamin Cooper, who came here from Utica in 1845. Benjamin Cooper and his two sons built a sawmill on 640 acres of land.

Historical Significance

The town was first called Polkton after James Polk, the sitting U.S. President. When the railroad came through in the late 1850s, Cooper offered the necessary land to the town, if they'd rename the town after him.

Local Landmark

Coopersville is perhaps most famous as the home of the Coopersville & Marne Railway. This small passenger line has played a major role in preserving some of the finest cars from America's railroad history. One of its most prized acquisitions is the Merlin, Car #8. It's an interurban car that ran through Coopersville on the electric Grand Rapids, Grand Haven and Muskegon Railway from 1902 to 1928.

Prominent People

The town's other claim to fame is one of rock & roll's earliest stars. He was born Charles Weedon Westover in Grand Rapids on December 30, 1934. But the boy who would become known as Del Shannon grew up in Coopersville.

His mother taught him to play the ukelele and by fourteen he was a guitar picker. Charles took that guitar everywhere — to school, to football games. At age 24 and married, the

Westovers settled in Battle Creek. Charles worked days as a carpet salesman, but at nights he played in a country-rock band at a local club.

One of the club's regular customers dreamed of being a wrestler under the name of Mark Shannon. Westover liked "Shannon" and got "Del" from his favorite car — the Cadillac Coupe De Ville.

His most famous hit is "Runaway" which became #1 in 1961. After many years of battling alcohol and depression, Del Shannon committed suicide in 1990. He was inducted into the Rock n' Roll Hall of Fame in March of 1999.

Tun-Dra-Kennels, a local company is the largest producer of dogsleds in the world.

Place Name

The town's name was changed from Crockery Creek to Nunica. Both names were derived from the Indian menonica, meaning clay earth, from which they made pottery.

Place Name

This small town was founded by Edward Craw in 1868. He named it Crawville, after himself. However, since the town was in the heart of a major fruit growing area (chiefly grapes and peaches) and it was also a port located on the shores White Lake, Fruitport it became.

Place Name

The settlement was named for a nearby river the French had called "Masquignon" or marshy river. It became Muskegon in 1838.

Historical Significance

Muskegon's earliest history dates back to the days of the Hudson Bay Company, when riches were found in furs. Trader Lewis Baddeau opened a trading post in the area in 1834 — just about the time that riches were found in the form of timber.

Many consider the time of the lumber industry here to be the most romantic in the region's history. Its peak years were from the late 1830s to the 1880s.

By the end of the boom, there were forty-seven sawmills on Muskegon Lake — and sixteen more on White Lake to the north.

Muskegon had become known as the "Lumber Queen of the World".

In just one year — 1888 — it had produced 665 million board feet. Chicago rebuilt itself with Muskegon timber after the great fire of 1871. And the city boasted more millionaires than any other town in America.

The end of the lumbering era could have meant disaster for Muskegon. But it had an excellent harbor and the city fathers were able to attract new industry. Manufacturing, tourism and recreational activities now are the leading industries in this town. Tank engines, used for fighting wars, were built here. And the city has long been a major part of the gas and oil industry.

The oil had, of course, been here for millions of years. It was discovered by accident. Gideon Truesdell was drilling for salt in 1869. His drillers punched wells up to 2,627 feet throughout Muskegon County. However, there wasn't enough brine to make retreiving the salt worth the investment. Besides, the salt was contaminated with oil — and who cared about that in 1886!

Stanley Daniloff noticed oil seepage near his home in 1922, but there still wasn't much interest. It would take him five years to raise enough funds to form the Muskegon Oil Corporation and start drilling.

They hit a gusher at 1,675 on December 27, 1927. Within a year, there were seventy oil rigs operating in the area. Muskegon enjoyed the boom, but it didn't last long. In 1929, Standard Oil dropped the price of a barrel of crude from $1.25 to fifty cents. Muskegon did keep its refineries and tank farms and was one of the largest distribution sites in the nation for many years.

Local Landmark

The romance of the lumber days is most evident in Muskegon at the Hackley and Hume Historic Site. The homes of Muskegon's most famous lumber baron, Charles Hackley, and his business partner, Thomas Hume, are the centerpieces of the site.

Visitors can see the incredible craftsmanship and get a glimpse into the lavish life of the 19th century. The homes' exteriors feature twenty-eight shades of paint, which highlight the many interesting details. Varied roof lines, elaborate chimneys and the variety of tools used make the houses exceptional examples of Queen Anne style architecture.

The Hackley House is the more elaborate of the two. It contains fifteen stained glass windows, detailed woodworking, and a fireplace surrounded by Italian ceramic tile. It is furnished both with original pieces and others of the period.

Thomas Hume's home was built for the comfort of his nine children. It features spacious living areas and nine bedrooms. A large Carriage Barn, used by both families, sits between the homes. The horses were housed on the first floor, the liverymen lived on the second floor.

* * * *

Perhaps the favorite thing here for visitors are the high rolling sand dunes. They are among the most impressive dunes in the country and shelter Muskegon from winds coming off of Lake Michigan.

The Gillette Sand Dune Visitor Center is located in P.J. Hoffmaster State Park. Exhibits tell the story of sand dunes and how they are created. There is also a hands-on classroom with seasonal displays of live animals who make their homes in the dunes. Visitors can be oriented to the ecology of the dunes and Lake through a multi-image slide show. Then they can get out on ten miles of trails and explore the towering dunes for themselves. A favorite place with tourists is the Dune Climb Stairway. At the top of one of the park's highest dunes, visitors get a panoramic view of Lake Michigan and the surrounding dunes. The beach is one of the most beautiful in the world.

* * * *

Muskegon State Park provides two miles of Lake Michigan shoreline, as well as one mile on Muskegon Lake. This gives visitors the opportunity to experience both a Great Lake and a smaller, inland lake. At this park are twelve miles of hiking trails, five miles of lighted cross-country ski trails — and one of only four luge runs in the United States.

* * * *

Another interesting site in Muskegon is the USS Silversides, a restored World War II submarine. Visitors get a glimpse of the cramped quarters the sailors worked and lived in while at sea.

The Silversides was built just after Pearl Harbor and was responsible for sinking twenty-three enemy vessels. That was the third highest for all U.S. warships.

General Trivia

Muskegon native David Rude, traveled eighty-one miles across Lake Michigan from Grand Haven to Milwaukee, Wisconsin. Suspended below a fourteen-by-sixteen kite the eighteen year old was towed by a seventeen-foot boat with a 200-horsepower motor. The journey took three-and-one-half-hours.

Prominent People

Muskegon native Jim Bakker, and his former wife, Tammy Faye learned first hand, "What the Lord giveth, he can taketh away" as they saw their multimillion dollar PTL (Praise the Lord) ministry crumble.

Bakker and his associates offered life-time partnerships to fund the building of christian facilities at "Heritage USA". However, the organization could not keep its promises towards them and was accused of deliberately refraining from building sufficient lodging space for regular guests plus Lifetime Partners. One of the most important allegations was that they oversold, which constituted a fraud.

Put on trial for fraud and conspiring to commit fraud Bakker was sentenced to 45 years in prison. He served almost 5 years in prison and was paroled for good behavior in 1993.

Industry

The nation's largest plant for manufacturing bowling alley equipment is located in Muskegon. Brunswick's passion for the game and dedication to improving the ten pin game has helped to create the $10 billion industry that it is today.

INTERSTATE
94

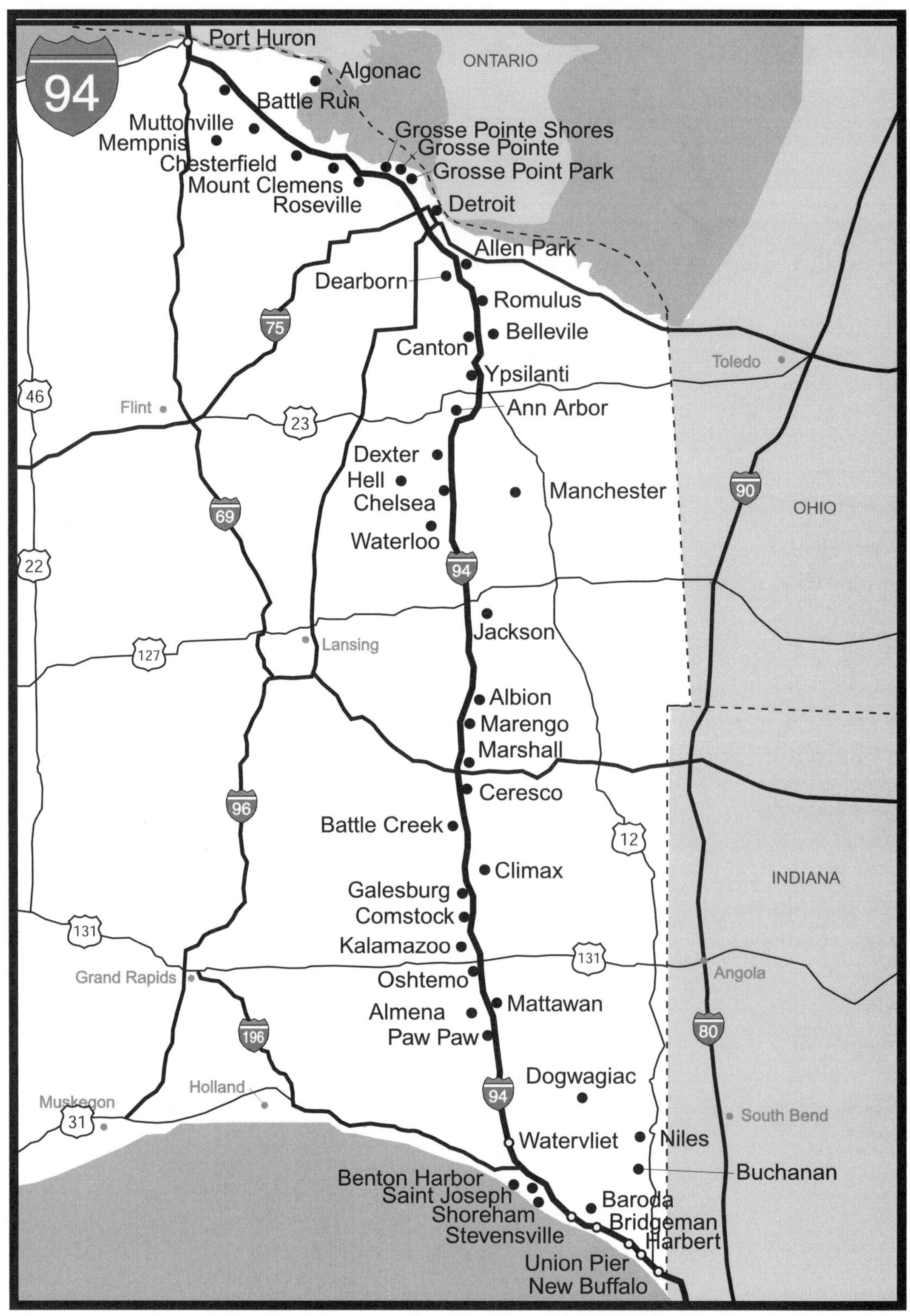
94
Port Huron
Algonac
ONTARIO
Battle Run
Muttonville
Mempnis
Grosse Pointe Shores
Grosse Pointe
Chesterfield
Grosse Point Park
Mount Clemens
Roseville
Detroit
Allen Park
Dearborn
Romulus
75
Bellevile
Canton
Toledo
Ypsilanti
46
Flint
Ann Arbor
23
Dexter
Hell
Manchester
Chelsea
90
OHIO
69
Waterloo
94
22
Jackson
Lansing
127
Albion
Marengo
Marshall
Ceresco
96
Battle Creek
12
Climax
INDIANA
Galesburg
Comstock
Kalamazoo
131
131
Grand Rapids
Oshtemo
Angola
Mattawan
Almena
Paw Paw
80
196
Dogwagiac
94
Holland
Muskegon
South Bend
31
Watervliet
Niles
Buchanan
Benton Harbor
Saint Joseph
Baroda
Shoreham
Bridgeman
Stevensville
Harbert
Union Pier
New Buffalo

Place Name

Capt. Wessel D. Whitaker was the first to notice the beauty and natural harbor of this area. He came here in 1834 by accident when his vessel ran aground and was destroyed. Fortunately, the captain was able to save his crew. He returned to his hometown of Buffalo, New York, but he couldn't get this place in Michigan out of his mind. He platted out a community and returned in 1835 with investors to create a new New Buffalo.

Place Name

The six McCartan brothers developed a business union with C.H. & John Gowdy to build a sawmill and pier, resulting in the name of the village.

Prominent People

Local track star Jackson Volney Scholz, won two gold, and one silver medals in the 1920, 24 & 28 Olympics. He used this experience for the topic of his book "Chariots of Fire," which was later made into a movie.

General Trivia

Bear Cave was the setting for a portion of the 1903 silent film classic, "The Great Train Robbery."

Town is named for the U.S. Senator, and later President, James Buchanan.

Place Name

This town named for Hezekiah Niles, the publisher of the Niles Register, a Whig paper in Baltimore, is the only community in the state that has been under four flags; including the French, English, Spanish and American.

Industry

Simplicity Patterns was started in Niles by James Shapiro in 1931. An advertising salesperson, Shapiro decided he could make and sell sewing patterns for as little as 15 cents each, when most companies were charging $1. Simplicity's straight forward and relatively easy to follow instructions enabled them to be a mid-sized worldwide company that designs, produces, markets, and distributes over 1,600 sewing patterns in a broad range of categories including fashion apparel, children's, home decorating, crafts, and costumes.

Prominent People

Writer Ringgold Wilmer Lardner, Sr., was born and started his journalism career in Niles. Lardner was hired as a baseball reporter for the South Bend Times. He then moved to writing for the Chicago Examiner where he was assigned to travel on the spring tour with the Chicago White Sox. By 1908 he was a baseball reporter for the Chicago Tribune. Ringgold left the Tribune to try his hand at being a managing editor for the St. Louis Sporting News.

Writing "In the Wake of the News" at the Chicago Tribune which made him an instant household name. Not only were his "Wake" columns becoming very popular, but also his short stories were well received in magazines such as The Saturday Evening Post and Esquire. Lardner wrote more than 4,500 columns and articles, and at the height of his popularity his work was syndicated in more than 115 newspapers.

Note: Lardner's achievements were favorably compared to those of Mark Twain.

* * * *

Ringgold's son, and namesake, Ring Wilmer Lardner, Jr., followed in his father's footsteps making his own mark as a Hollywood screenwriter. Ring won an Academy Award (Best Original Screenplay for 1942 with Michael Kanin) for "Woman of the Year."

Lardner also won an Academy Award and a Golden Globe award for "M*A*S*H" in 1970, when, ironically, very little of his original script "made it" into the film."

After the success of M*A*S*H, he was offered the opportunity to write for the TV series but declined. According to Lardner, "Frankly, I couldn't see how you would sustain a TV series based on a war that had just a few months of action. Shows you what I know. I also didn't think Selznick should buy Gone With the Wind." (Entertainment Weekly 28 FEB 96)

Harbert was home to Pulitzer Prizes winning poet Carl Sandburg from 1928 to 1943.

Place Name

Originally this barren and sandy area was known as Greenbush, because a small swamp kept the vegetation green throughout the year. The town's name was changed by the Chicago & Western Michigan railroad officials for a Chicago capitalist by the name of Harbert.

Place Name

Founded by a lumbering company, the area which previously was known as Plummer's Pier, was named Charlotteville, after Charlotte Howe, a wife of one of the owners. Fourteen years later, George Bridgman platted a townsite only a half mile to the east. When the railroad built their station there, the station and village took the name Bridman.

Place Name

This town was named for a city in India.

Place Name

The town's name is derived from the Native American word Ndowagayuk, meaning foraging ground. This was in reference that the area could fill all their basic needs for food, clothing and shelter.

Industry

Few tackle makers evoke the name recognition and the passion of James Heddon, a newspaperman and bee keeper who founded what became the most famous and enduring of American fishing tackle companies.

Legend has it that during the late 19th century, James Heddon supposedly was whittling a piece of wood near the Mill Pond in Dowagiac when he tossed the stick into the water. A bass came up, hit the wood, and Heddon came up with the idea for the Dowagiac, his first minnow-imitating plug.

He patented his first lure in 1902. One of the best paint schemes was the green "crackle back." Heddon was in such a hurry to dry the paint on a plug he put it in the oven, and the heat gave it a cracked appearance something like the skin of a frog.

Place Name

Town was named for Thomas Stevens, the person who gave the land used for the Chicago & Western Michigan railroad right-of-way.

Place Name

Englishman WIlliam Ducker built his home in this village along the shores of Lake Michigan. Because he wanted to keep the area residential; and being English liked the sound of the "ham" ending, called it Shoreham.

Saint Joseph

Place Name

The river here was the first thing to be named St. Joseph, after a patron saint of Canada.

The town was first called Saranac, after a Great Lakes ship, then Newburyport before becoming St. Joseph in 1833.

Historical Significance

Here in November 1679, on the Miami River, as the St. Joseph was then called, La Salle, the French explorer built a fort as a base for his western explorations. Here he awaited the Griffin, the upper lakes' first ship. When the ill-fated vessel did not come he made his way on foot to Canada through lower Michigan's uncharted wilderness. He returned in 1681 to prepare his great push down the Mississippi. A decade later the French built Fort St. Joseph, some 20 miles upriver near Niles.

(Historical marker located on Lake Blvd and Ship Street)

General Trivia

Augustus Moore Herring from nearby Benton Harbor may have flown the first airplane from Silver Beach in Saint Joseph in 1898, five years before the Wright brothers' famous flight.

Unfortunately a reporter for the Benton Harbor Evening News did not take an in-flight picture to accommodate his article. Unable to substantiate that Herring's plane indeed did leave the ground under its own power, Orville and Wilbur Wright were given credit for the first manned flight.

Industry

Entrepreneurs dream big, but it's unlikely that Louis, Frederick and Emory Upton ever imagined their homegrown washer company would become the world's largest appliance manufacturer.

Near the pleasant shores of Lake Michigan the Upton brothers created the Upton Machine Company in 1911 to produce electric, motor-driven wringer washers.

The company's first major order came almost immediately: Federal Electric requested delivery of 100 washing machines. A problem arose when a cast-iron gear in the transmission failed — in every single machine. At his company's own expense, Lou Upton replaced the defective parts with a new cut-steel gear. Impressed with the fledgling company's business ethics, Federal Electric doubled its order to 200 washing machines.

A watershed event took place several years later, when retail giant Sears, Roebuck and Co. began marketing two Upton-manufactured washers under the trade name "Allen." At a board meeting in October 1916, Lou Upton reported that this relationship was going so well, Sears was actually selling washers faster than the Upton Machine Co. could manufacture them.

> Whirlpool Corporation is the largest North American supplier of major appliances to Sears under the Kenmore brand.

Place Name

The town was named to honor Thomas Hart Benton, the senator from Missouri who had led Michigan's drive for statehood.

Historical Significance

Benton Harbor and St. Joseph were once rivals. However, they are so close together that today they have become partners in growth.

The town exists because a mile-long canal was built through the wetland between the St. Joseph River and the site of Benton Harbor. Developed by Sterne Brunson, the canal was opened in 1862.

In the 1870s, Benton Harbor was a busy port on Lake Michigan. Thousands of tons of fruit were shipped out of here. Sawmills and basket factories dotted the canal. By the time the city was incorporated in 1891, it was already popular with tourists, who liked to take mineral baths. They were said to have restorative powers.

Local Landmark

In the Spring of 1902, Mary and Benjamin Purnell had found a temporary home and resting place in Fostoria, Ohio, after 7 years on the road as itinerant preachers. Here they found the nucleus of the Seventh Church at the Latter-Day, the Israelite House of David, Church of the New Eve, Body of Christ, and finish the printing of their 780 page manuscript, of 7 years in writing.

By inspiration, Mary Purnell was given the actual home base for the newborn church to be at Benton Harbor, Michigan. In the Spring of 1903, a small party of Charles Norris, John Schneider, Cora and Paul Mooney, Mary, Benjamin and Coy Purnell journeyed from Fostoria to Benton Harbor, arriving on Saint Patrick's Day. Silas Mooney had been sent ahead to procure properties for housing and open ground for raising food, and to meet with the heads of the local circle of believers, the Louis and Albert Baushke families and a party of nine in Benton Harbor. The Baushke family being prominent citizens and carriage makers by trade, built in their down town Benton Harbor factory, America's first automobile of their own design.

Mary City of David is the third oldest practicing Christian community in America.

By 1910 the Star of Bethlehem was in its third edition, had circulated around the world to the churches/followers of the former six Israelite messengers, and had gathered into the fast growing Israelite House of David community over 700 people.

Eden Springs Park was in its second extra ordinarily successful season on its way to become America's premiere pre-Disney, theme park; the House of David schools would provide education and recreational activities for its children that would soon develop into legendary barn storming base ball teams, "Jesus Boys", and traveling jazz bands that would catch the attention of America in sweeping nationwide vaudeville circuit tours throughout the 1920s.

By the mid 1930s, and in spite of world wide economic depression, the Israelite House of

David and its reorganization, Mary's City of David, would come to dominate southwestern Michigan's economy, tourism and agricultural industries.

The Israelite House of David and its reorganization, Mary's City of David, over the century, has touched the lives of most of the local population, and also has had its significant effects upon American culture.

- Played in the first night baseball game in history at Independence, KS, April,1930.
- Ladies could vote and hold office in 1903, 17 years before the 19th Amendment.
- One of the founding families was one of America's earliest automobile makers, 1894.
- John Philip Sousa led their band in 1921 at San Francisco during our California/west coast tour.
- Invented the automatic pin-set for bowling, 1909-10.
- Jackie Mitchell, professional baseball's first female, pitched for us in 1933, and was the starting pitcher in their victory over the St. Louis Cardinals, in September of that year
- Walt Disney bought one of their original 1909 miniature steam locomotives in the early 1950s.
- Their final basketball tour of 1954 was an exhibition series throughout Europe against the Harlem Globetrotters.

> The sugar waffle-cone for ice cream was invented at Mary City of David

General Trivia

The Blossomtime Festival goes back to 1906. Reverend W.J. Cady told his congregation to get out and enjoy the blossoms in the orchards. Cady called them "symbols of life renewed". From this Blossom Sunday was born.

Prominent People

The comedian of the TV show, "Laugh In," Arte Johnson was born in Benton Harbor.

* * * *

Comedian Sinbad (aka David "Sinbad" Adkins) also comes from Benton Harbor where he had dreams of being a basketball star. That was until his knees gave out while playing ball at the University of Denver.

From college he joined and found his new career in the Air Force. Winning a talent show Sinbad toured with the Air Force Tops Blue program, which is a program of active duty Air Force members who perform shows around the world.

Later a finalist in Ed McMahon's "Star Search" talent contest whetted his appetite for stand-up comedy.

Hearing that a pilot for Different World was in the works, Sinbad was booked as a warm-up comic for an episode of "The Crosby Show." He hoped it would be a spring-board for the new show. However, seeing Sinbad's act, Bill Crosby came out of the audience and much to his surprise said, "This guy oughta be on TV every week." Sinbad went on to guest spots on the Cosby show, became a regular on "A Different World," eventually staring in his own show, "The Sinbad Show."

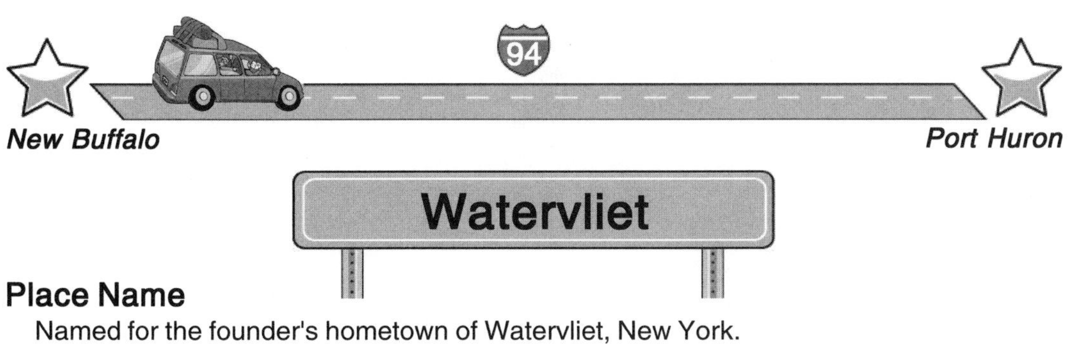

Place Name

Named for the founder's hometown of Watervliet, New York.

Place Name

The town gets its name from the Paw Paw River, which in turn was named by the Indians after the paw paw fruit growing along the banks.

Place Name

Legislative representative F.C. Annable named the town after an Indian princess when the townsite was platted.

Place Name

Attorney Nathaniel Chesbrough bought 40 acres in the area when the Michigan Central Railroad was being built through the area. His plat of land, which was the start of the village, was named for a New York town on the Hudson River.

Oshtemo

Place Name

The town's name comes from the Native American word meaning head waters.

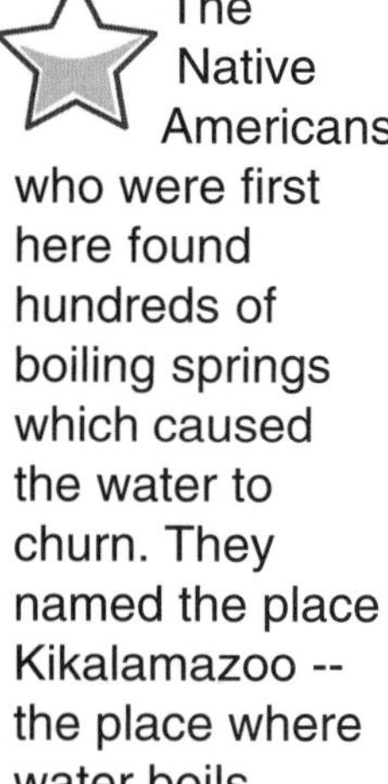

The Native Americans who were first here found hundreds of boiling springs which caused the water to churn. They named the place Kikalamazoo -- the place where water boils.

Place Name

Bronson was the original name of this town. Had it stayed that way, it would probably never have been immortalized in song.

Titus Bronson was the first settler here. He came from Connecticut in 1829, platted the village and named it after himself. He was not the most popular man in his town -- he was considered eccentric and unfriendly.

Just two years after starting his village, Bronson was accused of stealing a cherry tree. Unlike George Washington, Bronson didn't own up to what he had done. He was accused, tried and convicted. The townsfolk petitioned for a name change and Bronson was renamed Kalamazoo.

Historical Significance

There are many interesting elements to Kalamazoo's history, aside from its name. There's that song made famous by Glenn Miller, "I Got a Gal in Kalamazoo." It's hard to believe that "I Got a Gal in Bronson" would have been as popular.

Plus this is the only town in Michigan where Abraham Lincoln ever spoke. Then an obscure lawyer, Lincoln spoke to a rally for Republican presidential nominee, John Fremont..

Kalamazoo has a cooperative neighborhood called Parkwyn Village, which was designed by Frank Lloyd Wright.

The first open-air pedestrian mall was created here in 1959.

Local Landmark

One of the favorite attractions here is the Kalamazoo Aviation History Museum, popularly known as Air Zoo. It is considered one of the top aviation museums in the U.S. Rare planes from around the world, covering the time period of pre-World War II to Viet Nam, can be found here.

A truly unique feature of the museum is that visitors can fly a vintage aircraft. Seats are sold for flights in a classic Ford C-4 Tri-Motor. The plane was built in 1929 and is one of the five purchased by Northwest Airlines.

The Michigan Aviation Hall of Fame is also housed here.

* * * *

The largest nature center in the Midwest is located on 1,000 acres near town. The Kalamazoo Nature Center has an eleven-acre arboretum and a restored 1858 homestead. Author James Fenimore Cooper often walked in a glen on what is now the center's land.

Inventions

The nation's first electric dental drill was patented by Kalamazoo native George Green.

His designed never caught on because it was to heavy and the batteries were too expensive for general use.

* * * *

The Ingersoll plant under contract with the navy, constructed the first World War II amphibious cargo carrier here in 1942.

* * * *

Kalamazoo was once known as "the celery city". Originally planted by a Scotsman named Taylor, a new hybrid celery was developed in 1866 by a Dutch immigrant.

Celery was a cure for "everything" from nervousness, a cough, headaches, sleeplessness, and general depression! People used celery in lots of things from breakfast cereal, to chewing gum, plus for medicinal purposes such as a diuretic and in cough drops. Celery tonic bitters was even promoted as an aphrodisiac!

Some 400 farms planting approximately 5,000 acres of the crop made Kalamazoo the world's largest producer of this vegetable.

Industry

In his first few years of practicing rural medicine, Williem E. Upjohn interest slowly changed from that of a physician to working on an innovative, new pill making process.

In 1883 he began producing pills in the attic of his home in Hastings. Two years later he received a patent for his machine that produced "friable" pills, (dissolve). At the time most pills had hard coatings that often did not dissolve in the stomach - they simply passed straight through!

At aged 32, W.E. moved his family to Kalamazoo and together with his brothers, Henry, Frederick Lawrence and James Townley established The Upjohn Pill and Granule Company. By the end of 1886 it employed 12 people and manufactured 186 different "medicinal formulas", compounded from 56 different drugs: 30 botanicals, 20 chemicals, 5 alkaloids and 1 glucoside. The first year's sales were an impressive $50,000! Within four years Upjohn sales reached $132,500.

In 1902, because the company was producing liquid extracts as well, the name was shortened to "The Upjohn Company". This very successful company became one of Kalamazoo's largest employers.

* * * *

Over the years' Gibson, Inc. has symbolized high quality and excellence in the music industry. Gibson, Inc. played an important role in the development of stringed instruments and of the music industry in general.

Born in New York in 1856, Orville Gibson headed west to Kalamazoo, Michigan, in the 1880s. He spent every free moment hand-crafting mandolins.

Gibson was approached by five men who offered to provide money to establish a manufacturing facility for his instruments. Gibson accepted, and the Gibson Mandolin-Guitar Manufacturing Company was incorporated

The Gibson guitar honor roll reads like a "Who's Who" in music. Eric Clapton. Les Paul. B.B. King. Jimi Hendrix. The Beatles. The Rolling Stones.

in 1904. Under the agreement, Gibson would serve as a consultant, training workers in the fine art of instrument building. Apparently frustrated by this new arrangement, Gibson moved back to New York in 1909 where he died in 1918.

With an aggressive sales policy, the Gibson Mandolin-Guitar Manufacturing Company flourished despite the absence of its founder.

The company's success continued during the 1960s, when it manufactured over 1,000 guitars a day and employed nearly 1,000 workers, but a sharp nationwide decline in guitar sales contributed to Gibson's difficulties during the 1970s and 1980s. The company moved its headquarters to Nashville, Tennessee, in 1981, and three years later it closed the Kalamazoo plant.

* * * *

On a breezy day, the sweet smell of Albert M. Todd's legacy still wafts through downtown Kalamazoo. Building on a boyhood interest, Todd established the mint industry in this area in 1869 and was so successful at it that he became known as the "Peppermint King." Nearly seventy years after his death, the A. M. Todd Company still scents the air of the city and flavors the chewing gum and toothpaste of the world from its headquarters here.

Prominent People

Born in Kalamazoo,writer Edna Ferber grew up here and in Appleton, Wisconsin. Ferber began her career at 17 as a reporter in Appleton, later working for the Milwaukee Journal. She won a Pulitzer Prize for the novel "So Big" in 1925. After Show Boat became a popular play in 1926, critics hailed her as the greatest woman novelist of the period.

Place Name

The area was surveyed by (and named for) General Horace Comstock, who passionately tried to get his village named the county seat over Kalamazoo.

Place Name

Galesburg was founded by George Gale. Gale named it Morton, after John Morton, one of the orginal signers of the Declaration of Independence. However a committee of citizen's voted to change the name honoring their founding father.

Place Name

The town's name resulted because it was the climaxed ending of the search for a new settlement.

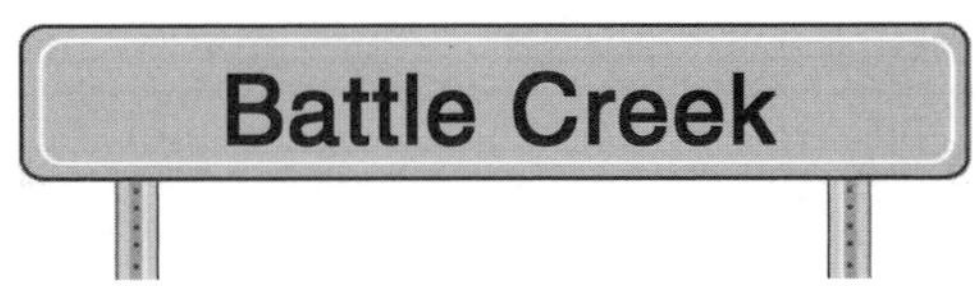

Place Name

The town's name comes from the neaby stream where two members of John Mullett's survey party battled it out with two Native Americans. As a result, Mullett referred to the river as Battle Creek.

Historical Significance

There are few cities in Michigan with a more interesting story than Battle Creek. The first thing that comes to mind, of course, is cereal. The city is home to the major companies who put breakfast on our tables -- Kellogg, Post and Ralston Purina. But this all came about because of a church! That's what makes it all so unusual.

William Miller was a Baptist preacher and had served as an army captain in the War of 1812. Between 1831 and 1844, he launched the "great second advent awakening". The movement spread through the Christian world. Miller studied the prophecy in the Book of Daniel 8:14 and predicted that Jesus would return to earth on October 22, 1844. When that failed to happen, Miller's followers experienced what was called "the great Disappointment".

Most who had joined the movement left in droves. But there were some who refused to give up. Out of this group came the Seventh-Day Adventist Church.

The name was chosen in 1860 in Battle Creek and the church was formally organized three years later. The denomination's headquarters moved out of Battle Creek to Washington in 1903.

Two of the original leaders were a couple named James and Ellen White. Ellen had many visions throughout her lifetime. The visions led to rules the Adventists live by today -- that they shouldn't eat meat, consume alcohol, tea or coffee, but should live on simple foods as the Bible instructs.

Local Landmark

The Western Health Reform Institute, later called the Battle Creek Sanitarium, opened in 1866. The Institute's director was Dr. John Kellogg. His brother Will served as business manager. The Sanitarium was part of the church's activities at the time. Because of its food restrictions, Kellogg looked for healthy substitutes.

On a historic day in 1894, Will Kellogg conducted an experiment with a new recipe. Meanwhile, a batch of boiled grain was forgotten. The next day Will discovered the grain. When he rolled it out, it turned into flakes. Bake and serve with milk, you have corn flakes for breakfast.

The new product was an instant success! Within eight years some forty cereal companies had opened in Battle Creek.

* * * *

The Midwest's newest attraction is Kellogg's Cereal City USA. See how cereal is made with a simulated production of the Corn Flakes production line. Take a step back through time in the historical timeline. Explore the world of marketing and advertising, the world's largest display of cereal artifacts, premiums and memorabilia. See the new home of Tony the Tiger.

Industry

Every June Battle Creek hosts the Cereal City Festival featuring the World's Longest Breakfast Table.

Will Keith Kellogg founded the Battle Creek Toasted Corn Flake Company in 1906. He manufactured the first boxes of cereal in a three-story building on Bartlett Street at the rate of thirty-three cases per day. In 1907 the original factory building was destroyed by fire, and part of the present structure was erected on this site.

Kellogg Company sold more than one million cases of cereal in 1909, and by 1911 the company's advertising budget had reached $1 million.

In 1917 production capacity reached nine million boxes per day. In 1980, United States production of Kellogg's ready-to-eat cereals required more than 110,000 bushels of corn, 225,000 pounds of bran, 9,000 bushels of wheat and 12,000 pounds of wheat germ each day. By its seventy-fifth anniversary in 1981, Kellogg Company had forty-seven plants operating in twenty-one countries.

(Historical marker located on Porter Street)

General Trivia

One of the more unusual novels and movies of the 1990s was The Road to Wellville, based on John Kellogg's running of the sanitarium. The book was written by T. Coraghessan Boyle. The movie starred Matthew Broderick and Bridget Fonda, with Anthony Hopkins as Dr. Kellogg.

Invention

In 1928 Otto Rohwedder designed a machine that would slice and wrap bread and later that year, a bakery in Battle Creek, Michigan, used his invention and began making and selling pre-cut loaves of bread!

Prominent People

Of course, Battle Creek does have history that isn't related to cereal. It played an important part in the abolitionist movement prior to the Civil War and was a stop on the Underground Railroad.

One of the most important people in the freedom movement has ties to the city. She was born a slave in upstate New York around 1797 and named Isabella. She was owned by five different masters before slavery was abolished in New York on July 4th, 1827. Legally free,

Isabella changed her name to Sojourner Truth.

Sojourner Truth moved to Battle Creek in 1858. It isn't known for sure if she actually helped slaves to escape. However, there is little doubt that she inspired them with her speeches. Her most famous being "And Ain't I a Woman?"

She encouraged social tolerance from whites and economic independence for freed blacks. When the Emancipation Proclamation was issued, she moved to Washington, DC. President Lincoln met with her and told her that he had heard of her speeches.

She campaigned after the Civil War for a land distribution system for ex-slaves. Despite her lobbying, Congress voted no. She went back home to Battle Creek and died there in 1883. Her funeral was the largest the town had ever seen. Sojourner Truth is buried in Oak Hill Cemetery and her gravesite still draws people who have read her words and share her vision.

* * * *

Betty Hutton, an energetic, "blonde bombshell" actress-singer of the 1940s was born in Battle Creek. She relocated to Detroit when she was two-years-old at the same time her father abandoned the family. Her mother ran a speakeasy where Betty and her sister Marion entertained customers, until into their early teens. Lived in near poverty during these years.

While still in high school, Vincent Lopez spotted her doing a guest spot at a night club and signed her. She toured with the band, did radio spots and vaudeville turns. This led to featured roles in several Broadway revues and then a role in the Merman musical "Panama Hattie". Paramount then signed her in 1941. In 1952, she left Hollywood to concentrate on stage and television.

* * * *

Dick Martin of the famous comedy duo of Rowan and Martin's Laugh In was from Battle Creek. They popularized such phrases as "Sock it to me," "Ring my chimes," and "You bet your bippy."

Place Name

Founders Isaac Cray and John Pierce named their village by combining the name (Ceres), the Greek goddess of growing grain, with the two letter (co) abbreviation of the word, company. It was believed that Ceres was responsible for the success of the miller's harvest.

Place Name

Town founders Sidney and George Ketchum named the community for Chief Justice John Marshall of Virginia whom they greatly admired. This occurred five years before Marshall's death and thus was the first of dozens of communities and counties named for him.

Historical Significance

As Agent Smart used to say, "missed it by that much!" This is the city that almost became the capital. In fact, its residents were so confident of winning the vote in 1847 that they already had the land set aside for it -- and they had built a mansion for the governor! The state Senate approved Marshall as the capital, but the House defeated it by the margin of one vote. Michigan's laws would be made in Lansing.

* * * *

Just a year prior to the capital decision, Marshall was involved in an incident that drew the nation's attention to slavery. Adam Crosswhite had lived in Marshall for two years, after escaping from his "owner" in Kentucky. However, slave hunters tracked him down and seized him for return to his master.

Marshall overwhelmingly supported Crosswhite and local abolitionists helped him and his family escape into Canada. The feelings here were so strong that the slave hunters were tried in federal court. They were acquitted.

The passions surrounding the issue on both sides led to the passage of the 1850 Fugitive Slave Act and served as another step toward the Civil War.

* * * *

After its disappointment over not becoming the capital, Marshall tried a variety of ways to stimulate economic growth. Nothing ever quite worked. The Michigan Central Railroad helped for awhile, but pulled out of town in 1872.

Marshall did become a major producer of patent medicine in the late 1800s, providing "pink pills for pale people". The medicine was made in places away from the public eye -- attics, sheds and other dark places. In 1906 the federal government shut the industry down.

* * * *

A touch of U.S. history was the founding of a union called the Brotherhood of the Footboard in 1863. A few months later the members realized that most people didn't know what a footboard was, so they changed the name of the union to the Brotherhood of Locomotive Engineers, still one of the country's strongest railroad unions.

Local Landmark

An unusual and fun museum in Marshall is the American Museum of Magic. It is housed on three floors of one of the city's restored buildings. The 1868 structure contains artifacts and props used by the greatest stage magicians of the 19th and 20th centuries. Nearly a half-million pieces of memorabilia can be found here and it is the only such museum in the world.

Among its most famous pieces is an escape apparatus used by Harry Houdini. It also features an archive on thousands of lesser-known magicians.

As an interesting sidenote, magician Harry Blackstone comes from Colon, Michigan, just forty miles away. Blackstone partnered with an Australian named Percy Abbott to start a magic manufacturing company. The partnership failed, but, oddly enough, it was Abbott who stayed in Colon to proceed with their plan.

The Abbott Magic Manufacturing Company is still there today and does business with magicians from around the world.

Every August it hosts the Magical Get-Together. Amateur and professional magicians alike come to Colon to exchange notes with each other and to stock up on needed supplies.

* * * *

The Butler-Boyce House is a handsome Italian Villa, with paired arched windows, adorned with combined cupola and railing. Edward Butler (1814-1881) merchant, banker and first treasurer of Calhoun County, built the residence in 1858 - 1861 on land once owned by author James Fenimore Cooper.

William D. Boyce founder of the Boy Scouts of America, purchased the house and sixty acres as a summer home in 1894.

Prominent People

William D. Boyce, a Chicago publisher, founded the Boy Scouts of America. Boyce first became acquainted with the scouting movement while in London in 1909. He lost his way in the midst of a heavy fog, and was rescued by a Boy Scout who took him to the address he was seeking. Offering the young boy a tip, he was told that Boy Scouts do not accept money for doing a good deed. Impressed by this organization, Boyce returned home with pamphlets, badges and a uniform. He incorporated Boy Scouts of America, now Scouting/USA, on February 8, 1910.

Place Name

When the village was established, the first town's meeting was held in the home of Seeley Neal. Discussing the town's name, they decided and chose the name of Napoleon's horse at the time of the battle of Waterloo.

Place Name

Joined together with a few other people, Jesse Crowell built the first grist mill business which was called the Albion Company, after Mr. Crowell's hometown in New York state.

General Trivia

On May 13, 1877, the second Sunday of the month, Juliet Calhoun Blakeley stepped into the pulpit of the Methodist Episcopal Church and completed the sermon for the Reverend Myron Daugherty.

According to legend, Daugherty was distraught because an antitemperance group had forced his son to spend the night in a saloon. Proud of their mother's achievement Charles and Moses Blakeley encouraged others to pay tribute to their mothers. In the 1880s the Albion Methodist church began celebrating Mother's Day in Blakeley's honor.

(Historical marker located at the corner of Ionia and Erie streets)

Albion is the original home of Mother's Day. Observing Mother's Day since 1877, thirty-seven years before it became a national celebration.

* * * *

The official observance of Mother's Day resulted from the efforts of Anna Jarvis of Philadelphia. In 1868 her mother had organized a Mother's Friendship Day in a West Virginia town to unite Confederate and Union families after the Civil War. Anna Reeves Jarvis died on the second Sunday in May 1905. In 1907 her daughter began promoting the second Sunday in May as a holiday to honor mothers. Following an act of congress in 1914, President Woodrow Wilson proclaimed the second Sunday in May Mother's Day.

(Historical marker located at the corner of Ionia and Erie streets)

* * * *

This is the birthplace of "The Sweetheart of Sigma Chi". Written in the spring of 1911 by two undergraduates at Albion College this song has become the most popular college fraternity song in history.

Many people ask "Who is the girl who was the inspiration?" But there was no one in particular, "The `Sweetheart' is the symbol for the spiritual ingredient in brotherhood.

* * * *

"The Old Rugged Cross," one of the world's best-loved hymns, was composed here in 1912.

Rev. George Bennard, the son of an Ohio coal miner, was a lifelong servant of God, mainly in the Methodist ministry. He wrote the words and music of over 300 other hymns. None achieved the fame of "The Old Rugged Cross," the moving summation of his faith.

"I'll cherish the Old Rugged Cross, Till my trophies at last I Lay down; I will cling to the Old Rugged Cross, And exchange it someday for a crown." Note: Albion is one of three towns that claim to be the birthplace of the hymn, The other town's claiming this honor includes Pokagon, Michigan or Sturgeon Bay, Wisconsin.

Local Landmark

In 1913 Floyd Starr purchased forty acres of land on Montcalm Lake to found Starr Commonwealth for Boys, a non-profit home and residential school for wayward, delinquent and neglected boys.

At that time, the only building on the property was an old barn in which Starr and the first two boys stayed until the first structure was completed. Today, 155 boys are served on a 300 acre campus encompassing facilities built with private contributions.

Services to youth were expanded with the founding of the Van Wert, Ohio, campus in 1951 and the merger with the Hannah Neil Center for Children in Columbus, Ohio in 1978.

Focusing on positive support in the character development of troubled children by providing a well-rounded academic, social and spiritual exposure, Starr Commonwealth is now a nationally recognized child care organization. They can focus on growth and learning.

(Historical marker located on Twenty-Six Mile Road)

Prominent People

Floyd Starr, originator of the credo "There is no such thing as a bad boy," was born in Decatur, Michigan, on May 1, 1883.

After graduating from Marshall High School, he worked for several half-way houses in St. Louis, Missouri. Returning to Michigan, he obtained his Bachelor of Arts degree from Albion College in 1910.

Fulfilling a lifetime dream to someday adopt fifty boys, Starr founded Starr Commonwealth for Boys in 1913. "Uncle Floyd," as he was affectionately called by his boys, earned the respect of court officials, co-workers and students for his successful work with homeless neglected and delinquent boys. He received numerous citations for his humanitarian efforts.

Starr retired from active leadership of Starr Commonwealth in 1967, but provided guidance until his death on August 27, 1980 at the age of 97.

(Historical marker located on Twenty-Six Mile Road)

Place Name

The first settler was Horace Blackman, who staked a claim on 160 acres in 1827 and built a log cabin. He named the place Jacksonborough for president Andrew Jackson. The name was changed to Jacksonopolis and finally (and wisely) to Jackson.

Historical Significance

Jackson is known as the "crossroads of Michigan" because of the number of highways which intersect here. I-94, US 127 and three state highways all come through Jackson. A number of railroad lines also liked Jackson. By 1910 there were ten lines passing through here.

Along with railroading, another important part of Jackson's economy has been prisons. In 1839 it was selected for Michigan's first prison. That institution still exists among a complex of six different facilities.

* * * *

On July 6 of 1854, Jackson Michigan hosted a convention that served as the first formal meeting place of the Republican Party.

Five thousand delegates came together here to oppose the Kansas-Nebraska Act. This bill allowed new states to settle the issue of slavery for themselves.

The first Republican platform denounced slavery, called for the repeal of the Kansas-

Nebraska Act, and demanded the prohibition of slavery in the territories.

It would be just six years before the party elected its first president, Abraham Lincoln.

* * * *

Jackson was also a stop on the Underground Railroad. Some of the homes used for transporting slaves from the south to freedom in the north can still be seen.

Jackson has the honor of being home to more U.S. astronauts than any other city in the nation.

Local Landmark

The Michigan Space Center honors their four native sons and all space pioneers. The Center is housed in a unique gold geodesic dome. Among the exhibits are the Apollo 9 command module, a memorial to the Challenger crew, space suits, satellites, a moon rock, and a model of the Hubbell space telescope.

Local Air Force Major Alfred Worden was the pilot of the Apollo 15 1971 mission when Colonel David Scott and Lt. Colonel James Irwin spent sixty-six hours on the moon's surface.

* * * *

The largest man made waterfalls in North America are found here. The Cascades were a gift to the city from William Sparks, a local industrialist and philanthopist. He also was the mayor for three terms.

Sparks loved his hometown and created The Cascades for his fellow citizens to enjoy, and to give visitors a favorable impression of Jackson. They're located in 465-acre Sparks Foundation County Park.

There are eighteen separate falls, of heights up to fifty feet. The falls have been illuminated and include six fountains of various shapes. A light and water show has been set to music.

A crowd of 25,000 people was on hand for the dedication on May 9, 1932, Sparks' 59th birthday. Upon his death, the park was given to the city. People from around the world still come to Jackson to see The Cascades.

Prominent People

Jackson composer, Hughie Cannon wrote the classic song, Bill Bailey Won't You Please Come Home.

Place Name

Town was named after the famous battle, the Battle of Waterloo.

Place Name

The Michigan Central Railroad built a station here in 1848. They were enticed by land concessions given up by brothers Elisha and James Congdon. They named the town for their old home near Chelsea, Massachusetts.

> Chelsea is the world headquarters for Jiffy Mix baking products, a brand name that was introduced in 1930.

Industry

Chelsea Milling Company is run by a family that has been in the flour milling business since 1802. The company handles the product throughout the entire process. It stores the wheat, mills it into flour, and uses that flour exclusively for its own prepared mixes.

Prominent People

Actor Jeff Daniels grew up in Chelsea, Michigan. He founded the Purple Rose Theatre Company in Chelsea, Michigan.

Daniels was cast as the philandering husband of cancer-stricken Debra Winger in the film "Terms of Endearment." Woody Allen made use of Daniels' restrained persona and clean-cut good looks by casting him as the movie star who steps out of the screen to help lonely Mia Farrow in "The Purple Rose of Cairo." He also appeared as Harry Dunner in "Dumb & Dumber."

Place Name

Nestled along the banks of the River Raisin, this friendly small town was named after Manchester, Ontario, from where the earlier settlers came.

Place Name

Founded by New Yorkers, who came to the area via traveling through the Erie Canal, established numerous businesses in the area, including as a sawmill, flourmill and distillery. Local tradition says the name of the town is attributed to the description of the drunken brawling by the Native American's in the area.

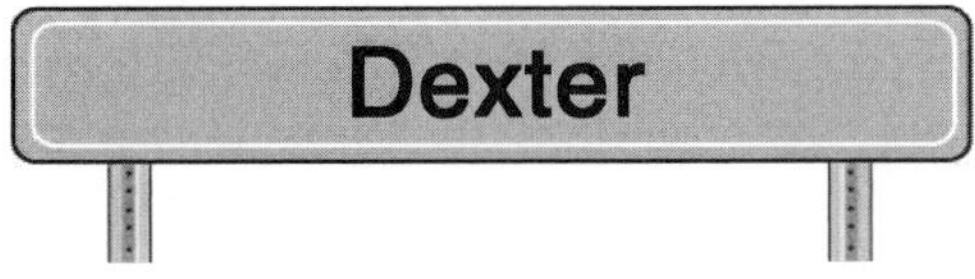

Place Name

Named after Judge Samuel Dexter, the areas first landowner, and postmaster.

Ann Arbor

Place Name

John Allen of Virginia and Walker Ramsey of New York came here with their wives in 1823 to become the first white settlers. Both of their wives were named Ann and the area was rich in natural grapes. They enjoyed the grape arbors as places to relax, to sit and visit, so the name of the town became Ann Arbor.

Local Landmark

Among the University of Michigan graduates are seven astronauts, three justices of the U.S. Supreme Court, several Pulitzer Prize winners and one president, Gerald Ford.

Ann Arbor has been the home of the University of Michigan since 1837, moving here from Detroit. The land had been offered to the city for a college by local Indians. State legislators at the time, trying to be cute, first called the school "The University of Michigania". It received its present and more dignified name when it moved to Ann Arbor.

Since the time of its arrival in town, the university has been the centerpiece of Ann Arbor's identity and growth. It's also a noted regional research and development center.

The University of Michigan boasts the largest pre-law and pre-medicine programs in the United States.

Among the "firsts " it is known for, the University of Michigan had the first professorship in education and started the first course of forestry offered at an American university. It also had the first university-operated hospital and, perhaps most significantly, was the first state university to allow women students. All states of the union and over one hundred foreign countries comprise today's student body.

* * * *

On the grounds of the university is the Gerald R. Ford Presidential Library. Unlike other presidents, who have their presidential archives and museums in one location, Ford separated his. The museum is in Grand Rapids in his former Congressional district. His papers are here at his alma mater in Ann Arbor.

President Ford donated the historical materials of his many years of public service to the federal government. However, his letter of December 13, 1976 to the president of The University of Michigan and the Archivist of the United States stated that he wanted the papers preserved in his home state of Michigan. He was the first president to give his papers to the country while still in office.

The library's groundbreaking took place in January of 1979 and former President Ford was on hand for the laying of the cornerstone that June. Papers in the collection cover Ford's years in Congress and as both vice president and president. Additionally, Mrs. Ford and a significant number of White House advisors have given their papers to the Library. It also contains records from the 1976 Ford Presidential campaign.

* * * *

On May 1, 1948 the Michigan Memorial-Phoenix Project was founded to honor the 585 University of Michigan alumni, students, faculty and staff who lost their lives in World War II. The Project is devoted to "peaceful, useful and beneficial applications and implications of nuclear science and technology to the welfare of the human race."

One of the first nuclear reactors to be built at a university came on line here in 1954. It is located on the north campus.

* * * *

The University of Michigan can also be proud of three museums located on its campus.

- The University of Michigan Exhibit Museum features displays on Michigan wildlife, biology, Native Americans, dinosaurs, anthropology, and astronomy.
- The University of Michigan Museum of Art is rated among the top ten university art museums in the country. It can be justly proud of a 13,000-piece permanent collection, including masterworks by Cezanne, Rembrandt, Monet, Picasso and others.
- The Kelsey Museum of Archaeology holds over 100,000 pieces in its collection, including Egyptian mummies and treasures from the Greek and Roman eras.

* * * *

And, of course, what is a university without football! Michigan Stadium draws over 100,000 fanatical Wolverine fans to their home games. Built in 1927, it is the largest college-owned stadium in the country.

Prominent People

One of rock's greatest singer, songwriters, Bob Seger of The Silver Bullet Band was born in Ann Arbor. His credits include seven platinum albums, and hit songs such as, "Nine Tonight" from Urban Cowboy, "Against the Wind" from Forest Gump and "Roll Me Away" from Armageddon.

* * * *

Before pursuing an acting career, Max Gail earned a master's degree in finance from the University of Michigan. Gail is well known for his role on TV's Barney Miller, as Detective Stanley "Wojo" Wojciehowicz.

Olympian Jesse Owens set six track and field world records in less than six hours in Ann Arbor in 1935.

* * * *

Kentucky born author Harriette Arnow, finished your greatest work, "The Dollmaker" after moving to a farm near Ann Arbor. The novel featuring a Kentucky family forced to move to Detroit during the war and their struggles trying to maintain their own family values remained on the best-seller list for 31 weeks.

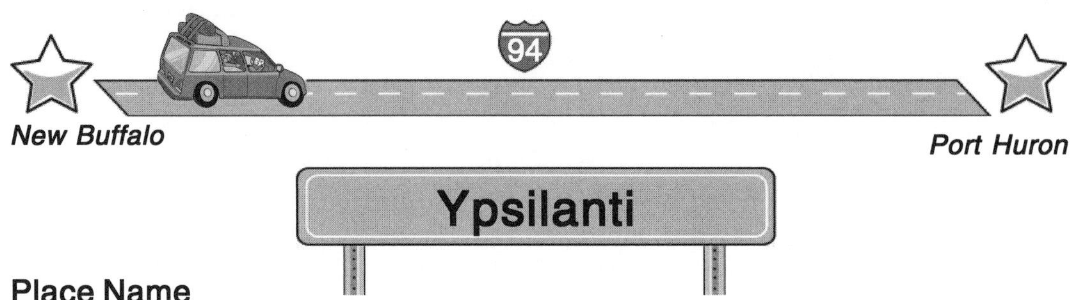

Ypsilanti

Place Name

At a meeting to select the name for their city, Judge Woodward suggested naming it for the Greek Patriot General Demetrius Ypsilanti.

In the struggle of the Greek people against Turkish tyranny appeared an outstanding heroic figure, Demetrius Ypsilanti. With three hundred men he held the Citadel of Argos for three days, against an army of thirty thousand. Having exhausted his provisions, he escaped one night beyond the enemy lines, with his entire command, having lost not a single man. He was admired by Americans for his part in a struggle for freedom so like their own. When a fire destroyed the school at Woodruff's Grove, that small settlement was abandoned in favor of Ypsilanti.

Historical Significance

In 1869, President Ulysses S. Grant made a speech at the train station in Ypsilanti.

* * * *

In 1881 Charles J. Guiteau, the assassin of President Garfield, was thrown off the train at the Ypsilanti station when the conductor found out he did not have a passenger ticket. History notes that he secretly boarded the train in Chicago and was thrown off in Ypsilanti. He then made his way to Washington D.C. and assassinated President Garfield at the train station. This journey was extensively researched and documented by the Secret Service.

General Trivia

In 1941, the Ford Freeway, which originally ran from Wyoming Avenue in Detroit to Carpenter Road in Ypsilanti, was built to bring workers from Detroit to Ypsilanti to work at the Willow Run Bomber Plant during World War II. That plant was quickly converted to wartime production when the U.S. entered World War II. The famous B-24 bombers rolled off the Willow Run assembly line one every 55 minutes. 8,000 B-24 Bombers were built.

* * * *

Ypsilanti was the home of the real McCoy

Engineer and inventor Elijah McCoy's first invention was a lubricator for steam engines. The invention allowed machines to remain in motion to be oiled, which revolutionized the industrial machine industry. Elijah would go on to establish his own firm and was responsible for a total of 57 patents.

The term "real McCoy" refers to the oiling device used for industrial machinery. His contribution to the lubricating device became so popular that people inspecting new equipment would ask if the device contained the real McCoy. This helped popularize the American expression, meaning the real thing. His other inventions included an ironing board and lawn sprinkler.

Industry

Some of Ypsilanti's more colorful early manufactured products included steel bustles for ladies' dresses and "Ypsilanti Health Underwear" -Long johns once known throughout the nation. The marketing slogan for the factory was "When Love Grows Cold Do Not Despair, There's Always Ypsilanti Underwear."

* * * *

Thomas Monaghan and his brother, James purchased DomiNicks pizza for only $900. Shortly thereafter, James sold Thomas his half of the business in exchange for a Volkswagen Beetle. Thomas went on to franchise his first store in Ysilanti seven years later and ultimately managed to build Domino's into the nation's second-largest pizza chain.

Today he often is credited with developing dough trays, the corrugated pizza box, insulated bags to transport pizzas and a unique system of internal franchising that rewards those franchisees, who, in turn, train their best restaurant managers to become store owners by sharing in the royalties of new stores.

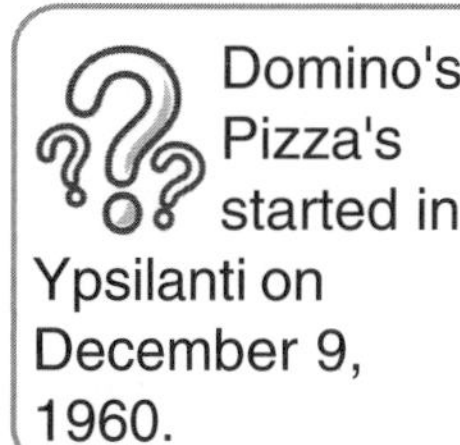
Domino's Pizza's started in Ypsilanti on December 9, 1960.

Prominent People

Rumor has it that Patsy Cline once lived in Ypsilanti as well as comedian Phyllis Diller who sang in the Presbyterian Church choir.

* * * *

In 1976, local 29-year-old Mark McPherson, an administrator at Wayne County Community College spent $3,000 looking for Scotland's Loch Ness monster. McPherson unsuccessfuly searched the 24-mile-long, 975-foot deep lake using sonar devices, binoculars and cameras.

Place Name

Named for a bustling community city in China known as Canton.

Place Name

The town's name, located along the shores of the lake by the same name, comes from belle ville, the French description for beautiful town.

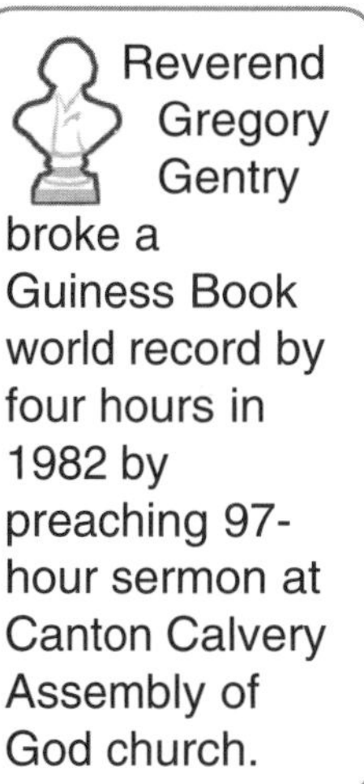
Reverend Gregory Gentry broke a Guiness Book world record by four hours in 1982 by preaching 97-hour sermon at Canton Calvery Assembly of God church.

Place Name

Located in Wayne County, this community was first settled by the family of Samuel McMath. McMath came from Romulus, New York, and named his new community after his old one.

Historical Significance

During World War II, nearly 5,000 German and Italian prisoners of war worked in Michigan's fields, lumber camps, and food processing centers. Romulus had prisoner-of-war camps operating in its area between 1943 and 1946.

Prominent People

Baseball player and coach Charlie Lau was born in Romulus in 1933. Lau was signed by the Detroit Tigers as an amateur free agent in 1952. Later traded to the Milwaukee Brewers. Charlie also played for the Baltimore Orioles, Kansas City Athletics and Atlanta Braves.

Place Name

Allen Park was named in 1926 after Lewis Allen. His father, Thomas, brought his family from New York State to Detroit in 1819. Lewis grew up to become a lawyer and a lumberman whose land holdings included 176 acres, part of which is in today's Allen Park.

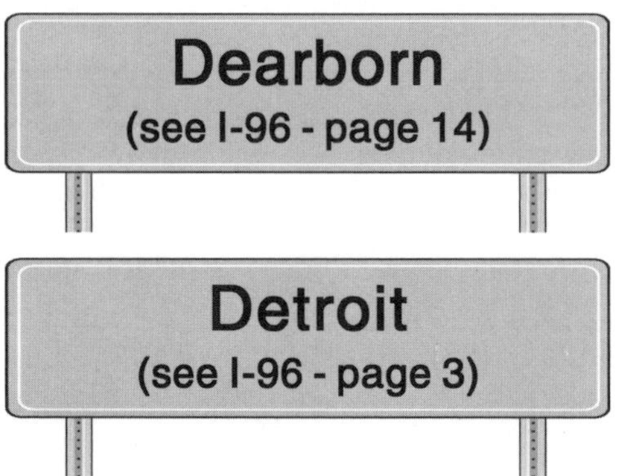

Dearborn
(see I-96 - page 14)
Detroit
(see I-96 - page 3)

General Trivia

Harry Houdini jumped off the Belle Isle Bridge on November 29, 1906 into the 30 degree fahrenheit river. Naked to the waist with his hands cuffed behind his back, snow falling, he plunged into the water twenty-five feet below. Within a minute, Houdini came to the surface, still locked in the handcuffs to waive to the applauding crowd as he swam to the rescue boat.

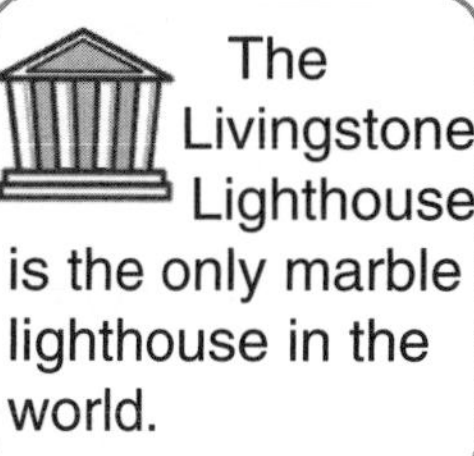

The Livingstone Lighthouse is the only marble lighthouse in the world.

Prominent People

Award winning actress Julie Harris was born in Grosse Point Park. Harris who wasn't very popular found solace in acting, becoming one the most honored performers in Tony history with ten nominations and five victories. She won the award as Best Actress in a Play for the following: "I Am A Camera"; "The Lark"; "Forty Carats"; "The Last of Mrs. Lincoln"; and "The Belle of Amherst". Her five additional nominations were for "Marathon '33," "Skyscraper," "The Au Pair Man," "Lucifer's Child," and "The Gin Game."

Julie Harris also appeared on the TV series "Knott's Landing."

Place Name

Given the name in reference to the point of land projecting out into Lake St. Clare.

Historical Significance

The history of the Grosse Pointe area differs slightly from that of its parent city, Detroit. About 50 years after the construction of Fort Pontchartrain on the present site of Detroit, the lakefront of the Grosse Pointe district was divided into ribbon farms, which although very narrow, extended back into the territory of the Huron and Ottawa tribes.

During English occupation of this area, Captain Alexander Grant bought a 640-acre farm on the present site of Grosse Pointe Farms. Grant, who was commodore of the British Navy on the great Lakes, erected a rambling hewn-log house, 280 feet long and two stories high, known as Grant's Castle. The castle was a favorite gathering place for British officers and Detroit society of that period. Thus, Grant was the first to establish an estate on this part of the lakeshore, and is regarded as the founder of Anglicized Grosse Pointe.

General Trivia

The four communities, Grosse Pointe Shores, Grosse Pointe Farms, Grosse Pointe, and Grosse Pointe Park all front Lake St. Clair. These collectively are known as Detroit's "Gold Coast." It is here that the estates and summer homes of many men and their descendents who profited by the industrial development of Michigan reside.

Local Landmark

Experience a refined style of elegant living in a bygone era at the Edsel & Eleanor Ford House, the magnificent estate of Henry and Clara Ford's only child, his wife and their four children.

Designed by renowned architect Albert Kahn, this architectural masterpiece is one of America's most outstanding estates. Witness centuries of history and elegance through the Ford's personal collection of antique furnishings. Stroll the magnificent gardens and grounds to experience the beauty of nature on your way to the enchanting Play House (miniature 2/3 scale house) and Gate Lodge Garage to view Edsel and Eleanor Ford's automobiles.

Place Name

When the French spread out from Detroit, they settled in the area they called L'Anse Cruise, meaning deep bay. At the suggestion of Conrad Hess the name was changed because of its location on the shores of Lake St. Clair.

Place Name

This community, named for tavern owner William Rose, developed as a result of an influx of Irish and German settlers.

Place Name

Christian Clemens was so impressed with the area when he surveyed it in 1795, that he returned here four years later to purchase John Brooks' distillery and help establish the town which would be named for him.

General Trivia

While working as a railway newsboy on the Detroit - Port Huron line, Tom Edison often stopped in Mount Clemens. He made friends with station agent J. U. MacKenzie and in 1862 saved MacKenzie's young son from death by a train. In gratitude Mr. MacKenzie taught Tom Edison railroad telegraphy.

From his training Tom became a qualified railroad telegrapher and worked during the 1860s at this occupation. Some of his earliest inventions were based on the telegraph.

(Historical marker located on Grand Street)

Local Landmark

Selfridge, Michigan's first real airport began operations as a training base in July, 1917. It has progressed to a leading role in America's air arm. It is often called "The Home of the Generals" because Selfridge has been a springboard to success in the careers of 145 Air Force generals.

It is named for Lt. Thomas E. Selfridge, the nation's first military pilot. In 1908 he was killed while flying with Orville Wright, becoming America's first military casualty of powered fight.

(Historical marker located on Hwy M-59)

The first airplane to exceed 200 mph. was piloted by Lt. Lester James Maitland on October 14, 1922 at an airplane show at Selfridge Field.

Local Landmark

Take a ride into the past and relive the Lionel model railroading story at the Visitor's Center, here in Chesterfield, where dreams span generations and enjoyment lasts a lifetime!

This Center features a ten-minute video on the production process and houses a 52-foot-long display of artifacts tracing Lionel's history since its founding. You will see a 14x40-foot operating layout with ten trains running simultaneously and accessories that visitors can operate by push button.

* * * *

When Lionel founder Joshua Lionel Cowen's immigrant family arrived in New York after the Civil War, the railroads were literally America's engines of progress. The "Golden Spike" meeting of the Union Pacific and Central Pacific lines in 1869 unified the continent and signaled the birth of a world power. Cowen was born in 1877, just before Edison's first electric light. He grew up with real trains, amid dizzying change. Around the time he founded Lionel in 1900, passenger lines like the peerless Twentieth Century Limited symbolized American technology and sophistication.

Cowen was already a successful inventor when he created his first toy train. But The Electric Express and its offspring soon became a sacred mission, and Cowen would spend a lifetime stoking America's imagination with the romance of the rails. He told boys that Lionels would prepare them for adulthood. Soon Dads too were encouraged to join Youngsters in model train enthusiasm, to further father-son bonding. With growing prosperity, Lionels layouts cropped up in more living rooms, especially at Christmas. Before mid-century, railroads were our economic lifeblood, as well as cultural icons -- but it was not to last.

And when Americans started driving to suburbia and flying cross-country, they stopped buying Lionel trains. By the 1960s, freight lines were being scrapped, and fathers and sons were on opposite sides of the "generation gap." That decade saw the tragic demise of New York's Pennsylvania Station, the retirement of The Twentieth Century Limited, and the passing of Joshua Lionel Cowen.

But now the Lionel dream is back and better than ever. America is renewing its relationship with the railroads -- building new high-speed passenger lines and even recreating historical landmarks like Penn Station. Joshua Lionel Cowen's legacy of family, friends, and shared enjoyment has endured and grown.

Industry

Henry Row Schoolcraft, an Indian agent, created the name from the Algonquin Indian tribe and by using the suffix, ac, meaning place.

For more than a century, Algonac has played a leading role in ship building, from sailing cargo ships to large pleasure craft, racing boats and World War II landing craft.

Between 1921 and 1932 Christopher Smith and Gar Wood built ten Miss Americas in Algonac. Smith and Wood worked together on the first; however, Wood was responsible for the rest. The Miss Americas held the Harmsworth trophy, symbol of the world's water speed supremacy, from 1921 to 1933. In 1932 Wood's Miss America X raced over a measured mile to establish the world's water speed record of 124.91 miles per hour.

During the 1930s Smith adopted the name Chris Craft Corporation. The firm became one of the world's largest builders of power pleasure boats. Headquartered in Algonac for many years, it had other manufacturing plants in Michigan, Ohio, Missouri, Tennessee, Florida and Italy.

(Historical marker located on St. Clair River Drive)

Place Name

Muttonville was founded (and named) as a predominately sheep raising area and slaughtering center.

Invention

Thomas Clegg (1863-1939) and his English-born father, John, built "The Thing," the first recorded self-propelled vehicle in Michigan (and perhaps the country) in 1884-85. The Thing, driven by a single cylinder steam engine with a tubular boiler carried in the rear, seated four. The vehicle was built in the John Clegg & Son machine shop here in Memphis. It ran about 500 miles before Clegg dismantled it and sold the engine to a creamery.

(Historical marker located at Cedar Street)

Place Name

Named after the nearby river, which was so named because on quiet evenings the water running over its pebbly bed made a rattling sound.

Port Huron

Place Name

Port Huron is tucked away in a corner at the south end of Lake Huron, where Michigan borders the Canadian province of Ontario. It is among the oldest settlements in the state.

Historical Significance

In 1686 the French built Fort St. Joseph here to ward off British attempts to steal the fur trade. The furs were the economic mainstay of the French settlers. However, it was 1790 before a true permanent colony was formed here.

Port Huron became another of Michigan's major lumbering areas when four villages combined to make up the town. As happened across the state, the timber eventually ran out. Fortunately, Port Huron had diversified its economy to include shipbuilding, railroading, and gas and oil distribution, so the town continued to grow.

Local Landmark

Located where Lake Huron empties into the St. Clair River, Port Huron sits at a strategic point for shipping. The river provides a connection between Lake Huron and Lake Erie.

The Blue Water International Bridge, just recently rebuilt, is a mammoth structure which rises 152-feet above the river and links Port Huron with Canada. From the bridge, it is possible to see oil tankers, bulk freighters and pleasure craft crossing the water.

The town today stretches out almost eight miles along Lake Huron. Across the river from Port Huron is a twenty-mile-long stretch of chemical companies, known as "Chemical Valley".

These companies wanted to build in Port Huron, but were rejected by citizens concerned about safety and the environment.

Prominent People

Thomas Alva Edison, was born in Port Huron in 1847.

At the age of fourteen Thomas Edison invented the first electric battery in Port Huron. He funded his youthful experiments by peddling fruit, nuts and newspapers on the local train. In fact, he printed and distributed his own paper, the Weekly Herald, on a train that ran between Port Huron and Detroit, about an hour to the south. He was the first publisher to attempt something like that.

Port Huron honors the life and work of Edison in Thomas Edison Park, which is located under the International Bridge.

* * * *

Legendary jazz singer Earl Coleman was born in Port Huron. Known as a fine ballad singer with a deep baritone voice, Earl was influenced by Billy Eckstine. Coleman made his place in history by recording "This Is Always" and "Dark Shadows."

General Trivia

The city seems to have had an unusual interest in leading the way in electricity. They started one of the country's first electrical utilities here in 1844 and built the first electrified underwater railway tunnel, which opened in 1891. The tunnel, built at a cost of $2.7 million, is 6,025 feet long.

* * * *

The Fort Gratiot Light stands 86-feet high in Lighthouse Park is Michigan's first lighthouse.

The Grand Trunk Western Railroad tunnel, linking Port Huron with Canada, passes underneath Military Street. This international submarine railway tunnel -- first in the world -- was opened in 1891. The tunnel's total length is 11,725 feet, with 2,290 feet underwater. The tunnel operations were electrified in 1908 and completely diesalized in 1958. Tracks were lowered in 1949 to accommodate larger freight cars. During World War I, a plot to blast the tunnel was foiled.

(Historical marker located on 16th Street)

INTERSTATE
75

75
Sault Ste. Marie
Dafter
ONTARIO
Rudyard
Kinross
Dryburg
Kincheloe
Saint Ignace
Mackinaw City
Topinabee
Indian River
Petoskey
Wolverine
Vanderbilt
Gaylord
31
23
Traverse City
Frederic
Grayling
Roscommon
75
West Branch
Cadillac
Alger
Sterling
Standish
Pinconning
Linwood
Kawkawlin
Essexville
131
25
Knowton
Bay City
Zilwaukee
Saginaw
Frankenmuth
Birch Run
Clio
Flint
Grand Rapids
Port Huron
75
Oxford
96
ONTARIO
Clarkston
Washington
Lansing
Pontiac
Rochester
Birmingham
Troy
69
Gross Pointe Shores
Southfield
Gross Pointe
Royal Oak
Hamtramck
Battle Creek
Highland
Detroit
94
Wyandotte
Kalamazoo
Flat Rock
Carleton
27
Newport
Coldwater
Monroe
Brest
Temperance
Erie
INDIANA
OHIO

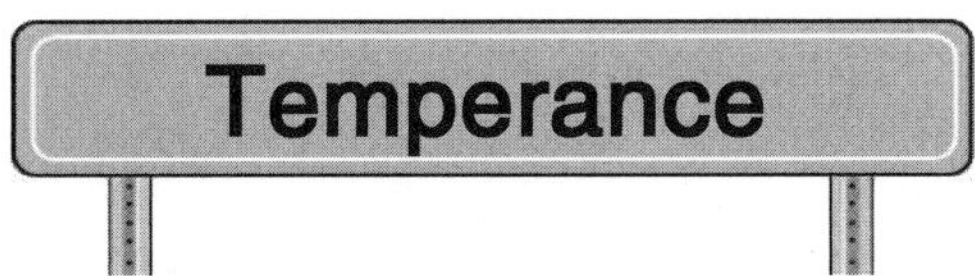

Place Name

Erie was named because of its location bordering Lake Erie.

Historical Significance

Founded by French settlers from the Frenchtown area (now Monroe) who cleared the walnut trees along the shores of Maumee Bay.

Place Name

Members of the Women's Christian Temperance Union, Lewis Ansted and his wife Marietta, own a 140 acre farm in the area. When they subdivided the land into lots, they included a clause that no liquor was to be either used, made or sold on property. This even went for the Ann Arbor Railroad when they obtained a right-of-way through the area. As a result of this ordinance the town was officially named Temperance.

Monroe

Place Name

A Frenchman named Francois Navarre left Detroit in 1780 and built a cabin here by the Raisin River. Within four years one hundred other French families had joined him. The settlement was called Frenchtown for obvious reasons. The name was Americanized to Monroe in 1813, to honor the new U.S. President.

General Trivia

Monroe County has more Native American archaeolgical sites than any other in Michigan.

Promient People

Christie Brinkley first "Sports Illustrated" swimsuit issue cover was in 1979. Christie also appeared on the cover in 1980 and 1981, making her the first model to appear on 3 consecutive covers.

Brinkley was one of three models featured as dolls produced by Matchbox Toys called "The Real Model Collection".

Christie played the "red-haired girl" in Billy Joel's "Keepin' The Faith" music video. She has also appeared as herself in various other Billy Joel music videos, including "River Of Dreams", "A Matter Of Trust", and "Leningrad".

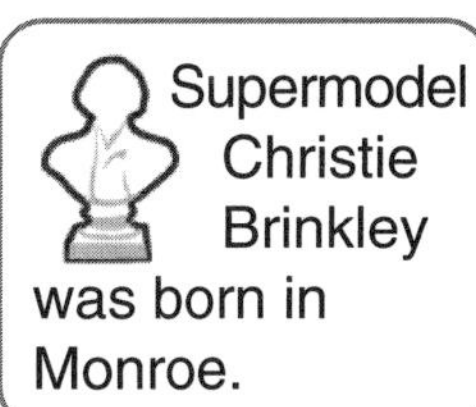

was born in Monroe.

* * * *

Its most noted native son was George Armstrong Custer. He was born in Ohio, but this is where the future general grew up. His half-sister raised him until he went off to West Point. He graduated at the bottom of his class in 1861 and was made a second lieutenant.

He entered the Civil War right out of West Point and fought with the 2nd U.S. Cavalry at Bull Run, Gettysburg, Chancellorsville and Culpepper Court House. He was wounded at Culpepper. By war's end he had attained the battlefield rank of General. With the end of the war, the title was revoked and he was made a Captain.

Custer married Elizabeth Monroe, daughter of the town's judge, and continued his army career. He became colonel of the newly authorized 7th Cavalry and remained its commander until his death.

He was part of the 1867 Sioux and Cheyenne expedition. However, an unauthorized visit to his wife led to a court-martial and he was suspended from duty for a year. The two lived for a time at Fort Lincoln near Bismarck, North Dakota.

Custer's army career ended on June 25, 1876, at the Battle of the Little Big Horn. His entire command was exterminated, with a loss of 266 officers and men. The bodies were buried on the field of battle. The next year remains were disinterred that might have been Custer's and given a military funeral at West Point.

Place Name

Town was settled and named by the French, after one of their great seaports.

Historical Significance

American promotors organized the Gibralter & Flat Rock Company in 1836 to develop Gibralter into a city (10 miles north) and Brest into its lake port, but the venture failed.

Place Name

Called Riviere aux Signes by the French, and later Swan Creek, the town would receive its name for its new location on Swan Creek near Lake Erie.

Place Name

Town given the name of Michigan poet, Will Carleton. Graduating from college in 1869,

Will Carleton first worked as a newspaper journalist in Hillsdale. He had been in the habit of writing poetry as a youngster. His first significant work published was “Betsy and I Are Out,” a poignant tale of a divorce which was first published in the Toledo Blade, but then reprinted by Harper’s Weekly. This poem was soon followed in 1872 by “Over the Hill to the Poor House” developing the plight of the aged and those with indifferent families. This piece captured national attention and catapulted Carleton into literary prominence, a position he was to hold the rest of his life as he continued to write and to lecture from coast to coast.

Place Name

The Gibralter & Flat Rock Company changed the town's name from Smooth Rock, so named because of the smooth rock bed of the Huron River which ran through it, to the City of Flat Rock when they platted the area.

Prominent People

Prior to getting his big break, Wyandotte born Lee Majors was the limo driver for producer Jim Barnett, the man who created the TV show "World Championship Wrestling."

Majors starred concurrently in two TV shows at the same time - Playing Jess Brandon in Owen Marshall and Colonel Steve Austin in Cy'borg and Six Million Dollar Man TV movies.

In 1976 Lee and Farrah Fawcett made TV history - a husband and wife each starring in separate top rating shows.

His cousin Johnny Majors was the 1956 Heisman Trophy runner-up at Tennessee, and became a great college football coach; from 1968-96 he coached at Iowa State, Pittsburgh, and Tennessee, winning the 1976 national championship with Pittsburgh.

Wyandotte is named for the Native American tribe who lived in the area.

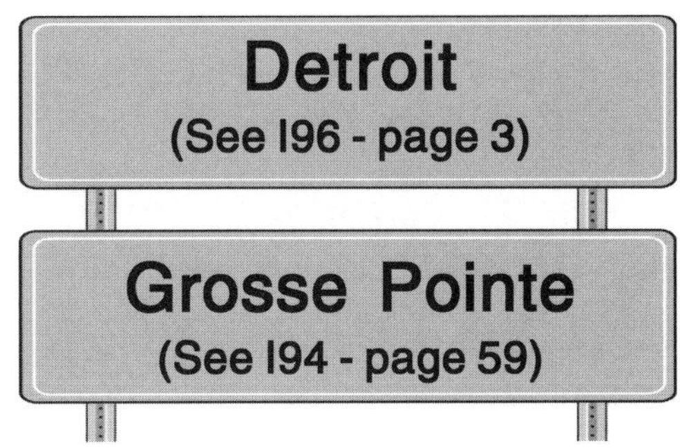

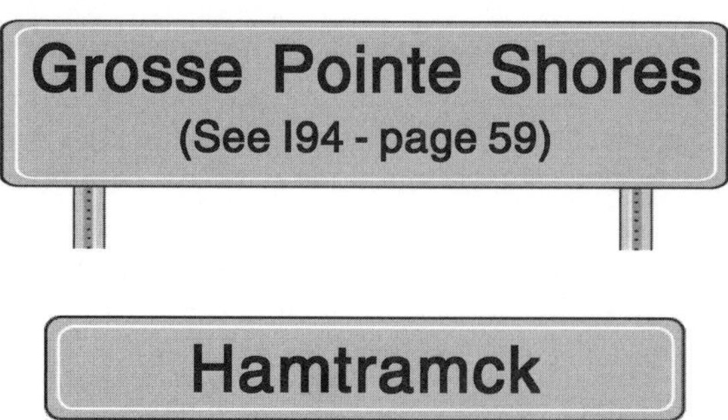

Hamtramck

Place Name

This township was named for Colonel John Francis Hamtramck. Colonel Hamtramck, under General Anthony Wayne, commanded the troops which took possession of Detroit upon the evacuation of the British in 1796.

Highland Park

> Henry Ford began mass producing automobiles in Highland Park on a moving assembly line in 1913.
>
> Two years later Ford built a million Model Ts.
>
> Within ten years over nine thousand were assembled daily.

Industry

On June 6, 1925, the Chrysler Corporation was founded here after a reorganization of the Maxwell and Chalmers automotive companies by Walter P. Chrysler. The first cars to bear the Chrysler name were manufactured in the Maxwell plant which was built here in 1909 and which is now the center of the corporation's worldwide administrative and engineering headquarters. Chrysler had its origin in some 130 auto companies founded as early as 1894 and today is one of the few survivors in an industry that has included approximately 1,500 companies. By 1930 Chrysler had become the world's third largest producer of automobiles; during World War II its production of war materials helped make Detroit the world's "Arsenal of Democracy."

(Historical marker located on Oakland Avenue)

* * * *

Henry Ford began mass producing automobiles here on a moving assembly line in 1913. Two years later Ford built a million Model Ts. Within ten years over nine thousand were assembled daily.

Southfield

(See I96 - page 17)

Place Name

The town's name comes from when Governor Lewis Cass camped under an oak tree in the area he was inspecting in 1818. Cass remembered the story of the Royal Oak of Scotland under which the Pretender to the throne hid to escape his pursuers.

Prominent People

Glen Frey of "The Eagles" rock group was born in Royal Oak.

Beginning as Linda Ronstadt's touring band in 1971, The Eagles later released four consecutive #1 albums between 1975 and 1979. They collectively topped Billboard's album chart for twenty-seven weeks. They won four Grammy awards, one each for "Heartache Tonight" (1979), "New Kid In Town" (1977), "Hotel California" (1977) and "Lyin' Eyes" (1975).

Frey's song "Smuggler's Blues" was turned into a script for the TV smash Miami Vice. Frey played a role in the TV show.

Birmingham

Prominent People

Tim Allen of ABC's "Home Improvement" lived in Birmingham

Two years after the death of Timothy Allen Dick's father, Gerald, who was killed in a collision with a drunk driver while driving his family home from a University of Colorado football game, his mother Martha, remarried her high-school sweetheart, an Episcopalian deacon. Shortly thereafter Tim along with his eight siblings moved to Birmingham, Michigan.

In high school, Tim's favorite subject was shop, of course. Following high school he attended Western Michigan University where he graduated in 1975 with a degree in Television Production .

Allen was arrested in 1975 on drug charges. Upon his release two years later, he had a new outlook on life and on a dare from a friend started his comedy career at the Comedy Castle in Detroit.

Tim Allen went on to do several cable specials before becoming the star of his own hit television series on ABC called "Home Improvement", receiving $1,250,000 per episode during the 1999 season.

* * * *

Noel Paul Stookey, came to Birmingham with his family in 1949. Paul is best known as a member of the folk trio, "Peter, Paul, and Mary."

Place Name

When the town was platted it was named Hastings in honor of Eurotas Hasting, then president of the Michigan Bank. It was later changed to Troy after the city in New York state where many of the early settlers came from.

General Trivia

Troy native Karl Thomas, suspended in a five-by-five foot wicker gondola, flew his hot-air balloon solo for a record setting eighteen days in 1979 from Arcadian, California, to Jacksonville, Florida.

Place Name

There are almost 250 suburbs surrounding the city of Detroit. Pontiac stands out because of the fascinating history of the Indian chief the city is named for.

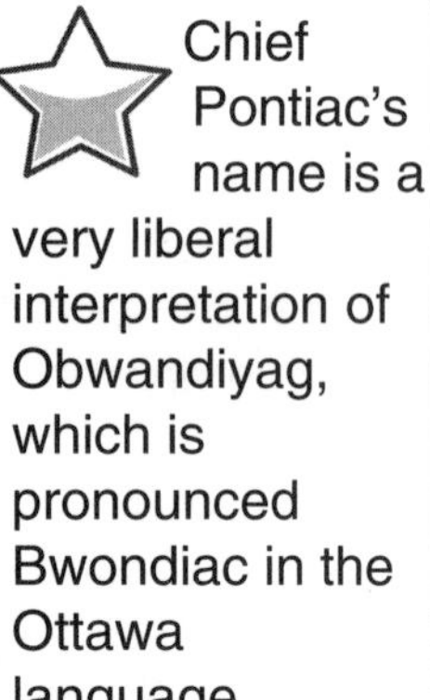

Chief Pontiac's name is a very liberal interpretation of Obwandiyag, which is pronounced Bwondiac in the Ottawa language.

Most of us know Chief Pontiac primarily as a hood ornament for Pontiac cars. But he ranks among the greatest of Native American leaders.

Prominent People

Chief Pontiac was both a fearless warrior and an intelligent, gifted speaker. He organized a confederacy of the tribes in the Ohio Valley and Great Lakes region.

Pontiac specified a particular day in 1763 when each of the tribes was to attack the British garrison closest to them. All but four of the fourteen posts were captured.

When the attack on Detroit failed, Pontiac laid siege to it for five long months. British reinforcements brought an end to the siege and Pontiac made a formal peace agreement with the red-coated enemy in 1766.

A Peoria brave murdered the chief just three years later. No one is sure of the reason -- whether it was jealousy, revenge, or simply a desire to destroy a powerful leader -- but an assassin was chosen. He acted friendly to Pontiac, but when the two left a store, the chief was clubbed from behind and then stabbed to death.

An Indian burial mound on Apple Island on Orchard Lake is said to be that of Chief Pontiac, the man who led the fight against those who would change forever the Indian way of life and the face of their land.

* * * *

NBC sportscaster, Dick Enberg grew up near Pontiac. He went to college first at Central Michigan University, graduating from Indiana University. Dick moved to Los Angeles to become an assistant baseball coach at Northridge State University.

Shortly thereafter Dick became a sportscaster. At first Enberg called local minor league sports, but then became the play-by-play man for the (then) Los Angeles Rams, the California (now Anaheim) Angels, and the UCLA Bruins.

Enberg rose to become NBC's top play-by-play announcer, calling during the late '70s, the '80s and '90s such sports as college and NBA basketball; golf, including many U.S. Opens in the '90s; tennis, including Wimbledon and the French Open; baseball; and, of course, NFL football, including 8 Super Bowls.

Local Landmark

From the king of rock to the kings of gridiron, the Pontiac Silverdome has established itself as a world-renowned facility hosting some of the most celebrated entertainers and athletes since 1975.

The Silverdome was Home to the Detroit Lions from 1975 until the start of the 2002 season.

The two highest attended events at the Silverdome were in 1987 when 93,682 people visited the stadium to hear Pope John Paul II conduct mass and 93,173 fans packed the stadium for Wrestlemania III in 1987.

The Silverdome was built at a cost of $55.7 million dollars. According to the 1992 Guinness Book of World Records it has the largest air-supported roof in the world. It takes 5 pounds of air pressure per square inch to keep the translucent fiberglass roof from falling in.

Place Name

This community lies between the high bluffs of the Clinton River on the south and the banks of winding Paint Creek on the north. Many automobile workers in the city of Detroit are attracted to this scenic community named after Rochester, New York.

The 110-room Meadow Brook Hall is a Tudor-revival style mansion inspired by English country manor houses of the Tudor and Elizabethan periods.

Local Landmark

A castle-like mansion called Meadow Brook Hall built between 1926 and 1929 at a cost of approximately $4 million by Alfred Wilson and Matilda Wilson, widow of the auto pioneer John Dodge.

This magnificent 88,000 square-foot mansion carefully preserved with original furnishings and art, beautifully exemplifies the lavish lifestyles and era of the American industrialists of the early 20th century. The house features 39 uniquely designed brick chimneys, solariums, a large library, hidden staircases, sculptured ceilings, courtyards, and gardens.

Place Name

This town was named for the first president of the United States, George Washington.

Invention

When the deputy surveyors entered Michigan's copper and iron country, they found that their magnetic compasses were nearly useless. In response to this problem, Washington native William Austin Burt—a deputy surveyor from 1833- 1855, who was self-taught in mathematics and astronomy—invented the solar compass, without which accurate surveying of much of Michigan's Upper Peninsula would have been impossible.

* * * *

America's first patented typewriter was constructed by William Austin Burt in 1829 in a workshop located in Washington.

It was also here that William Austin Burt built the solar compass, patented in 1836, which was the prototype for those used today. Burt's compass became an indispensable instrument for surveying because it used the sun instead of the magnetic north as a fixed reference and was therefore unaffected by the magnetic fields of iron ore deposits.

Burt also received a patent for an Equatorial Sextant. Among Burt's other accomplishments include the establishment of the northern point of the Michigan principal meridian in 1840; the discovery of the Marquette iron ore range in 1844 and the establishment of the northern portion of the Michigan - Wisconsin boundary in 1847. In 1852 he assisted in surveying the route for the Soo Canal.

(Historical marker located on Main Park Road)

Brace Beemer, the hearty voice announcer who thrilled Long Ranger radio audiences with his, "Hi yo, Silver, away" died of a heart attack at Oxford on March 1, 1965.

Place Name

The Clark brothers, Jermiah, Nelson, and Milton platted the town that would be named after them.

Place Name

The town's name comes from Otis Thompson, who said, "since nearly all the settlers had ox-teams and probably would hold on to them for some years to come."

Place Name

The town was named for the beautiful holly which grew in the area as well as for the fact that Jonathan Allen came from Mount Holly, New Jersey.

Flint

Place Name

The river that flows through the area was named Pawanunking or "river of flint" by the Indians. The name of the river and the town became simply Flint, although its original name was Grand Traverse or "great crossing".

Historical Significance

Flint, from its earliest days, was a transportation center. It began as a stop on the Pontiac Trail, one of a network of Indian trails which criss-crossed the wilderness.

When Michigan became a state in 1837, there were already three hundred settlers here. Flint incorporated as a city in 1855 and, like most other towns in Michigan, was affected by the logging boom.

This little town in the wilderness was the place where katydids, carts and wagons were made. Katydids were two-wheeled vehicles used to transport logs.

Industry

The origins may seem a bit too humble, but it was that early cart and wagon building that led to what became General Motors.

Auto manufacturing started in Flint in 1904 with the creation of the Buick Motor Company. William Durant, who later became president of General Motors recognized talent and hired people whose names became legendary in the auto industry -- names like Chrysler, Nash and Chevrolet. Durant also tried to buy Ford Motor Company, but was told by short-sighted bankers that Ford wasn't worth the price they were asking!

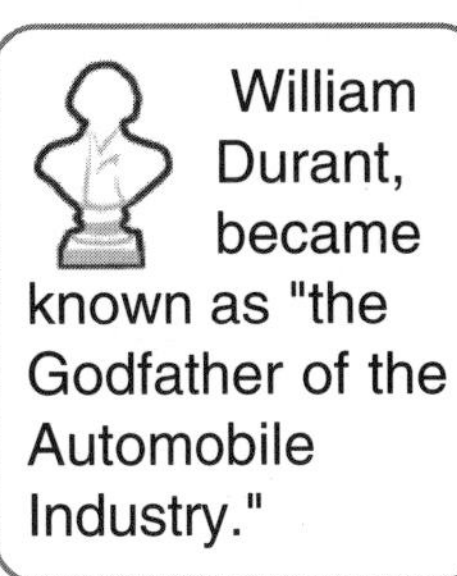

William Durant, became known as "the Godfather of the Automobile Industry."

* * * *

Flint is still one of the largest manufacturers of cars and other vehicles in the world. It is a blue collar, company town, with G.M. the company. It is also known as a workers' town and is famous for the strike of 1937. The workers showed up for their jobs, but they sat down and refused to work until the company's officials would talk with them.

National Guard troops came in and tear gas and riot guns were used to control the workers. Eleven policemen and sixteen strikers were injured.

But, as a result of this strike, thousands of auto workers benefited for many in higher wages and benefits. Flint became known as the birthplace of the modern labor movement.

* * * *

Perhaps one of the most popular assembly plants is the GM Truck and Bus factory built in 1947. Its products are mainly Chevrolet, including the whimsical Corvair of the 1960s and military vehicles used in all major conflicts since World War II. Employment here has dropped from a one-time high of 8,000 workers to today's 3,500 -- primarily due to the use of automation and robots.

Local Landmark

There is more to Flint, of course, than automobile factories. Museums here cover a variety of topics. A collection of vintage automobiles, including the oldest production Chevrolet, and an exhibit on Flint's Native American history can be found at The Alfred P. Sloan Museum.

A unique facility is The Labor Museum, where retired auto workers serve as docents.

Thanks to the philanthropy of the auto tycoons, Flint is home to Michigan's second most prominent museum of the arts, the Flint Institute of Arts. It contains over 5,000 permanent pieces and features rotating special exhibits.

For a taste of the 19th century, there's the Crossroads Village and Huckleberry Railroad. The complex includes thirty restored buildings, including a grist mill and cider mill, as well as a carousel, ferris wheel and locomotive-powered steam train.

Lloyd G. Coleman of Flint invented the first rubber ice cube tray.

General Trivia

Three men from Flint, Richard and Ray Moore, along with Lorne Matthews set a world record by traveling 6,000 miles in 42 days from Flint to Alaska by snowmobile.

Prominent People

Brian Roberts son of the founder of the Comcast Corp. empire began his career as assistant manager of the company's office in Flint, then Comcasts' largest market. Roberts eventually became president of the Philadelphia-based cable empire, which now includes QVC, a home-shopping channel; Comcast SportsNet, a 24-hour cable sports network; and two professional sport teams, the Philadelphia Flyers and Philadelphia 76ers.

* * * *

Mark Farner, Don Brewer, and Mel Schacher formed the Grand Funk Railroad Band in Flint in 1969 and became one of the era's biggest American rock bands.

* * * *

Sandra Bernhard - actress and comedian- was born in Flint. She played a role in "The King of Comedy" with Robert De Niro, worked in television as Nancy Bartlett on the "Roseanne" show, and earned the National Society of Film Critics Award for best supporting actress.

* * * *

Andre Rison who grew up in Flint, Michigan and attended Northwestern High School, played wide receiver for the Kansas City Chiefs. While attending Northwestern he played eight different positions on the football team.

* * * *

Major League Baseball player Jim Abbot, grew up in Flint. A left-handed pitcher born without a right hand, played for the California Angels, New York Yankees, Chicago White Sox, and Milwaukee Brewers.

Abbott wore a right-handed glove over the stump on his right arm, rapidly putting the glove on his left hand after finishing his pitching motion in order to field any ball that might come his direction. He would then remove the glove and make the throw with his left hand. In spite of his disability, Abbott's fielding statistics matched or slightly bettered the league average most seasons.

Jim was a member of the 1988 U.S. Olympic baseball team and received the Sullivan Award.

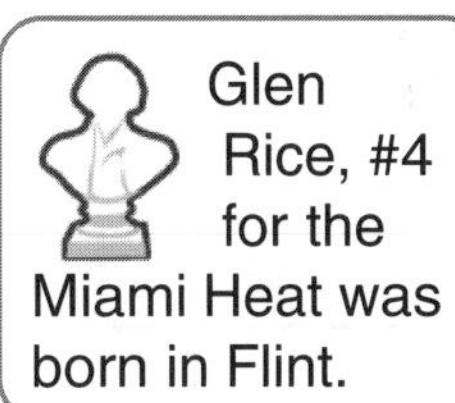

Glen Rice, #4 for the Miami Heat was born in Flint.

* * * *

Courtney Hawkins who plays for the Tampa Bay Buccaneers attended Beecher High School in Flint. He attended Michigan State (majoring in criminal justice) and finished his college career second place on the school's all-time receptions list.

Place Name

The meaning of the name "Clio" is lost in history. This is rather ironic, as Clio, pronounced "kl-ee-oh", was the Muse of History.

Since the residents of Clio pronounce it "kl-eye-oh", however, this basis for the origin of the name is unlikely. This leaves room for "humouros" stories of the origin.

One such story is based on the fact that Clio rests very near County Line 10 of Michigan on maps. This line is abbreviated CL10.

Place Name

The town's name is in reference to the station on the Pere Marquette Railroad that runs through the birch region of the state.

Frankenmuth

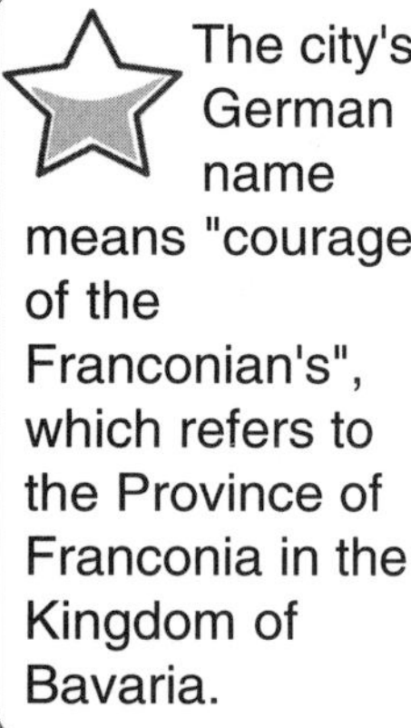

The city's German name means "courage of the Franconian's", which refers to the Province of Franconia in the Kingdom of Bavaria.

Historical Significance

A group of young Lutherans from Neudettelsau, Germany created the town in 1845. They came here as missionaries, both to convert the Chippewa Indians to Christianity, and to minister to other Germans who had settled in the Saginaw Valley.

The Indians weren't very interested in the new arrivals' message. But most of the missionaries chose to stay and make their home here, buying farms and starting families.

The Germans, like almost everyone else in Michigan, were loggers when they first arrived, but concentrated more on farming when the forests became depleted.

General Trivia

There wasn't much in this simple farm town to attract visitors for the first half-century or so of its existence. What started the tourism industry here was something very basic -- a good old chicken dinner.

Traveling salesmen were the first to discover this wonderful home cooking. Frankenmuth's location between Detroit, Flint and Saginaw made it a convenient stopping place.

Word of mouth is the best sales tool and it brought families here in the 1920s and 1930s, as they were out for Sunday drives. Today people from across the country travel to a small town in Michigan for chicken dinners.

Two of the largest restaurants in the United States, Zhender's and the Bavarian Inn, serve a combined two million plus meals a year. They sit across the street from each other in downtown Frankenmuth and may just comprise the "eatingest" block in the world!

Local Landmark

Broner's Christmas Wonderland is known as "The World's Largest Christmas Store."

But, of course, the town would have to have more than a good chicken dinner to attract three million visitors a year. This phenomenally successful "store" today covers an area the size of more than four football fields. Shoppers can find hundreds of Christmas trees, a variety of nativity scenes from around the world, and more than 50,000 Christmas ornaments.

If you collect Hummel figurines, Bronner's is something like mecca!

Broner's, started as a sideline to Wally Broner's sign business. Signs are one of the ways that the store has been marketed, with billboards as far away as Florida and Pennsylvania.

An exact replica of the "Silent Night" chapel in Oberndorf, Austria, where the famous hymn was written and first performed, was added to the complex in 1993.

* * * *

Frankenmuth is also known for the quality of its hand-crafted items and locally produced products.

A special favorite is Frankenmuth Brewery, the largest in Michigan. Pilsner, Dark, Bock, and Old Detroit Amber Ale are made here by a traditional German brewmaster in the traditional way.

If wine is more to your liking, Michigan's largest winery, St. Julian Winery, has a small branch here in Frankenmuth. Wine from the main winery in Paw Paw is made here into solera cream sherry. A variety of wines and sparkling fruit juices can be sampled in the tasting room.

German sculptor Georg Keilhofer is considered one of Frankenmuth's finest artists. He has been awarded commissions for sculptures for churches and other institutions around the world. The figures are created in his small workshop on South Main Street.

Quilters are drawn here by Zeilinger's Wool Company. A self-guided tour allows visitors to watch the process of refining wool -- from washing and air-drying it to carding and then making hand-stitched products, such as comforters and quilts. Zeilinger's has been in existence for more than eighty years.

And for those who can't pass by an outlet mall, Birch Run, Michigan's largest, is located nearby with nearly two hundred stores.

Place Name

The town's name, Saginawe or Saugenah, was given to the entire river valley, meaning place of the Sauks.

Prominent People

Steveland Judkins Morris Hardaway was born in Saginaw in 1951. Blind since birth, the boy would become known later as Stevie Wonder. His family moved to Detroit before Stevie found fame as a singer, songwriter and musician. Stevie was introduced to Motown Records in Detroit by a friend of his brother's. The friend just happened to be part of the singing group, the Miracles.

"Little" Stevie Wonder mastered every instrument he played (from piano, bongos, guitar and harmonica) by the time he was ten and recorded his first album at age 12. His first hit was "Fingertips". He has won a large number of Grammy's for his albums with hit songs such as "Ebony and Ivory," and "I Just Called to Say I Love You."

In 1999 at the age 49, Wonder was the youngest-ever recipient in 22-year history of annual Kennedy Center Honors, to recieve an award presented by President Clinton for his lifetime contribution to arts and culture.

Stevie Wonder's personal quotes include, "Just because a man lacks the use of his eyes doesn't mean he lacks vision."

* * * *

Saginaw has a tie-in with another famous person who goes further back into history. Dr. Richard Mudd, now 92, is a grandson and Laura Chapelle a great-great granddaughter of Dr. Samuel Alexander Mudd, the man who set the leg of John Wilkes Booth after he assassinated Abraham Lincoln. The two Michigan citizens have worked for many years to clear the name of their relative.

Dr. Samuel Mudd was a slave owner and Confederate agent in Maryland. He had hosted Booth, one of the most famous actors of his time, in the fall of 1864. When his friend showed up at his door needing assistance the next spring, Mudd helped. He set Booth's leg and gave him a room in his home. It wasn't until the next day that Mudd went to town, heard the news, and realized that he was harboring an assassin. Mudd claimed that he didn't recognize his visitor and did not give him up to the authorities.

Stories differ wildly as to what happened next, depending on whether it's a Lincoln historian or a Mudd descendant doing the telling. In any event, Mudd was convicted and sentenced to life imprisonment, narrowly escaping the death penalty. He was pardoned in 1869 by President Andrew Johnson, after helping to stop a yellow fever outbreak at his prison.

His descendants and other sympathizers are still trying to get his conviction overturned. They have found a friend in Rep. Steny Hoyer, a U.S. Congressman from Maryland. He introduced the "Samuel Mudd Relief Act" in June of 1999 to exonerate the doctor.

* * * *

Poet Theodore Roethke was born in Saginaw. As a child, he spent much time in his fathers and uncles greenhouse resulting in his use of natural imagery in his poetry. This American poet published several volumes of poetry and awarded the Pulitzer Prize for poetry in 1954 for his book "The Waking."

* * * *

Because of his age and that many of his early fights were in Saginaw, George LaVigne earned the nickname, "The Saginaw Kid."

Pound for pound, lightweight boxing champion George "Kid" LaVigne was one of the greatest fighters who ever lived.

LaVigne turned pro in 1886 at the age of 16 in Saginaw. Although he began boxing early, he went unbeaten in 46 fights including defeating (British) Dick Burge with a 17th-round knockout to win the World Lightweight Title in 1896. A terrific puncher, Lavigne retained the title with knockouts against Jack Everhart, Eddie Connolly and Walcott.

The "Kid" did not suffer his first loss until 1899 when he moved up in weight in a bid to capture the welterweight title and was knocked out by champion "Mysterious" Billy Smith.

Local Landmark

The Japanese Cultural Center and Teahouse -- Awa Saginaw An -- offers guests a once-a-month opportunity to see a true Japanese tea ceremony in an authentic Japanese teahouse.

Tokushima, Japan is a sister city to Saginaw and is honored by the Friendship Garden behind the teahouse. Many of the garden's bridges, trees and stones were imported from Japan.

* * * *

Michigan's most famous sculptor is celebrated at the Marshall M. Fredericks Sculpture Gallery. Over two hundred items are here, including plaster models, drawings and actual sculptures. The Gallery also features pictures of Fredericks' sculptures as they are displayed around the world.

* * * *

The Flint, Titabawassee, Shiawassee, and Cass Rivers all come together here to form the Saginaw River.

In 1953 a refuge, the Green Point Environmental Learning Center, was established at the confluence. It covers over 9,500 acres and serves as a wetland to attract migrating waterfowl. Late fall finds over 30,000 ducks and 25,000 geese making a temporary home here. Over 500 tundra swans also come through here each year and owls, hawks, eagles and other feathered creatures can be seen throughout the year.

Invention

A product was created in Saginaw that has been used by most American families over the years. Proctor & Gamble bought Spic & Span in 1945 and still market it today.

Elizabeth McDonald and her chemist aunt developed Spic & Span during the Great Depression.

* * * *

Anti-Theft Steering/Column Lock were developed in Saginaw. This invention won the product of the year given out by the Great Michigan Foundation in 1968.

* * * *

The inventor of the no-nail picture hanger was Saginaw inventor Jack Rabinovitch. Jack made the familiar by attaching a small metal hook into a rectangular piece of cloth with an adhesive-backing.

Place Name

New York City residents Daniel and Soloman Johnson named the township where they established a steam sawmill, Zilwaukie*. They named it in the hope of luring German immigrant workers here by confusing them with a name similiar to Milwaukee.

* Note the spelling of the town was later changed to Zilwaukee.

Bay City

Place Name

The town is appropriately name for its location near the shores of Saginaw Bay.

Historical Significance

Leon Tromble was the first white man to homestead here in what was once an Ojibwa Indian camp. Tromble arrived in the mid-1800s on a government assignment. He built a log home by the Saginaw River and Bay City was created, a place destined to become a major and rather rowdy lumber town.

Lumberjacks by the thousands would come to town during the winter to work in the city's more than fifty mills. Logs were constantly floating down the rivers until the Saginaw Valley had little timber left to give up. More than four billion board feet of lumber was cut here before 1888.

Local Landmark

Timber left its mark here, however, as the mansions built by lumber barons still stand. In fact, the town has more than 250 buildings on the National and State Historic Registers.

A 125-foot clock tower rises above Bay City's majestic City Hall. This stone building has a classic design and serves as the focal point for the city.

Defoe built cargo carriers and hundreds of ships for the navy during the two World Wars.

Industry

Unlike many of the lumber towns, Bay City diversified its economy early on, with such things as coal mining, beet sugar crops and fishing. Boat building was another important industry.

The Honey Fitz was crafted along the Saginaw River at the Defoe shipyard in Bay City in 1931. It went on to serve Presidents Dwight Eisenhower, John F. Kennedy, Lyndon Johnson and Richard Nixon under a variety of names.

General Trivia

Once 94,000 wild turkeys roamed the area in the days before white settlers. Indians didn't think the meat was fit to eat, so they used the birds only for their feathers. When the settlers cleared away the trees, the birds left.

* * * *

Local schoolteacher, Annie Edson Taylor was the first person to survive a barrel ride over Niagara Falls. She took the plunge in 1901 in a self-designed, wood barrel made by a Bay City cooperage.

Prominent People

Today a musical "bird" is the most famous export of Bay City. Louise Veronica Ciccone, known to the world as Madonna, was born here in 1959. She has called her hometown "the armpit of the U.S.", which has not made her popular with the residents. No Madonna Music Festival is planned here in the near future.

Never-the-less Madonna has had a number of musical hits such as "Vogue" and "Like a Prayer." Plus the superstar also appeared in several films including "Dick Tracy," "A League of Their Own" and "Evita."

* * * *

The town also figures into pop music history in another way, giving its name to the Bay City Rollers, a group from Scotland. The band wanted an American name, they stuck a pin into a map and Bay City won!

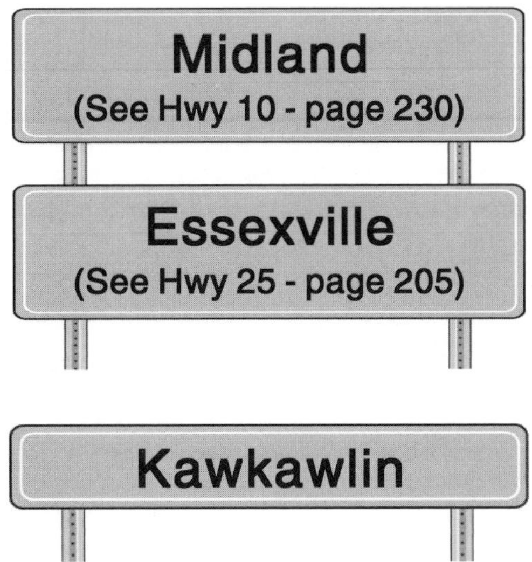

Place Name

Named for its location on the Kawkawlin River, which Native American's referred to as Oganconning, or place of the pike fish.

Place Name

Linwood is a combination of the words, line and wood, because it lays on the dividing line between Kawkawlin and Fraser townships, and it was heavily wooded.

Originally named for O-pin-cin-conning, a Native American word meaning potato place.

Place Name

This township was named for its proximity to the Pinconning River.

Place Name

Named for Detroit native, John Standish, who built a mill here in 1871.

Place Name

This town is named for James Sterling, whose sweetheart, Catherine Cuillerier, fearing that her lover might fall victim to the Indian fury, warned him of Chief Pontiac's plot to infiltrate and destroy Detroit in 1764, and he in turn relayed the warning* to Major Henry Gladwin.

Note: Catherine Cuillerier's father, Antoine, was a friend of Pontiac and it is known that the Chief held at least one council in the Cuillerier home.

* Wacousta is also credited with having given the warning and, of course, both may have.

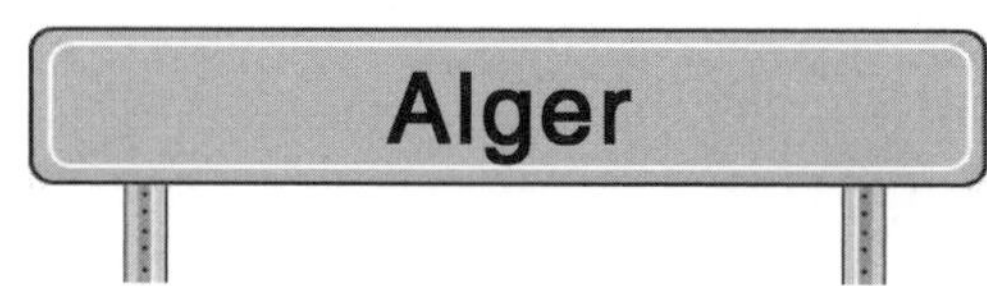

Place Name

This village was platted in 1884 by former Congressman John Newberry (1879-80) and named for co-founder, Russel Alger, who would became governor a year later. (1885-86).

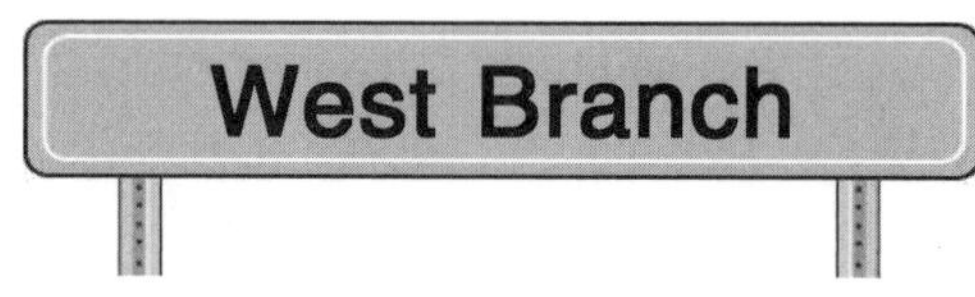

Place Name

The town was named for its location on the west branch of the Rifle River.

Place Name

This town as well as the county were named for a county in Ireland.

Place Name

Grayling was named for the grayling trout, which was fished out of existence here. The trout were found in the Au Sable River, which flows through town enroute to Lake Huron.

Historical Significance

In the 1800s, natural resources were thought to be endless. There were so many trees and so many fish that there would always be enough. Anglers would throw hundreds of fish ashore and take home the best. Over-fishing and over-lumbering destroyed spawning beds and the grayling disappeared. The Au Sable is still here, however, and today's fishermen are a bit more careful (and more regulated) in their fishing.

With the Au Sable flowing to Lake Huron and the Manistee River just a mile away flowing west to Lake Michigan, Grayling's location was ideal for the shipping of furs and timber. It also became a transportation hub when the railroad came to town.

When the timber was gone, Grayling developed its natural beauty and resources into one of Michigan's top outdoor recreation areas.

The Au Sable River Canoe Marathon requires 55,000 paddle strokes (or thereabouts).

General Trivia

The Au Sable River Canoe Marathon is run each June from Grayling to Oscoda on Lake Huron. It requires more than 14 hours to complete.

Local Landmark

One of Michigan's largest remaining stands of virgin white pine harbors the Hartwick Pines Lumbering Museum. Visitors can tour a forest visitor center and lumber-camp log buildings. The loggers, river men, mill hands and lumber barons who made Michigan the leader in sawed lumber production all have their stories told here. A paved trail leads to the three hundred-year-old Monarch Pine, one of the few remaining examples of the ancient forests that disappeared by the 20th century.

Place Name

This village began as a wooding-up stop on the Mackinaw division of the Michigan central Railroad known as Forest. The name was eventually changed in honor of pioneer settler Frederic Barker.

Gaylord

Place Name

With the arrival of the Jackson, Lansing and Saginaw Railroad in the area in 1874, the town was named for A.S. Gaylord, an attorney for the road.

General Trivia

Looking for a touch of Switzerland in Michigan? This is where you'll find it. Pontresina, Switzerland is a sister city to Gaylord and the town truly does have the feel of an Alpine village. An annual snowfall of 150 inches certainly helps!

Gaylord actually has more citizens of Polish and German descent than Swiss. But all of the community joins in to celebrate Alpenfest every July. They wear traditional garb, eat Swiss food and play Swiss games.

Local Landmark

The largest free-range herd of elk east of the Mississippi is in the Gaylord area. They were reintroduced here in 1918, after disappearing from the Lower Peninsula in the 1870s.

Place Name

The town was settled and given the name of the New York Vanderbilt family who owned a good portion of the land in the area.

Place Name

This town takes the name of the state animal, the wolverine.

Place Name

This small town is named for the river which runs nearby. Indians used the river, now crossed by I-75, to avoid the Mackinac Straits.

Local Landmark

The cross created by sculpture Marshal Fredericks stands 55-feet high and 22-feet across. Cast in Norway, it is made of California redwood and bronze and weighs in at seven tons. It is part of a 13-acre site which is dedicated to Kateri Tekakwitha, who some believe may become the first American Indian saint.

Indian River is home to the world's largest crucifix.

Place Name

This town was founded by officials of the Michigan Central Railroad who wanted to see a resort located on the shores of Mullett Lake. Hotel owner H.H. Pike named the new town after Potawattomi Chief Topinabee, or: "Great Bear Heart."

Chief Topinabee, signed a treaty giving white men the site of Fort Dearborn, which is now Chicago.

Historical Significance

The straits of Mackinac separate Michigan's upper and lower peninsulas, and also serve as an intersection for Lakes Michigan and Huron. This natural water highway made an ideal place for the area's first inhabitants, American Indians, to find the fish and game they needed to sustain them.

The first Europeans to come to the straits were French explorers in 1634. They were looking for a water route to the Orient, but instead they found riches here in the hides of furs.

In 1715 the French built Fort Michilimackinac to help them expand their fur trade, as well as to barter with the native peoples and protect their territory from other European countries.

The French presence was significant here. But their fortunes were about to turn. The British won the French and Indian War, took control of Canada, and Fort Michilimackinac became theirs.

Fur trade continued at the fort. However, the American Revolution was coming. When it did, the British found the site vulnerable, so Michilimackinac was abandoned in 1781 in favor of the new Fort Mackinac. Located on the cliffs of Mackinac Island, not far from the mainland, the new outpost was easier to defend. With America's victory, Fort Mackinac was taken over by U.S. soldiers in 1786.

War between the United States and the British broke out again in 1812. Fort Mackinac was captured by the Brits in a surprise attack. The Treaty of Ghent, which officially ended The War of 1812, gave the Fort back to the Americans. After the Civil War, the fur trade pretty much came to an end.

Tourism, brought by luxury cruisers and trains, took over as the #1 economic activity of the area and it still is today.

* * * *

Mackinac Bridge is designed to withstand 600-mile-per-hour winds, the upper towers, which soar 552-feet into the sky, can sway as much as 15 feet.

A major boost to the area was the Mackinac Bridge, otherwise known as "Mighty Mac." The idea of a bridge across the Straits of Mackinac was first proposed in 1884.

Until the bridge, the only way to cross the straits was by ferry. The wait was often several hours and the lines sometimes were as long as twenty-three miles.

But "the bridge that couldn't be built" finally was. It took three years of construction and $99 million ($400 million in today's dollars). Stretching for five miles, the bridge permanently brought together the upper and lower peninsulas of Michigan. It is the longest suspension bridge in the United States and third longest in the world.

* * * *

Today around Mackinaw City, visitors can view a reconstructed Colonial Michilimackinac.

The other major park in the area is Mill Creek State Park, which is the oldest 18th-century industrial site in the Great Lakes. A 1790 visionary saw that there would be a need for lumber. He built a water-powered sawmill, blacksmith shop and grist mill.

By the mid-1800s, however, the site had been abandoned and was soon largely forgotten. It wasn't until the 1970s that archaeologists redisovered the site. They continue to explore it today. Visitors to the park can watch the work, as well as see how sawyers of old cut lumber with a pit saw and how the water-powered mill mechanized the cutting.

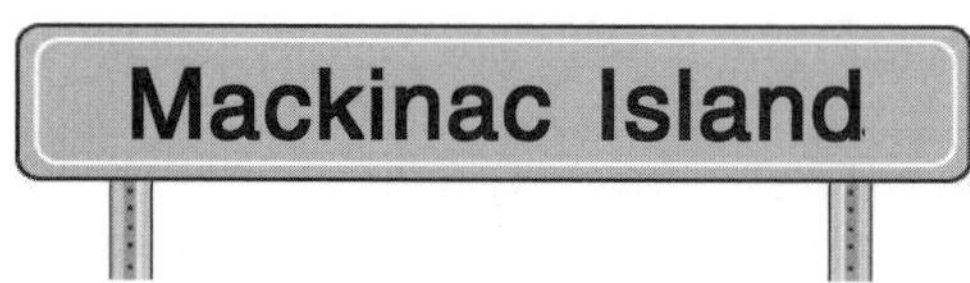

Place Name

Mackinac Island was called the "Great Turtle" by Native Americans, who considered it sacred ground. French fur trappers used it, calling it Michilimackinac, a translation of its Indian name.

And, of course, what sets Mackinac Island apart is that there are no cars on the island. Residents and visitors alike ride bicycles, take horse-drawn buggies -- or they walk.

Historical Significance

A restored replica of the Fort, with its whitewashed exterior, is still an important part of the landscape. It can be seen from many miles away. The fourteen buildings reflect the period and are filled with historic artifacts. Re-enactors bring the history to colorful life, with authentically costumed guides demonstrating musket and cannon firings.

Fort Mackinac was of great importance to both the British and the Americans.

Fort Mackinac was first built by the British in 1780-81. It was not until 1796, thirteen years after the end of the Revolutionary War, that the British relinquished this fort to the Americans. At the outbreak of the War of 1812 the British seized the island and built Fort George. This fort was renamed Fort Holmes by the Americans who reoccupied the island in 1815. Troops garrisoned Fort Mackinac until 1895.

(Historical marker on Mackinac Island)

* * * *

The Treaty of 1836 was one of the earliest attempts to consider the Indian problem in a humanitarian way. The treaty provided for "a dormitory for the Indians visiting the post." The Indian Dormitory building, completed in 1838, was designed by Henry R. Schoolcraft, author of the treaty. For ten years it served as a guest house for Indians, mostly Chippewa, who came to the island to receive their annual allotments. From 1848 to 1867 the building was used for a variety of purposes, including that of a U. S. Customs House. In 1867 it became the Mackinac Island School, serving in this capacity until 1960.

(Historical marker located on Huron Street)

* * * *

During the peak of the fur trade Market Street bustled with activity. Each July and August Indians, traders and trappers by the thousands came here with furs from throughout the Northwest. In 1817, John Jacob Astor's American Fur Co. located its headquarters here. After 1834 the trade moved westward.

(Historical marker located on Market Street)

Furs valued at $3,000,000 went through the Market Street offices in 1822.

Local Landmark

Of course, the most famous of the local landmarks is the Grand Hotel. Built in 1887, the Grand is the largest summer resort in the world, and served as the setting for two movies. "This Time For Keeps" was filmed here in 1947 and starred Esther Williams and Jimmy Durante. "Somewhere in Time" starred Christopher Reeve and Jane Seymour and was filmed here in 1980.

- It takes 500,000 gallons of water to fill the Grand Hotel's swimming pool, which was named for actress Esther Williams.
- This renown hotel features the world largest porch. At 660 feet, the front porch is as long as two football fields.
- More than 105,000 bedding plants (annuals) are used to create the many

The Grand Hotel porch includes 260 boxes with 2,000 geraniums planted with seven tons of potting soil.

gardens on the ground's, along with the one ton of bulbs that are planted each fall, including 24,000 tulips and 3,000 daffodils.

- Five U.S. Presidents have stayed at the Grand Hotel over the years including Clinton, Bush, Ford, Kennedy and Truman.
- One of the hotel's most popular desserts are the Grand Pecan Balls, with over 50,000 consumed each season.

* * * *

The Union Congregational Church, affectionately called Little Stone Church, was established in 1900 by eleven charter members. Local residents and summer visitors donated funds for its construction. The cornerstone was laid on August 2, 1904.

This structure was built of Mackinac Island stones in an eclectic Gothic style. Its handsome stained glass windows, installed in 1914, tell the story of the Protestant movement on the Island.

(Historical market located on Cadott Street)

* * * *

According to tradition, Skull Cave is the cave in which the English fur-trader Alexander Henry hid out during the Indian uprising of 1763. The floor of the cave, he claimed, was covered with human bones, presumably Indian.

(Historical marker located on Garrison Road)

General Trivia

When Alexis St. Martin was accidentally shot in the stomach, Fort Mackinac army surgeon Dr. William Beaumont was called to treat him. While St. Martin had fully recovered except for his abdominal wound wouldn't heal, leaving an opening through which his stomach could be seen. Dr. Beaumont persuaded St. Martin to participate in a number of experiments, observing his digestive system. After a year of observations, Dr. Beaumont reported his findings, many which remain accurate to this today. St. Martin continued to live a normal live until his death at age seventy-six.

Historical Significance

Although still a small community, St. Ignace has never lacked in importance. This was evident from the time of its first explorer, Father Jacques Marquette, who came here in 1671. Partnering with Louis Joliet, Marquette would be one of the first two white explorers of the Mississippi River.

Local Landmark

The importance of Father Marquette to the city's history is honored today with two attractions.

The Father Marquette National Memorial and Museum depicts his extraordinary life through artifacts and displays. Visitors can also explore trails through the 52-acre park which provide views of the nearby Mackinac Bridge.

Also in St. Ignace is Marquette Mission Park and the Museum of Ojibwa Culture. Although not known for sure, it is presumed that Marquette is buried here, where a statue and garden honor his memory.

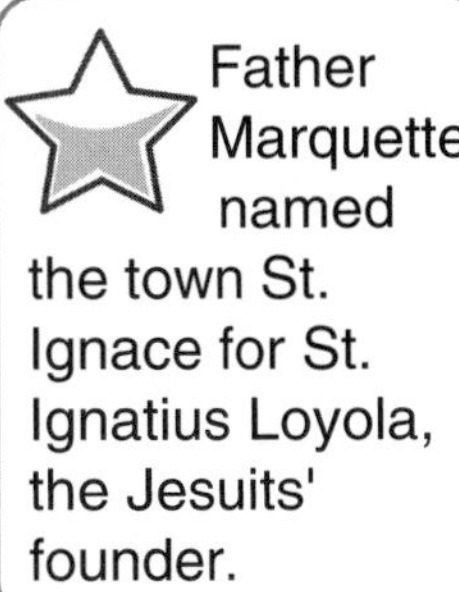

Father Marquette named the town St. Ignace for St. Ignatius Loyola, the Jesuits' founder.

General Trivia

Motor-route newspaper carrier, Otto Hyslop has traveled over 260,000 miles in his 1978 Cherolet pickup truck. Traveling farther on its original six cylinder than any other General Motors Company. The company offered to buy the vehicle from Hyslop and use it in their advertisement, but he declined their offer.

Place Name

The town's name was given when the residents agreed to banish strong drink from the community.

Place Name

The original name of the town in 1833 was Pine River. However, the name wasn't all that original, as a number of other Michigan towns had already claimed it. It wasn't until 1896, however, that the city received its present name of Rudyard.

A general manager for the Baltimore & Ohio Railroad by the name of Fred Underwood was given the assignment of naming villages created by the railroad's expansion. A lover of literature, he renamed Pine River to Rudyard and another U.P. village Kipling. Rudyard Kipling appreciated the honor and wrote a poem for the Michiganders.

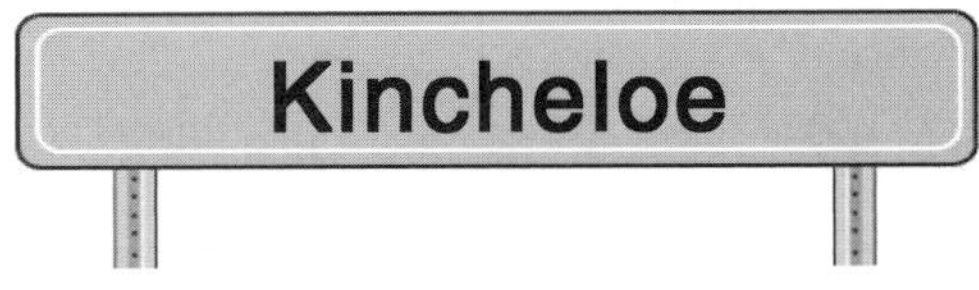

Place Name

This town was founded by the U.S. Army Air Force in 1941 as Kinross Auxiliary Field. In 1947, the Air Force became a separate branch of the services and it became Kinross Air

Force Base. In 1959 it was renamed in honor of Captain Iven Kincheloe, a native of Cassopolis. Kincheloe was a jet ace in the Korean conflict and later a test pilot for the X-2 experimental rocket-powered aircraft. Captain Kincheloe died attempting to eject from a F-104 in July, 1958. He is buried in Arlington National Cemetery.

Place Name

Scottish-immigrants who emigrated here by way of Canada gave the name of Kinross, Scotland to their new home.

Place Name

When the first mission was started, the settlement's original name of Sault du Gastogne was changed to Sault Ste. Marie in honor of the Virgin Mary. The word Sault (pronounced "Soo") means "to jump" and refers to having to jump the St. Mary's River here. At one time treacherous rapids and cascades made the river unnavigable.

Historical Significance

Sault Ste. Marie is the "granddaddy" of Michigan's cities. Not only is it the state's oldest community, but it is the third oldest city in the United States. It was established in 1668.

It sits at a strategically important point, between Lake Huron and Lake Superior. Highway and railroad bridges connect it to its Canadian sister city -- Sault Ste. Marie, Ontario.

First here were the Ojibwa Indians in the 1500s. But incursions of warring tribes from the east, as well as early European settlers, forced the Ojibwa's out.

As in most areas of what would become Michigan, it was the French who came first -- both missionaries and fur traders, arriving in the early 1600s.

The area first came under U.S. control in 1820, after years of competition between the British and French for the fur trade. The Americans built a fort and the area started to grow -- especially when it was discovered that the region was rich in copper and iron.

The problem was how to get these resources out to the rest of the world. There were constant back-ups of goods, due to the rapids in the river. The solution was locks, which allowed ships to pass between the two Great Lakes.

The first two American locks (approximately 5,674 feet long) date to 1853. Constructed of two tandem locks, each were 350 feet long, 70 feet wide and 11 1/2 feet deep, with a life of 9 feet. The locks were completed in two years at a cost of almost one million dollars ($999,802).

> Four locks handle over ninty-five million tons of freight annually.

Local Landmark

Sault Ste. Marie provides other ways of learning about its river heritage and the life that has resulted for those who work the river.

The Valley Camp, a retired Great Lakes freighter, can be toured to see what it was like to live aboard such a vessel. One of the most famous recent disasters on Lake Superior was the loss of the Edmund Fitzgerald in 1975. Two of the ship's lifeboats are exhibited here.

The River of History Museum features life-sized dioramas, depicting the many elements of over 8,000 years of St. Mary's River history.

And rising twenty-one stories above Sault Ste. Marie is The Tower of History. Visitors to the top can get 360-degree views of the American and Canadian cities, the Soo Locks, Lake Superior, and the countryside.

General Trivia

In 1964 a 45-year old, 200-pound lumberjack from Sault Ste. Marie, Tony Calery,left his hometown in a fifteen-foot rowboat and rowed 2,200 miles in seventy-five days to arrive at the New York World's Fair.

INTERSTATE
69

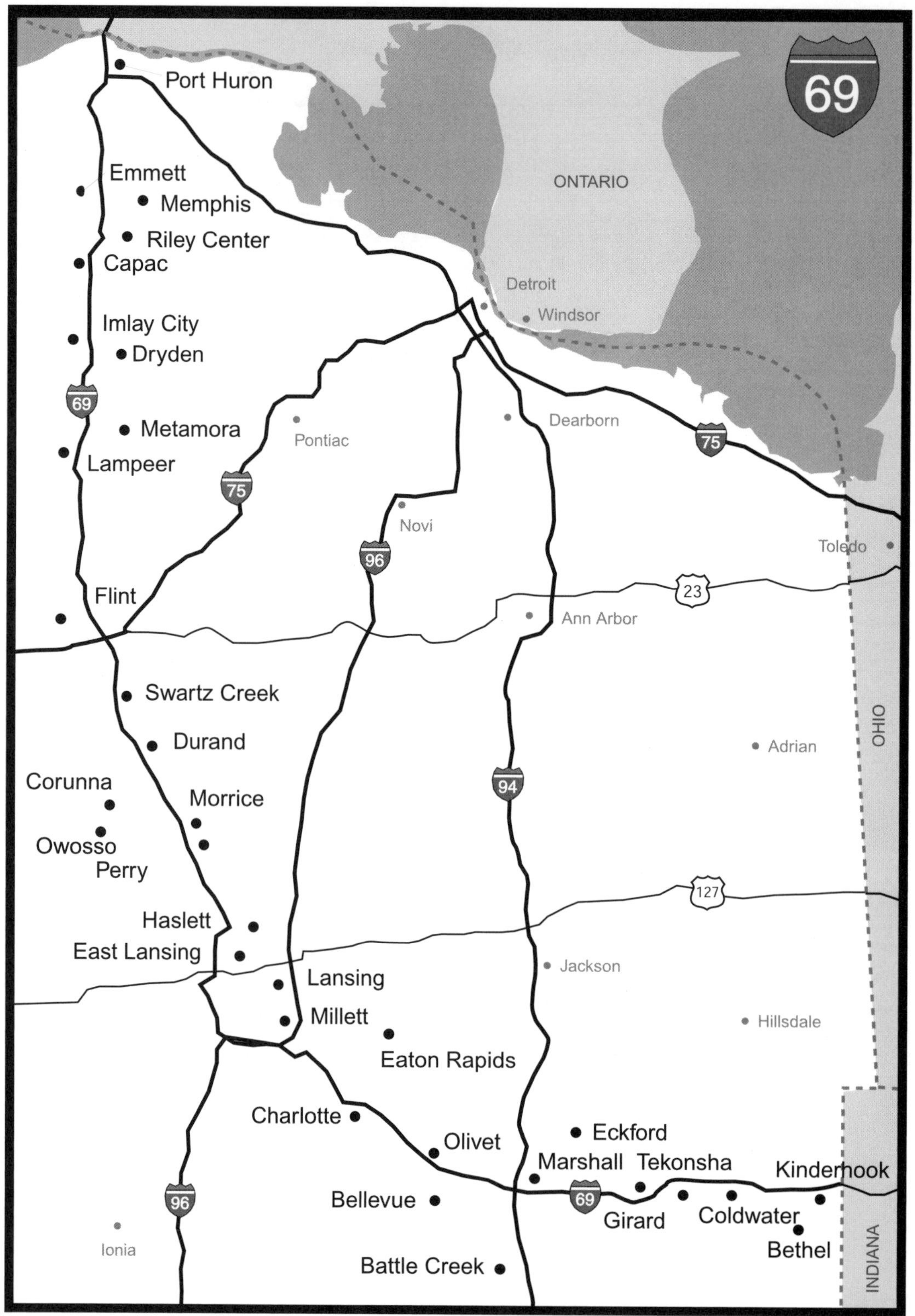
69
Port Huron
ONTARIO
Emmett
Memphis
Riley Center
Capac
Detroit
Windsor
Imlay City
Dryden
69
Metamora
Pontiac
Dearborn
75
Lampeer
75
Novi
96
Toledo
Flint
23
Ann Arbor
Swartz Creek
Durand
Adrian
OHIO
Corunna
Morrice
94
Owosso
Perry
127
Haslett
East Lansing
Jackson
Lansing
Millett
Hillsdale
Eaton Rapids
Charlotte
Eckford
Olivet
Marshall
Tekonsha
Kinderhook
69
96
Bellevue
Girard
Coldwater
Ionia
Bethel
INDIANA
Battle Creek

Place Name

The towns name honors the birthplace of President Martin Van Buren, Kinderhook, New York.

Place Name

For some unknown reason, the town's name was changed from Elizabeth to Bethel, the Old Testament Hebrew word for House of the Lord.

Place Name

The Potawatomi Indians ceded Coldwater Prairie to the United States in 1827. The Indians called it "Chuck-sew-ya-bish," meaning "cold spring water." (Historical marker located at intersection of US 12 and US 27)

Local Landmark

It was never a very exciting or bustling place, but residents were justly proud of its Tibbits Opera House. The theatre, built in 1882, was acclaimed for the quality of its acoustics and state-of-the-art backstage equipment by the performers who played here.

Prominent People

Harriet Quimby, was the first woman in the United States, and the second in the world to obtain a pilot's license.

Harriet Quimby was born in the Coldwater area on May 11, 1875 to Ursala (Cook) and William Quimby. The Quimby family moved to Arroyo Grande, California, in 1884, then to San Francisco.

In 1902, Harriet became a journalist for the San Francisco Dramatic Review. She later wrote features for the San Francisco Chronicle and worked for the Call-Bulletin. In 1903 she went to New York City as a drama critic and a feature writer for Leslie's Weekly.

At the Belmont Park Aviation Meet in October 1910 she became fascinated with flying. At the Hotel Astor, mingling with the theatre crowd, she met John Moisant, who was celebrating his victory at the meet.

She soon began taking lessons at the Moisant School of Aviation in Mineola, New York. She later toured the United States, Mexico and Europe with the Moisant Fliers.

* * * *

On April 16, 1912, Quimby became the first woman to cross the English Channel, flying from the Cliffs of Dover to Hardelot, France. She returned in triumph to the United States after being feted in Europe.

In June, she shipped her plane to Boston so that she could fly in the Harvard-Boston Aviation Meet. On July 1 she flew the manager of the meet, William A.P. Willard, around the Boston Light. During the flight, her Berliot plane was caught in turbulent air and nose-dived, plummeting both Willard and Quimby to their deaths in Dorchester Bay.

(Historical marker located at Branch County Memorial Airport)

General Trivia

One of the more amusing pieces of Coldwater's history made the town the "butt" of many jokes. A local man stole a cow bell. Upon being found guilty, he was sentenced to bend over a log and allow every person who attended the sentencing to whack him on his backside. The town's citizens couldn't ignore such an unusual opportunity. Most of them turned out to cheerfully administer the punishment with a board that was four feet long by six inches wide. The defendant, taking affront to this activity, sued his fellow citizens who had "whacked" him. The Cow Bell Suit was moved from court to court until it finally disappeared from the legal records. The defendant would feel right at home in today's litigious society.

Place Name

This town was named for American philanthropist, Stephen Girard. His influence was evident in shipping, construction, banking, and even in politics, later into coal mining and railroads.

Place Name

This village was named for Tekon-qua-sha, a local Pottawattomi chief who may be buried in the area.

Place Name

A Rochester, New York surveyor by the name of Oshea Wilder platted the town that he would name for Henry Eckford, a friend he met while traveling in England.

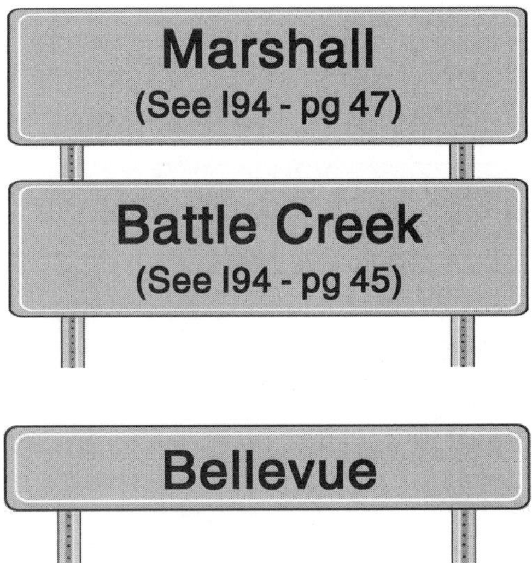

General Trivia

Twenty-five year old Billy Page, appeared on NBC's television show Real People. The unemployed handyman mimiced perfectly a fire and ambulance siren.

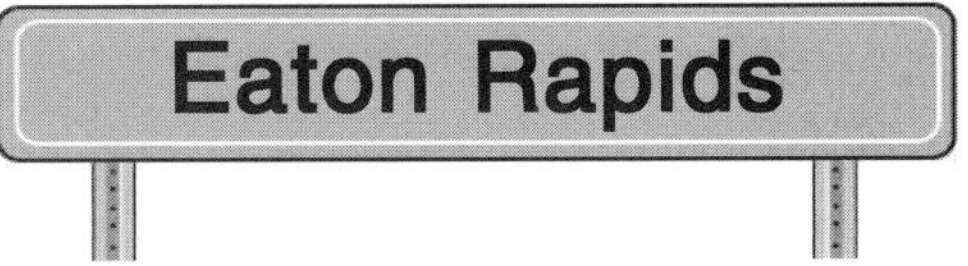

Place Name

Reverend John Shipherd, the founder of Ohio's Oberlin College, led a colony of 39 people westward intending to start a Congregational college and community in the Delta valley. Unfortunately the group became lost in the wilderness and arrived here instead. Believing it was divine intervention, they remained in the area they would name after Mount Olive of the Bible.

Eaton Rapids

Prominent People

Civil War governor Austin Blair (1818-1894) came to Jackson, Michigan, from New York in 1841. In 1842 he moved his law practice to Eaton Rapids. At that time the area was made up mostly of farmers, and Blair was paid for his services with produce and firewood. He lived in a frame house that once stood near this site. In 1843, while a resident of this town, he was elected Eaton County clerk. Poverty and the deaths of his infant daughter and his wife led him to resign as county clerk and return to Jackson.

This town gets it name from its location on the Grand River and from the county, which was named after John Eaton, President Andrew's secretary of war.

* * * *

Austin Blair began his political career in 1842 as Eaton County clerk. In 1846 he was elected to the Michigan House of Representatives. He was selected as Jackson County prosecutor in 1852 and from 1855 to 1856 he served in the state senate.

In 1861 Blair became governor of Michigan, a post he held for two terms. While in office he personally raised about $100,000 to equip the 1st Michigan Volunteer Infantry Regiment. He represented Michigan as a U.S. congressman from 1867 to 1873 and was a University of Michigan regent from 1882 to 1890.

(Historical marker located on East Main Street)

Place Name

Edmond Bostwick, H.I. Lawrence, Townsend Harris and Francis Cochran developed the village they would name for Mr. Bostwick's wife, Charlotte.

Place Name

The town was established on land around coal and clay beds of S.E. Millett.

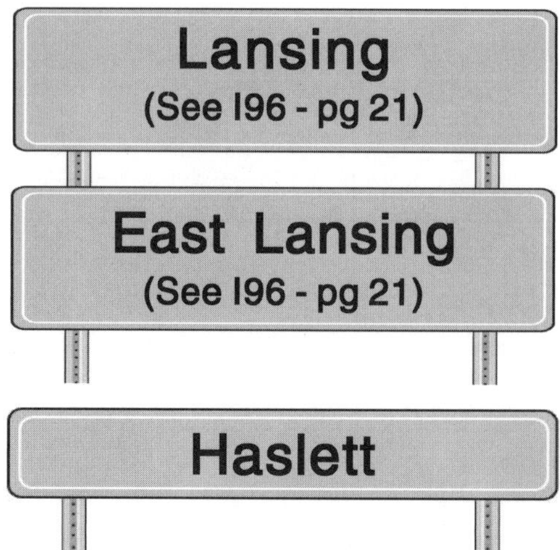

Place Name

The town was started by James Haslett as a Spiritualist summer camp. He had visions of making it their national headquarters but the program ended with his death.

Place Name

Village named for Oliver Hazard Perry, a American naval commander who wrote the famous report, "We have met the enemy and they are ours..." after the defeat of the British at the Battle of Lake Erie.

Place Name

Scottish immigrants from Aberdeenshire, William Morrice founded this community and later joined by his brothers John, George and Alexander.

Prominent People

Former governor of New York, Thomas Dewey was born in Owosso. Dewey was also a two-time Republican presidential nominee, losing to Franklin Roosevelt's and Harry Truman.

The town was named in honor of Chief Wasso.

Place Name

This town was originally settled in the early 1840s by a group of businessmen called the Shiawassee County Seat Company. Andrew Mack, a member of the group, named this town after Corunna, Spain, after traveling there to purchase sheep.

Place Name

The town is named for the congressman from the 6th district, George Durand.

Historical Significance

If there is one word which sums up the history of Durand, it would be railroading. The economy of this town was fueled by the railroads in the 1870s.

By the start of the twentieth century, Durand was known as Michigan's largest railroad center outside of Detroit. Up to forty-two passenger trains, twenty-two mail trains and seventy-eight freight trains passed through Durand daily.

Its Union Station served nearly 3000 passengers every day -- almost as many people as lived in the community at the time.

Local Landmark

At the turn of the century, railroad depots were often the main focal point for a town and were often the largest structure there.

Durand's Grand Trunk Railroad Depot, known as Durand Union Station, was built in 1903. Today it is one of America's most photographed stations. Its architecture is a unique Chateau Romanesque design. It captures the vibrant history of American railroading at its peak.

The station is now home to the State Railroad History Museum, a facility which interprets Michigan's rich railroad lore. Exhibits are changed throughout the year. They depict the colorful heritage of the men who built and operated the railroads, as well as how trains contributed to the growth of the lumber, mining, agricultural and manufacturing industries of Michigan. Railroading historians, geneaologists or just plain old train buffs will especially treasure the Museum Information Center and Archives. It features photographs, ledgers, technical information, union materials and many other documents of great interest to researchers.

Place Name

German immigrant Adam Miller founded the town that was named for the small Swartz Creek which flowed nearby. Swartz is a German word for black.

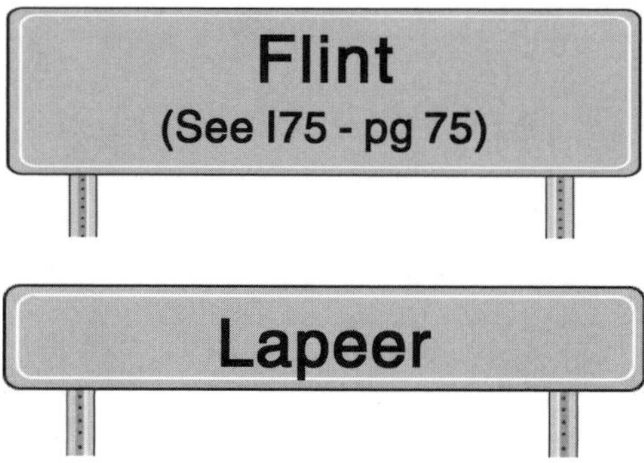

Place Name

Early French traders traveling in the area noticed the rocky river bed and gave the name French word (La Pierre*) for stone, to the village which developed where Alvin Hart and his family settled. Note: Lapeer is the Americanized word.

Place Name

Metamora, an indian name meaning among the hills. It is also the name of an Indian hero, a son of Massosoit.

Massasoit,a chief of the Wampanoag tribe,also known as Ousamequin, or "yellow feather," was born about 1590 in the village of Pokanoket, which was near the present-day Bristol, Rhode Island.

He was one of the most powerful native rulers of New England. In 1621 Massasoit went to Plymouth to sign a treaty with the Pilgrims, which he faithfully observed until his death. Because of this agreement, the Wampanoag and Pilgrims lived in peaceful coexistence including during the Pequot War of 1636.

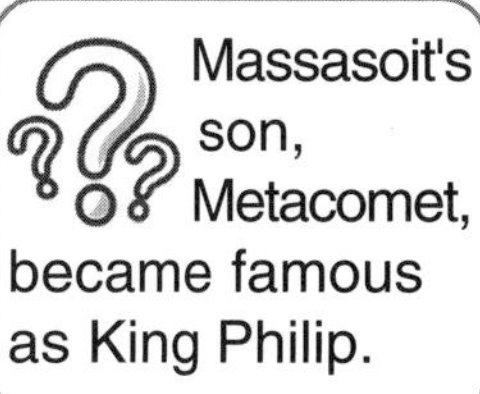

Massasoit's son, Metacomet, became famous as King Philip.

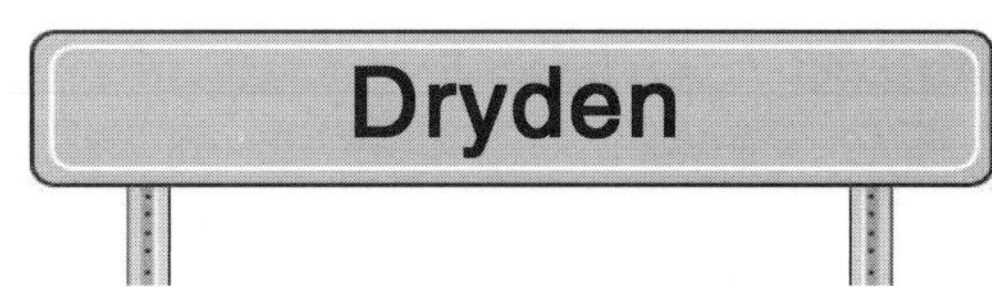

Place Name

Sanford Kendrick changed the name of the town known as Lamb's Corner (named after John Lamb, one of the first owners of the area) to Dryden, in honor of the English poet and dramatist John Dryden, who would dominate literary efforts of The Restoration.

John Dryden died in London on May 12, 1700, and was buried in Westminster Abbey next to Chaucer. He left behind almost 30 works for the stage as well as a major critical study (An Essay on Dramatic Poesy) and a number of translations including the works of Virgil.

Place Name

Connecticut capitalist, William Imlay purchased the pine forest land in the area in 1836. When the town was organized in 1850 it was named for him.

Place Name

George Funstand and the Judge DeWitt Walker leading a group from Romeo founded and platted the city named by the Honorable Walker after Huayna Capac, head of a Peruvian line of Inca Indian emperors. (d. 1527) However, local historians disagree and feel that it was Manco Capac, the first Inca ruler, that gave birth to Capac's name.

Prominent People

Capac was the hometown of Preston Thomas Tucker, the automotive industry innovator, before he made Ypsilanti his hometown where he had a dream for a new kind of car.

Anticipating World War II, Tucker develops a light mechanized bullet-proof vehicle for the army. Unfortunately it was rejected because it was considered "too fast." However the military did like his turret.

After the war, Tucker saw his chance to accomplish his dream of building a new kind of car. It would have innovations such as safety glass, seat belts, disk breaks, and (his personal favorite feature) a rear-mounted engine. He sold the idea to the whole country-even before his prototype was built.

Place Name

John Riley, for whom the town was named, was a half-breed Chippewa Indian whose father purchased land and gave John a life time lease on it for only six cents a year.

Place Name

This township was named for the Irish patriot, Robert Emmett.

Irish patriot, Robert Emmett lead an armed rebellion against Dublin, Ireland, in 1803. Before reaching the castle his small band of men was dispersed by British troops. Emmet was captured, convicted of treason, and hanged.

Emmet became a hero of Irish nationalists, largely on the basis of his stirring speech from the scaffold.

"Let no man write my epitaph...When my country takes her place among the nations of the earth, then, and not till then let my epitaph be written."

INTERSTATE
196

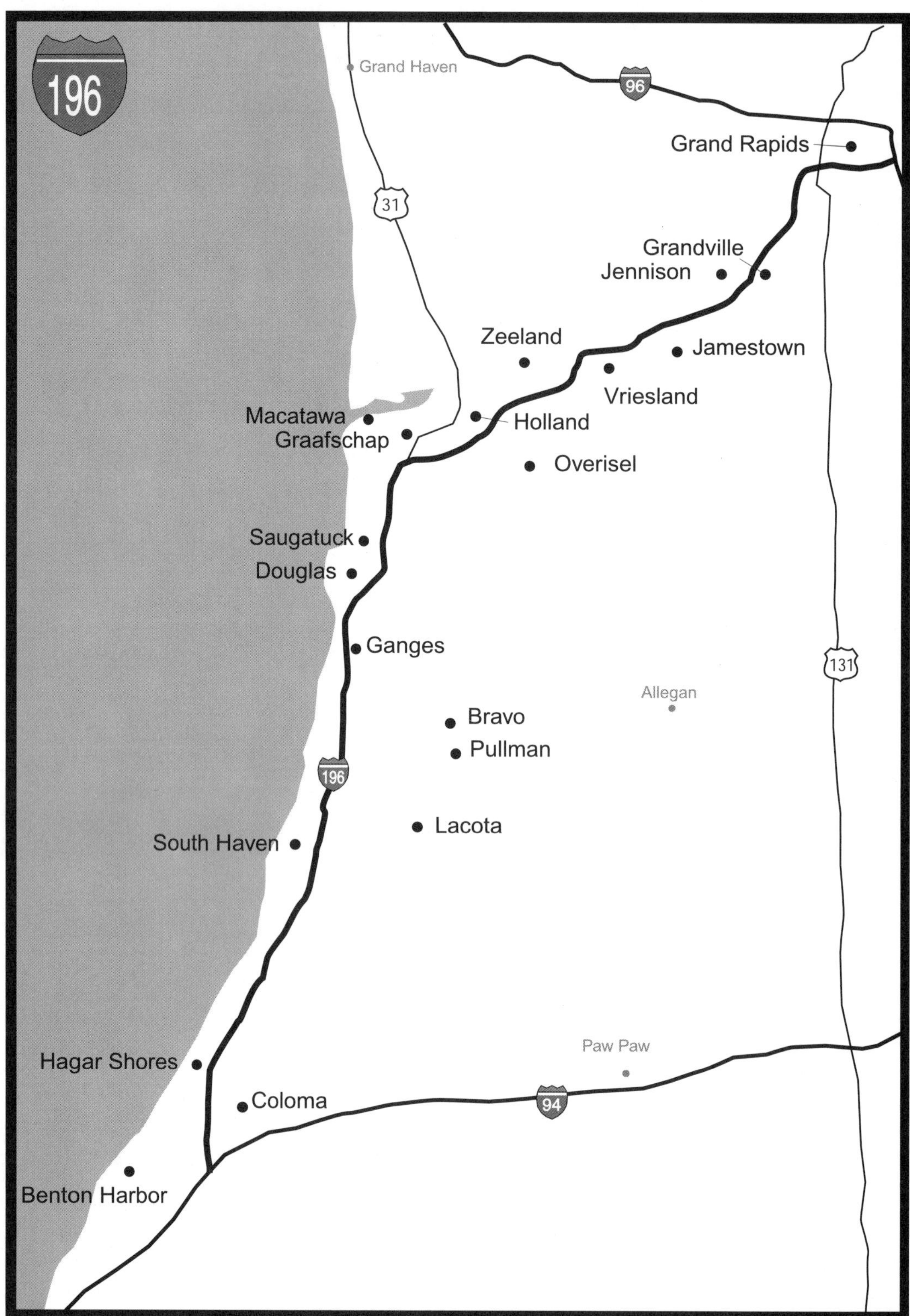
196
Grand Haven
96
Grand Rapids
31
Grandville
Jennison
Zeeland
Jamestown
Vriesland
Macatawa
Graafschap
Holland
Overisel
Saugatuck
Douglas
Ganges
131
Allegan
Bravo
Pullman
196
Lacota
South Haven
Paw Paw
Hagar Shores
Coloma
94
Benton Harbor

Coloma

Place Name

When shingle maker, Stephen Gilson came to the area from Chataqua, New York, the village was known as Dickerville because since money was scarce local business people had to dicker or barter for goods and services. The name was later changed to Coloma, after the Gilson hometown in California.

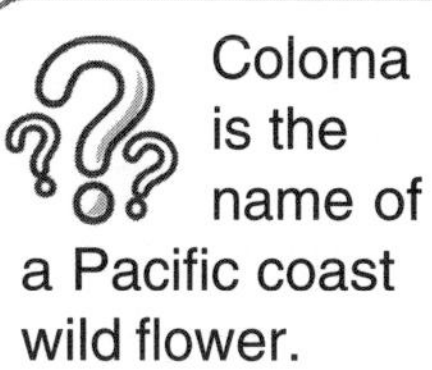

Coloma is the name of a Pacific coast wild flower.

Hagar Shores

Place Name

Established as a summer resort community, the town's suggested name of Lake Michigan Beach was rejected by the post office.

By a vote of the citizens it was named Hagar Shores for its location on Hagar Road and for its boundary along the Lake Michigan shoreline.

South Haven

Place Name

South Haven was named because it is south of Grand Haven.

Historical Significance

Jay R. Monroe settled the town in 1831. A sawmill was built by Joseph Sturgis in 1850. Not long after, A.S. Dyckman purchased the mill and started to really promote the town. He is credited with being the true father of the town.

Local Landmark

The South Haven Light has been welcoming travelers for over 125 years. The original wooden tower was built in 1872. It was reconstructed of steel in 1903. Today it is 12 feet in diameter at the base and stands 35 feet tall.

The adjacent pier has gone through a number of changes through the years. The first pier was, naturally, made of wood. It started at a length of 300 feet and was eventually extended to 700 feet. A steel elevated walkway of 800 feet was built in 1925. The current concrete pier, which runs 1200 feet, was constructed in 1940.

General Trivia

Redhaven was the first red-skinned commercial peach variety. It is now the most widely planted freestone peach variety in the world.

South Haven is "the blueberry capital of the world." The fruit is celebrated each August with the National Blueberry Festival. There's a parade, entertainment, and lots of yummy treats made with blueberries. The picking season runs from July to September and the blueberries cover acres upon acres.

But blueberries are not the only favorite fruit of the commercial growers in the area.

The Haven peach varieties were developed here by Michigan State University's South Haven Experiment Station, under the direction of Professor Stanley Johnston.

From 1924 to 1963, eight yellow-fleshed freestone varieties were selected from more than twenty-one thousand cross-bred seedlings. They were named Halehaven, Kalhaven, Redhaven, Fairhaven, Sunhaven, Richhaven, Glohaven and Cresthaven.

Haven peaches have provided an orderly supply of high quality peaches extending over a seven-week period. Prior to the development of Haven peaches, harvests had been restricted to a three-week period.

(Historical marker located on St. Joseph Street)

Place Name

The town's name was suggested by V.D. Dilley for the chief character of a novel his father, Varnum Dilley, was reading. Lacota was an Indian maiden.

Place Name

This town was named for George Pullman, known as the inventor of the railroad sleeping car. Pullman originally developed it to transport the dead body of Abraham Lincoln.

Place Name

Named for the accolades applauding the early pioneers spirit in establishing the settlement here in the wilderness.

Place Name

Named by a state legislaturer from Otsego, Dr. Joseph Coates, after the holy river of India.

Place Name

There are two explanations on where the town's name originates. Founded by Jonathan Wade, one explanation given by his son-in-law Colonel Fred May suggest the name was given after the town of Douglas, on the Isle of Man, the Mays ancestors homeland. Fred Wade, Jonathan's nephew, says that he recalls the name given for the American statesman, Stephen Douglas.

Historical Significance

The Ottawa Indians also were drawn here. It has a special natural beauty, nestled in beautiful woodlands at the mouth of the Kalamazoo River. For centuries it was a popular area for both fishing and trading villages.

Things became more formalized in the 1830's when the local fur traders built a sawmill and started an actual town.

Most of the lumber used to rebuild Chicago after the 1871 fire came out of the Saugatuck area.

The area's economy was severely affected by the "bust" of the timber economy. The nearby village of Singapore totally disappeared.

The trees had protected the village from Lake Michigan's winds. Without the trees, blowing sands covered up the village.

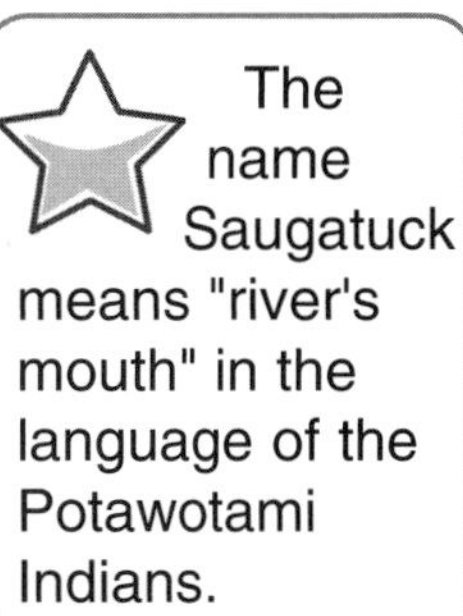

The name Saugatuck means "river's mouth" in the language of the Potawotami Indians.

Saugatuck rebounded somewhat when commercial fishing and boat-building became important in the late 19th century.

The railroads, however, bypassed Saugatuck, which has turned out to be a blessing. Saugatuck has maintained a charming, non-industrialized look, somewhat like towns in New England.

And it found new sources of life. In 1914 the Art Institute of Chicago founded an art colony here. It is located on the Ox-Bow lagoon between Saugatuck and Big Lake. The artists had been inspired by tourists who had returned to Chicago and raved about a quaint town on Lake Michigan. So the artists started coming, looking for a quiet place to create. Saugatuck became Michigan's "art coast".

The former home of gangster Al Capone is located in the area.

Local Landmark

One of the last of the Great Lakes steamships is located here. The SS Kewatin was so large that it had to be cut in half to get through the channel that links the Kalamazoo River and Lake Michigan.

Place Name

When members of the Dutch Reform Church organized this village, it was given the name Graasschap. This name refers to regions in their homeland of Hanover and the Netherland where small principalities were ruled by graafs, otherwise called counts, whose districts were known as graafschaps.

Place Name

The town's name is an Ottawa word for black. A description given to the dark color of Lake Macatawan.

Place Name

Named for Rotterdam, Holland the fatherland of the areas first settlers.

Historical Significance

The town started as a refuge for religious freedom by a group who came here in 1847 from Rotterdam, Holland. They were led by Rev. Albertus Christian Van Raalte. He envisioned

an American colony modeled after his homeland, where people could build new lives. Van Raalte arrived here in the middle of winter with sixty followers and knew that he had found the place. Twenty years later Holland was incorporated as a city.

The year 1871 was a pivotal one for Holland. Two railroads fueled economic growth when they announced that they would extend their lines to the city. But the year brought disaster as well. Strong winds off of Lake Michigan fueled a brush fire that all but destroyed the city. However, the Dutch are known as a persistent and industrious people. Like a phoenix, Holland was rebuilt from its ashes.

The city continued to grow and is unique in having had its very own municipal sailing ship. The A.E. Knickerbocker traveled between Holland and Chicago, transporting goods. That Dutch industriousness was also crucial when the federal government refused to build a shipping channel linking Lake Michigan and Lake Macatawa. The people just built it themselves.

Right before the Great Depression hit, Holland was a prosperous, growing community, with its population still ninety per cent Dutch.

Local Landmark

Today visitors come here for the Dutch atmosphere and look which permeates the town. The centerpiece is the "DeZwaan" (The Swan), the only working Dutch windmill in the United States. Located on Windmill Island, it is more than 275 years old and stands twelve stories high. The sails span eighty feet and the mill cranks out flour that is sold within Windmill Island Municipal Park.

Other sites on the Island are the Post House Museum, housed in a replica of a 14th-century Dutch wayside inn; "Little Netherlands", a miniature Dutch village; and a carousel.

DeZwaan was the last windmill ever to leave the Netherlands, as they are now considered historic monuments.

* * * *

The most popular time for visitors is during tulip time in the spring. The Veldheer Tulip Gardens come to life in a mosaic of color and beauty. More than one hundred varieties of tulips and other flowers can be seen among a setting of windmills, drawbridges and canals. It gives people the feel of being in The Netherlands.

Artisans in the adjoining DeKlomp Wooden Shoe demonstrate the art of carving wooden shoes. Known as klompen, this peculiar wooden footgear is well suited to the soggy soil of the Netherlands. Not only do these shoes keep the farmers feet warm and dry, but when he comes inside, it is a simple matter to step right out of them, keeping the house clean.

Artists mold, hand-paint and glaze delftware in the old fashioned manner at the Delft Factory. See the art of painting the beautiful blue and white delft china.

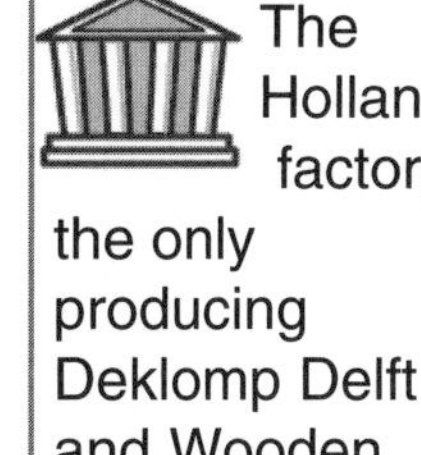

The Holland factory is the only producing Deklomp Delft and Wooden Shoe Factory in the United States!

* * * *

Klompen Wijsheid (Wooden Shoe Wisdom)

- Put your klompen on backwards before advising your friend where to fish or whom to marry. A klomp carved from green wood dries without cracking - a child disciplined while young grows up even-tempered.
- Marriage is like new klompen, one must learn to walk in them.
- Should a child address you in hard words, apply a klomp to his soft parts.
- A man without a wife walks but one klomp.
- Father, tuck your temper in a klomp outside the door, give your family tenderness and they'll ask for little more.

General Trivia

The idea of Tulip Time was introduced at a meeting of the Women's Literary Club in 1927. Miss Lida Rogers, a biology teacher at Holland High School, suggested that because of Holland's many ties with the Netherlands, it should adopt the tulip as its flower and set aside a day or days for a festival. The next year the city funded the importing of 100,000 tulip bulbs from Holland.

Tulip Day was celebrated in 1929 and the next year the festival began. Today it is ranked as the country's 5th largest annual festival attracting 500,000 visitors from around the world during a ten-day period in mid-May.

Streets are scrubbed in the traditional Dutch way and there are bands, parades and Klompen dancers, all set against the backdrop of millions of blooming tulips.

Industry

The only location that produces Life Saver candy in the world is in Holland, Michigan.

Over 120 million rolls of Life Saver mints are made each year at the Holland plant.

Invented in 1913, by a small chocolate maker from Cleveland, Ohio. Clarence Crane invented Life Savers as a "summer candy" as an alternative to chocolate, which melted in the warm summer months. Since the mints looked like miniature life preservers, he called them Life Savers.

Mr. Edward Nobel, an advertising salesman, was so impressed with the taste, clever shape, name and package of the Lifesaver that he tried to convince Mr. Crane to do more in the way of promotion- but, he refused. Mr. Crane's real love was chocolate. Instead Mr. Crane sold the mint candy idea to Mr. Noble for $2,900.

Noble created tin-foil wrappers to keep the mints fresh, instead of cardboard rolls. Pep-O-Mint was the first Life Saver flavor. Since then, many different flavors of Life Savers have been produced. The five-flavor roll first appeared in 1935.

* * * *

The Heinz plant located on the southern shore of Lake Macatawa processes over 1 million pounds of pickles per day during the green season.

* * * *

Squirt was the first soft-drink in the United States sweetened only by aspartame. The Holland based company replaced saccharin in 1983, which has been linked to cancer, with the more expensive artificial sweetener.

Place Name

Dutch settlers from the province of Overisel, Holland established their colony here in 1848.

Place Name

Zeeland is name for the first colonists hometown province in the Netherland.

Industry

Howard Miller was schooled in the fine art of clockmaking by his father, Herman, in the Black Forest region of Germany. Howard developed into a visionary whose keen sense of innovation spawned a tradition of excellence that has been uncompromised through three generations.

While the early years focused on the manufacture of chiming wall and mantel clocks, Howard Miller also produced trend-setting avant garde clocks that stand today in collectors' galleries.

During World War II, Howard Miller joined forces with the Ford Motor Co. to produce anti-aircraft covers.

Zeeland is home to Howard Miller Clocks, the nation's largest clockmaker.

In the 1960s, the company turned its attention to grandfather clocks, eventually earning the company the title of "World's Largest Grandfather Clock Manufacturer."

Place Name

Town is named for the Netherland province of Friesland.

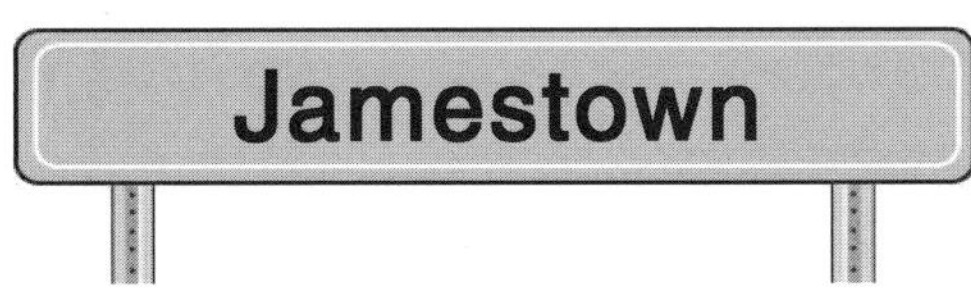

Place Name

Town named for Eben James, who partnered with Cornelius Ruggles to establish what later became the site of the Manistique Pulp and Paper Company.

Place Name

This town was named for the twin brothers Luman and Lucius Jenison, the founders of a large grist mill.

Place Name

Located in Kent County, Grandville was first settled in 1832 by Luther Lincoln. He named the town by describing its location on the Grand River.

General Trivia

Make sure to keep your eyes open and your wits about you while traveling near Grandville, because money has been known to fall from the sky! Two Holland men stole $2,000 at knifepoint from a convenience store and approached a police roadblock on I-96 near Grandville on November 1, 1984. As they approached, they threw the cash out of the car window.

Many fortunate passers-by stopped their vehicles and stuffed the bills into their socks, pants, and coats. The robbers then eased through the blockade. One suspicious motorist, however, reported the strange incident to the police, and the robbers were caught. However, only $587 of the money was recovered.

HIGHWAY
131

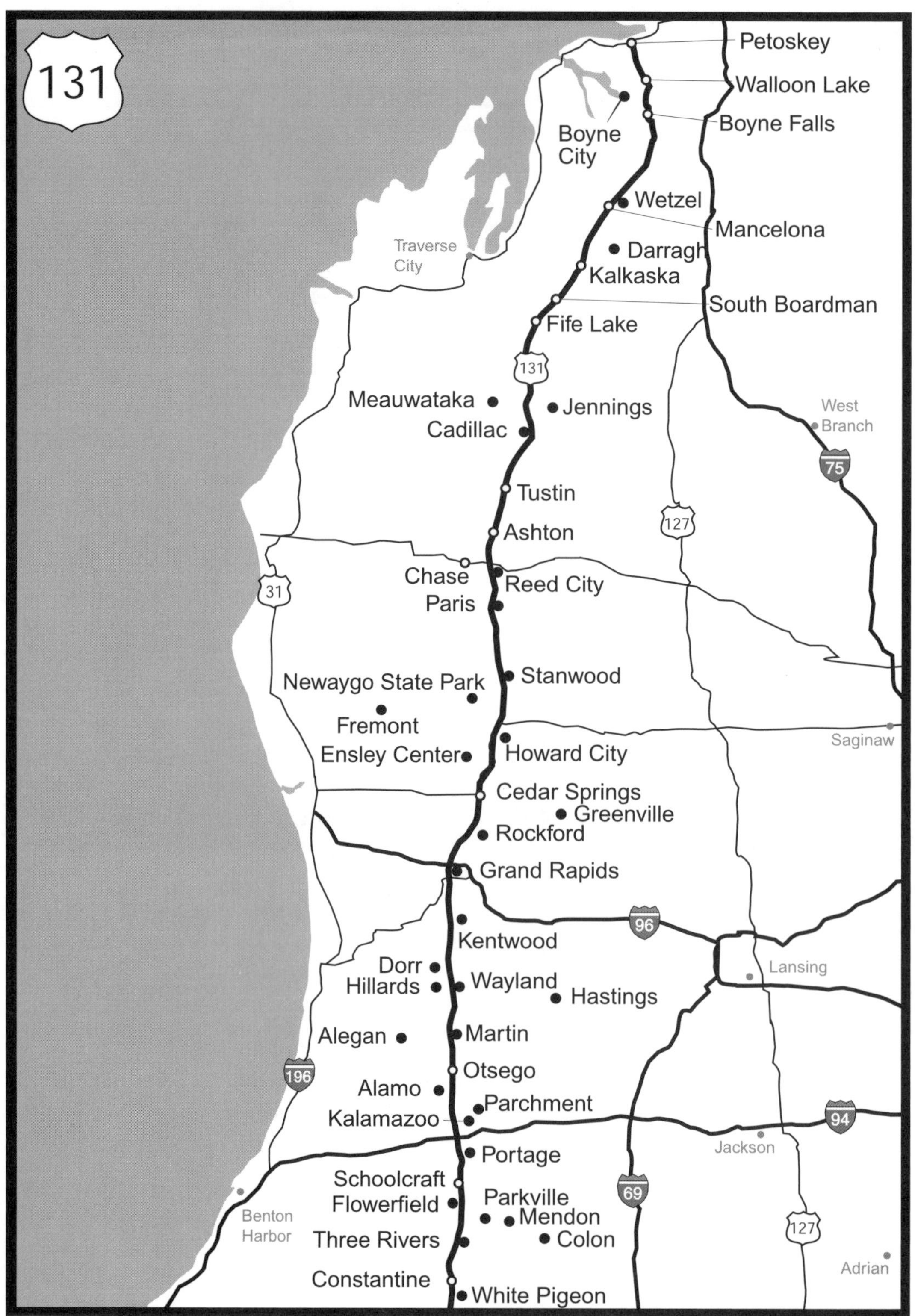

131
Petoskey
Walloon Lake
Boyne Falls
Boyne City
Wetzel
Mancelona
Darragh
Traverse City
Kalkaska
South Boardman
Fife Lake
131
Meauwataka
Jennings
Cadillac
West Branch
75
Tustin
127
Ashton
Chase
Reed City
31
Paris
Stanwood
Newaygo State Park
Fremont
Saginaw
Ensley Center
Howard City
Cedar Springs
Greenville
Rockford
Grand Rapids
96
Kentwood
Lansing
Dorr
Hillards
Wayland
Hastings
Alegan
Martin
196
Otsego
Alamo
Parchment
Kalamazoo
94
Portage
Jackson
Schoolcraft
Parkville
Flowerfield
Mendon
69
Benton Harbor
127
Three Rivers
Colon
Constantine
Adrian
White Pigeon

White Pigeon

Place Name

Named in honor of Chief White Pigeon, "Wahbememe", the Indian chief who gave his life to save the settlement in 1830.

Place Name

Local businessman and lawyer, Niles Smith, changed the Meek's Mill (named in honor of Judge William Meeks) to that honoring Constantine the Great. Constantine was the first Roman emperor to convert to Christianity.

Place Name

John Bowman named the town Three Rivers because it sits at the confluence of the St. Joseph, Portage and Rocky Rivers.

Three Rivers has enjoyed a diverse economy during its history. In earlier days, it was a major hub for the fur industry. Today much of its manufacturing is auto related.

Local Landmark

Langley Covered Bridge was constructed in 1887 and is one of the few remaining in Michigan. With three spans totaling 282 feet in length, it is also Michigan's longest.

* * * *

Little River Railroad restored, preserved and operated historic railway cars such as Steam locomotive No. 110 is a 4-6-2 Pacific. It was custom built in 1911 by the Baldwin Locomotive Works for the Little River Railroad in Townsend, Tennessee. It is the only one of its kind.

Prominent People

Television newscaster Charles Collingwood comes from Three Rivers. CBS correspondent Charles Collingwood played a leading role in organizing the program, "A Tour of the White House with Mrs. John F. Kennedy." Three out of four television viewers tuned in on February 14, 1962 to watch the documentary.

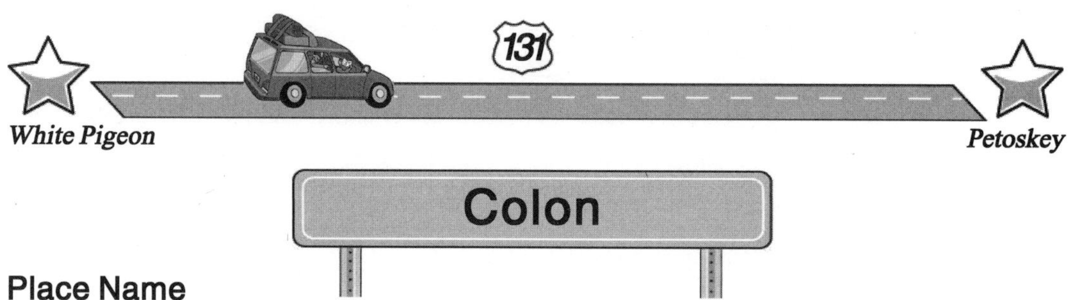

Place Name

When it came time to name this city, one of the early settlers was said to have opened the dictionary, flipped through a few pages randomly until he dropped his finger and pointed to a word in the middle of the page.

> Michigan's most famous magician was not born here, nor did not die here, although Harry Blackstone is buried here.

General Trivia

Harry Blackstone, was one of the nation's foremost magicians for years called Colon his home. The speed and flash of his performing made his act legendary.

Harry invited Australian magician Percy Abbott, who would have further impact on the town and the world of magic. Abbott came for the fishing and relaxation, but stayed and helped form the Blackstone Magic Company. However when the partnership dissolved, Abott remained here to continue building the Abbott's Magic Manufacturing Company into the largest manufacturer of magical implements in the world.

General Trivia

The unmarked grave of Potawatomi Chief Sawauguette is located in Mendon. He was poisoned for selling tribal lands for $10,000 and attempting to persuade them to leave for the rich hunting grounds he promised them in Kansas.

Place Name

When the first settlers visited the area, they noticed its park like appearance, which resulted in the name of the township.

Place Name

In the early days of this township, it was often viewed as a picturesque village, known for its lovely appearance. Thus it was given the name Flowerfield.

Place Name

Founded by surveyor Lucius Lyon, who named the town after his friend, a Michigan Indian agent, Henry Rowe Schoolcraft.

Place Name

Town was given the name of the primary stream, Portage Creek.

Place Name

Parchment was founded by Jacob Kindleberger and named for Kalamazoo Vegetable Parchment Company paper mill.

Place Name

Named for David Crockett and his comrades who "so heroically defended themselves at the famous castle of the Alamo" in the revolt of Texas from Mexico.

Place Name

Otsego, New York native Horace Comstock was responsible for giving the city its name.

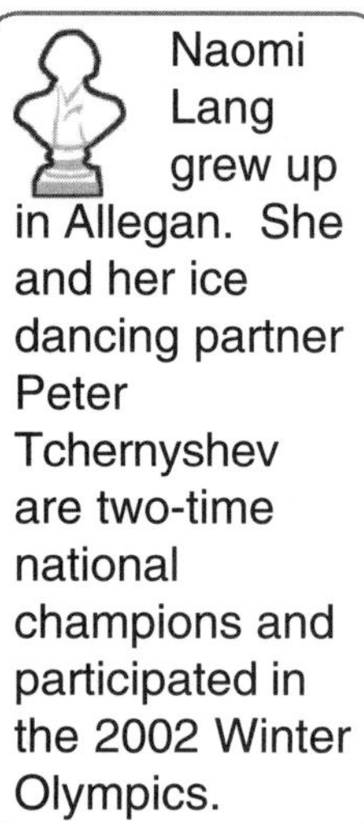

Naomi Lang grew up in Allegan. She and her ice dancing partner Peter Tchernyshev are two-time national champions and participated in the 2002 Winter Olympics.

Place Name

Michigan Indian agent, Henry Rowe Schoolcraft named this town after the Allegan or Alleghen Indian tribe which inhabited the area prior to its settlement.

Place Name

State representative George Barnes named this town in honor of President Martin Van Buren.

Prominent People

Dr. William Upjohn, founder of the pharmaceutical firm that bears his name, established his practice here after the Civil War and perfected a process for the commercial manufacture of the friable pill.

(Historical marker located on West State Street)

Place Name

Colonel Isaac Barnes first settled this area in 1836 and built a sawmill here. His son George became a state representative for the area. As is the case with so many Michigan towns, Wayland got its name from a town in New York. That's where most of the early settlers had come from.

Place Name

Named for Canadian lumberman, Lonson Hilliard who bought a large tract of timber land in the area.

Place Name

This town is supposedly named for principal leader of the Dorr's Rebillion. Thomas Wilson Dorr encouraged Rhode Islanders to take up arms against the State to force a repeal of its law refusing to franchise to all who did not own $134 worth of real estate.

Place Name

Kentwood was given a describing name for the county. The county's name was suggested by Lucius Lyon for New York jurist James Kent. Active in the Federalist party, Kent served several terms in the New York legislature. In 1793, Kent moved to New York City, where his reputation for learning established him as first professor of law at Columbia College.

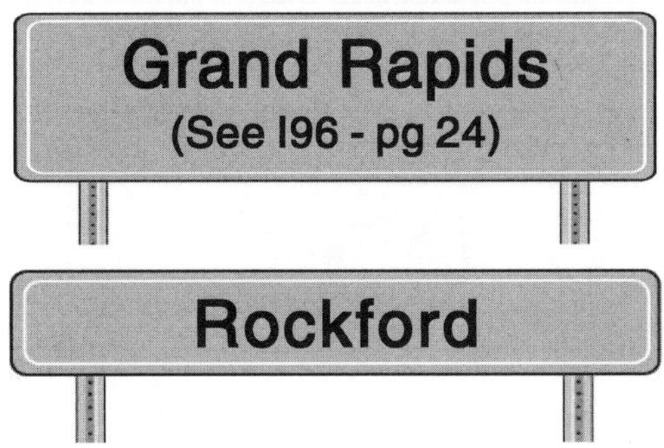

Industry

In 1958, when Wolverine World Wide invented soft pigskin suede and the Hush Puppies shoe, something amazing happened: the world discovered comfortable, casual style. Hush Puppies headquartered in Rockford, can be seen on the feet of celebrities, in movies, and in 80 countries around the globe.

Place Name

The town was named for the founder, John Green.

Historical Significance

The first glider to land on Normany on D-Day was purchased by students of Greenville High School through a sale of $72,000 in war bonds.

The Gibson Refrigerator Company built the first glider to land on Normany on D-Day.

Place Name

The town got its name because the area was both, abounding with springs and covered with a dense growth of cedars.

Place Name

The town was named in honor of Benjamin Ensley, who built a half-way house on the state road between Grand Rapids and Grand Traverse.

Place Name

William Howard, a Detroit railroad attorney was honored with the naming of this city.

The town is named in honor of western explorer John Fremont, a Republican presidential candidate on the Free Soil ticket in 1856.

Industry

Fremont is home to the world's largest baby food company, Gerber Products. The Gerber family had moved to Fremont in the mid 1870s establishing a tannery, which became a major industry. In the 1890s, the lumbering industry, the source of a major raw material for tanning, ran out of trees and the Gerber family turned to processing area farm produce and formed the Fremont Canning Company.

In 1928 Dan Gerber started to manufacture baby foods as a result of impatiently waiting for his wife to strain vegetables for their own child.

Test marketing their new product Gerber ran an ad in Good Housekeeping. Offering readers six cans of baby food for only a $1. In addition he asked for the name of their local grocery store on the order blank. With the list in hand the Fremont Canning Company soon became Gerber Baby Foods, selling 590,000 cans at 15 cents in the first year.

Gerber, with over 180 products today, now controls over 70% of the U.S. baby food market. The Gerber Fremont plant produces baby food for over 20 foreign countries.

* * * *

John B. Whitlock, director of public relations for Gerber said it appears that the Humphrey Bogart story, arose from the fact that his mother was an accomplished artist and frequently sold drawings and illustrations for commercial purposes. It is entirely possible and, in fact, probable that an early drawing of Humphrey Bogart was used for some baby food advertisement or some baby need illustration early in the 1900s. Gerber baby foods, however, were not introduced until 1928, at which time Humphrey Bogart would have been approximately 29 years old. We are sure, therefore, that the Bogart illustration has never been used for a Gerber baby food ad.

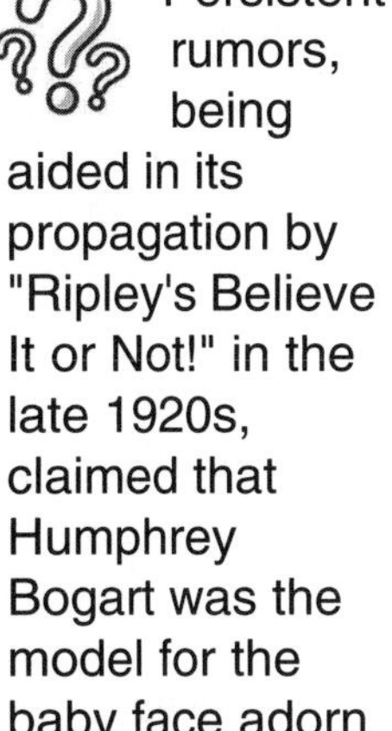

Persistent rumors, being aided in its propagation by "Ripley's Believe It or Not!" in the late 1920s, claimed that Humphrey Bogart was the model for the baby face adorn by millions. Which simply wasn't true.

In 1928, when company officials sought an illustration for a proposed national ad to introduce Gerber prepared baby foods, leading artists of the day were invited to submit their work for consideration. Artist Dorothy Hope Smith, then living in the Boston area, sent in a small charcoal sketch of her neighbor's baby asking if this were about the age and size illustration desired. That charcoal sketch became the now famous Gerber baby which is literally known around the world.

For many years, at the request of the family, the identity of the original model has not been general public information. However, in recent years the model herself, Mrs. Ann Turner Cook of Tampa, Florida, has granted several local newspaper interviews in which she is identified as the "Gerber Baby."

Place Name

This state park is the name for the Chippewa chief, Naw-wa-goo, who was influential in the signing of the Treaty of Saginaw.

Place Name

The Big Creek post office was relocated here when the Grand Rapids and Indiana Railroad established a station in the area. The name was given as a description of the splendid stand of timber in the region.

Place Name

John Parish, a fisherman and hunter, was the first settler to build a hut here in the county. The town that was platted was given the name, Parish. A few years later it was shortened to simply Paris.

Reed City

Place Name

Reed City, named for James Reed, one of the city founders, is located in Osceola County. The county was named after the native Seminole Chief Osceola.

General Trivia

Back in 1895, a farmer in Reed City made quite a discovery in one of his fields. He found a 43 pound meteorite!

"The Old Rugged Cross." church hymn was written by local minister Reverend George Bennard.

Prominent People

Many people know the church hymn, "The Old Rugged Cross." Few, however, know that the author of the hymn, Reverend George Bennard, lived in Reed City for several years. In 1954, the town's Chamber of Commerce had a cross built in his honor.

Another interesting note about the good Methodist minister, is that he preached in every state in the country except for Utah and Louisiana at some time during his ministry.

Place Name

The first settlement in this area was known as Grendale. (Actually, thanks to a clerical error, the settlement first appeared as Green Dell.) The current name of Chase came from John Bigbee. He named the town in the late 1800s after the one-time governor of Ohio, Salmon Portland Chase.

Prominent People

Ashton is the childhood home of the reformer and suffragist Anna Howard Shaw. Shaw an ordained Methodist minister, was a friend and colleague of Susan B. Anthony. Anna was the first woman to receive the Distinguished Service Medal (the highest civilian Presidential citation) for her international efforts on behalf of world peace.

General Trivia

Village is located at the highest point on the Lower Peninsula of Michigan.

Place Name

The Grand Rapids & Indiana Railroad sent Dr. J.P. Tustin, a medical missionary to Sweden to recruit laborers. Acquiring 40 acres of land, approximately 300 people settled here, establishing a colony known as New Bleking. The village later changed its name to honor Dr. Tustin.

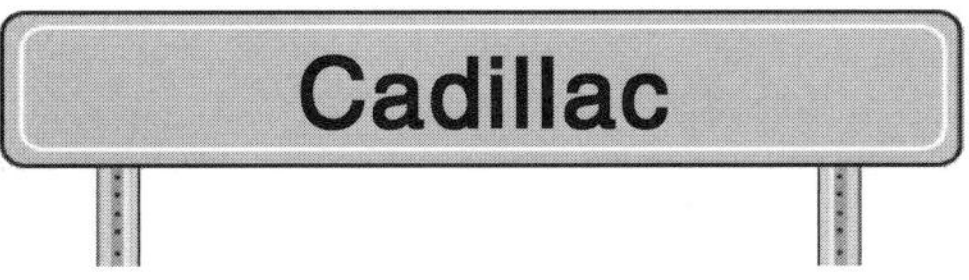

Historical Significance

A lumber camp was built here in 1871. Four sawmills were operated in Cadillac, manufacturing about four million board feet of lumber per month.

Named in honor of Antoine de la Mothe Cadillac, the French explorer.

Place Name

Founders Austin and William Mitchell named the new townsite after William Jennings Bryan. Bryan, U.S. congressman, three-time democratic presidential nominee, and secretary of state, was a gifted orator. He once said, "Destiny is not a matter of chance; it is a matter of choice. It is not a thing to be waited for; it is a thing to be achieved."

Place Name

Meauwataka is a Native American word meaning half-way.

Place Name

Town is named for William Fife, a state highway commissioner from Acme.

Place Name

The town gets its name for the location where the railroad line crossed over the south branch of the Boardman River.

Place Name

Kalkaska, a Native American name, is said to have the meaning of "Table Land" or "Burned Over Land".

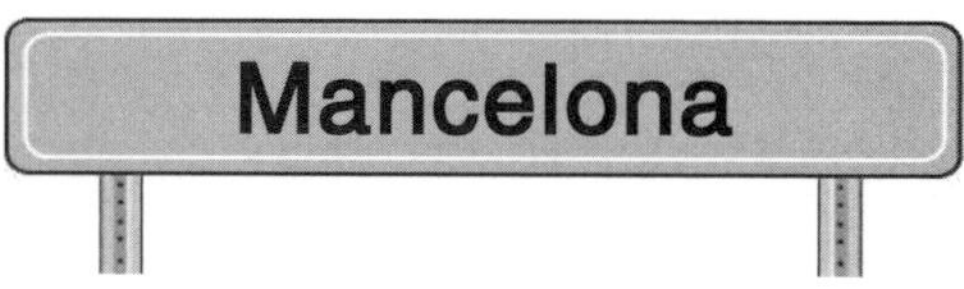

Place Name

This township was named for the honorable Congressman Archibald Barragh.

Place Name

Mancelona was named for the youngest daughter of, Perry Andress, the areas first homesteader.

Wetzel

Place Name

The town takes its name from the Wetzell Turning Works.

Place Name

The small village is named for the falls on the nearby Boyne River.

Local Landmark

It is perhaps best known for Boyne Mountain, the first downhill ski resort in the Midwest. The ski area was developed by Everett Kircher, an auto dealer from Detroit. He felt that the wealthy auto barons would want a place to play in the winter.

Boyne Mountain became a leader in skiing technology. Modern snowmaking was perfected here; the quad lift was invented here; and the first high-speed, six-passenger lift debuted here.

Everett Kircher also developed resorts in Montana, Utah and Washington.

Place Name

John Miller settled at the mouth of the Boyne River, naming his town after the river; which was named for a river in Ireland.

Place Name

A local butcher gave Walloon Lake its name after seeing it on an old railroad map. The railroad looked into the name and found that a group of Walloons had come from Belgium and settled here. There has never been any traces of the Walloons found in the area.

Local Landmark

The lake is the twenty-sixth largest in Michigan, with a shoreline of thirty miles. It was created by glacial activity, which re-shaped and deepened it. It extends over nine miles at its longest point and has a maximum depth of 100 feet.

Note: This is the lake that Ernest Hemingway made famous in his stories, after spending summers here with his family.

* * * *

When the Ironton Ferry was first started in 1876, it was horse-drawn. Thirty-five feet of cable on the lake bottom guide the small ferry. It can only transport four cars at a time and covers a distance of just 575 feet. It has been featured in "Ripley's Believe It or Not."

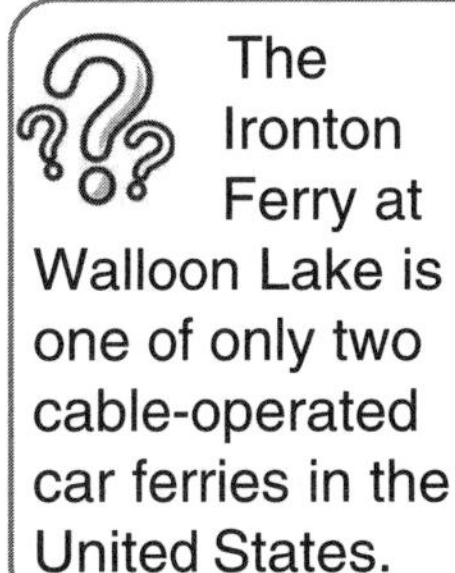

The Ironton Ferry at Walloon Lake is one of only two cable-operated car ferries in the United States.

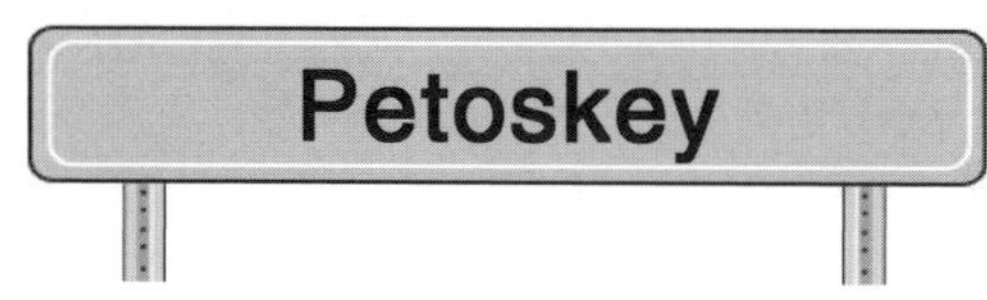

Place Name

The first name of the town was Porter's Village. The name was chosen by the first permanent white settlers, who came here in 1865. The community developed, thanks in great part to lumbering, and the railroad came through in 1873. That's when the name was changed to Petoskey. Where that name came from makes a fascinating story.

Legend has it that a man named Antoine Carre came here as a fur trader with the John Jacob Astor Company. Carre was a descendant of French nobility. After he met and married an Ottawa Indian princess, the Indians called him Neaatoshing. He made his home with the tribe and eventually became their chief.

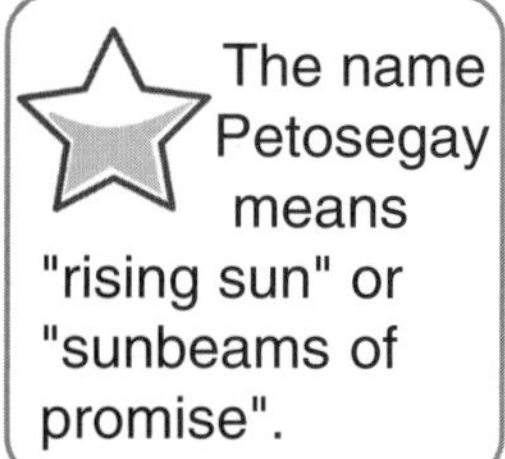

The name Petosegay means "rising sun" or "sunbeams of promise".

Neaatoshing and his family spent the winter of 1787 in Chicago. On their way home the next spring, they camped on the banks of the Kalamazoo River. A son was born to the chief and his princess that night.

As the sun rose, the rays fell on the baby's face. Noting this, the chief declared that "His name shall be Petosegay. He shall be an important person.

His father predicted correctly. Petosegay became an important fur trader and merchant, acquiring a great deal of land and wealth. He was also handsome with smooth skin and sharp, deeply set eyes. He spoke English well. He took for a bride the daughter of Chief Pokuzeegun, a great Ottawa chief from the Lower Peninsula. She gave him eight sons and two daughters.

In 1873 a nondescript town started to build on Petosegay's land along the bay at Bear Creek. The name of Porter's Village became Petoskey, an English adaptation of Petosegay. The settlers honored the man who gave his land and name and a heritage of "sunbeams of promise". Petosegay died a few years later.

Historical Significance

Sitting on the edge of Lake Michigan gave Petoskey an advantage during the lumbering boom of the late 1800s. Pine, maple, elm, ash and hemlock were all available in great quantity here. Landowners became wealthy and manufacturing grew. Freighters off the Great Lakes ferried lumber throughout the Midwest. The first sawmill in the region dates to the 1840s at L'Arbe Croche.

Small wood manufacturing plants were built throughout the county between 1885 and 1915. Michigan Maple Block Company, one of the oldest, is still in operation. It is the world's largest manufacturer of meat butcher blocks.

Prominent People

Ernest Hemingway spent the first twenty-two summers of his life here (except for the famous one spent in Italy). He called it "a priceless place" and enjoyed his time on Walloon Lake and Horton Bay.

His experiences here would later become the background for some of his most famous short stories: Up in Michigan, The Nick Adams Stories, and The End of Something. One of

his earliest novels, The Torrents of Spring, was set here. It was published in 1926.

Geological

Petoskey stones were created by a coral that lived 350 million years ago during the Devonian Age. At that time the northern part of Michigan was covered with warm sea water. The stones are found today in gravel pits, road beds, and from the shores of Traverse City across the state to Alpena. The best place to look for them, though, is right around Petoskey.

The stones found here are generally very smooth. This is caused both by the wave action of the water and by tumbling against other stones and being smoothed by the sand. Some Petoskey stones have very distinct fossil imprints.

On June 28, 1965 -- nearly a century after Petoskey was founded -- Governor George Romney made the Petoskey Stone Michigan's official state stone. Petosegay's only living granddaughter, Miss Ella Jane Petoskey, was present for the signing.

Local Landmark

There's one unusual attraction in Petoskey that not everyone can get to. The Skin Diver's Shrine is an eleven-foot high statue of Christ that sits thirty-four feet under the Bay.

HIGHWAY
127

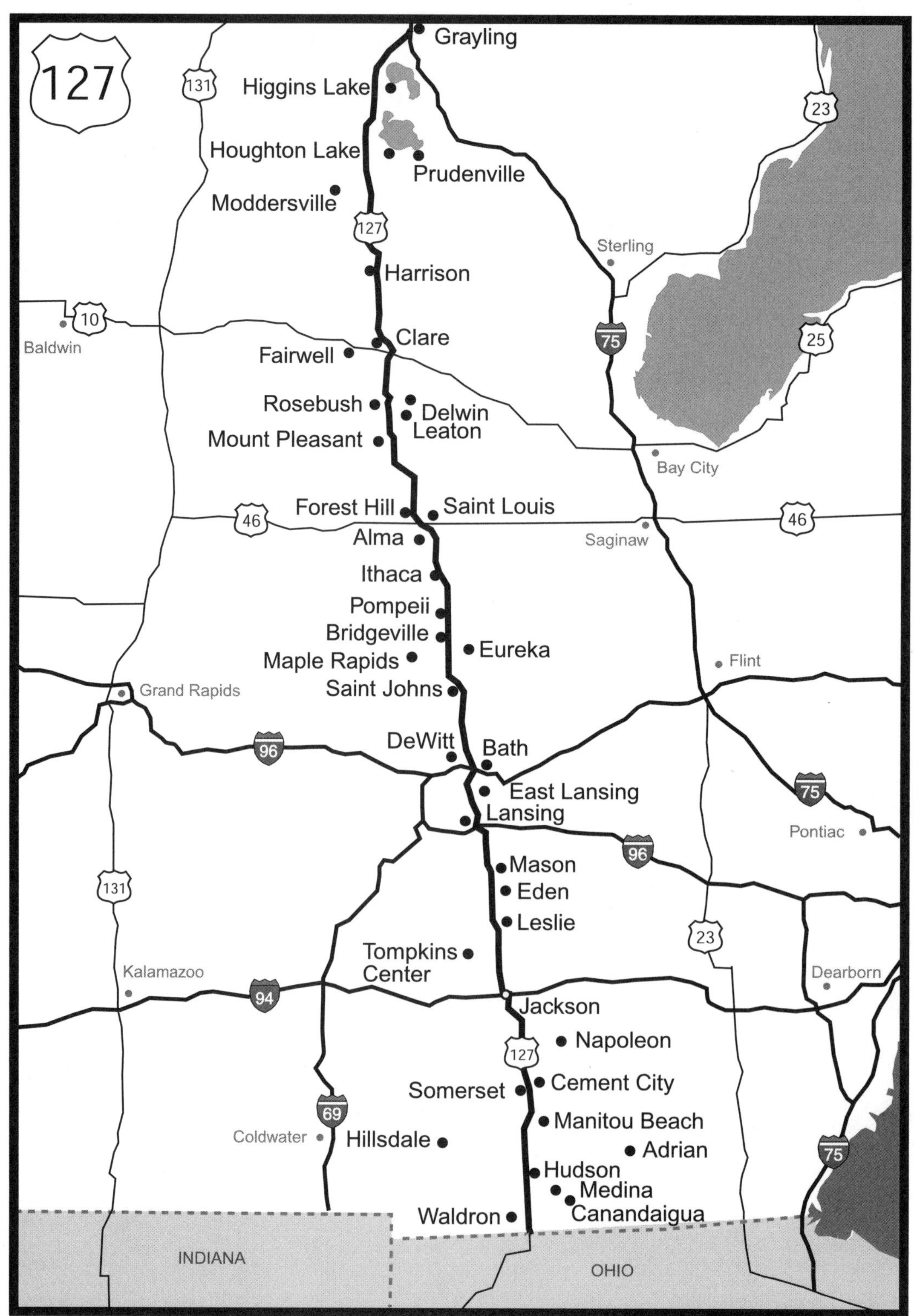
127
131
Grayling
Higgins Lake
Houghton Lake
Prudenville
Moddersville
127
Harrison
Sterling
23
10
Baldwin
Clare
Fairwell
75
25
Rosebush
Delwin
Leaton
Mount Pleasant
Bay City
Forest Hill
Saint Louis
46
Alma
Saginaw
46
Ithaca
Pompeii
Bridgeville
Eureka
Maple Rapids
Flint
Grand Rapids
Saint Johns
DeWitt
Bath
96
East Lansing
Lansing
75
Pontiac
96
Mason
Eden
131
Leslie
23
Tompkins
Center
Kalamazoo
94
Jackson
Dearborn
Napoleon
127
Cement City
Somerset
Manitou Beach
69
Coldwater
Hillsdale
Adrian
75
Hudson
Medina
Canandaigua
Waldron
INDIANA
OHIO

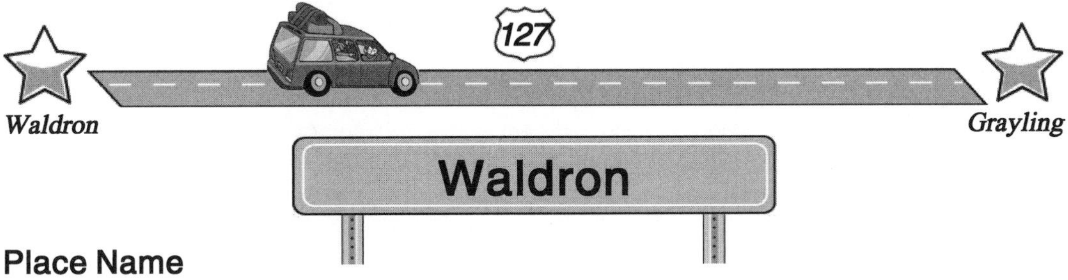

Place Name

Named for the Hinsdale Congressman, Henry Waldron who represented the district.

Place Name

Most of the first settlers came from Canandaigua, New York, giving the town its name.

Place Name

Many of the original settlers came from the state of New York and as a result, the name of the town is believed to be named after Medina, New York.

Place Name

When Hirman Kidder came here from Yates County, New York, the area was first known as Bean Creek. The name was given in reference to its location by a nearby stream, with the same name, where a substantial quality of bean timber grew along the banks.

Adrian

Place Name

Addison Comstock came to the area in 1825 looking for land, whereby he acquired 1,100 acres. Return from New York with fellow settlers they platted the town which his future wife pursuaded him to name for her hero in history, the Roman emperor Hadrian.

Invention

Using a grain drill with cavities to deliver seed at a regulated volume, Adrian native Joseph Gibbons patented the nation's first practical seeding machine.

Local composer, James Royce Shannon wrote the classic song, Too-ra-loo-ra-loo-ra.

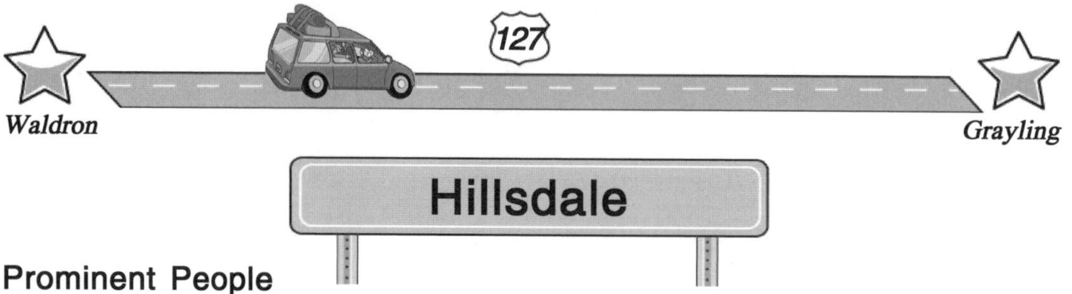

Prominent People

Hillsdale native, Jason Robards, Sr., and husband of Actress Lauren Bacall, appeared in over 100 films as the leading man.

His son, Jason Robards, Jr. followed in his footsteps as an actor winning an Oscar for his role in "All the President's Men."

Place Name

Located on Devil's Lake, the town of Manitou Beach name comes from the Indian word "Manitou" meaning great spirit, good or evil, and was given as a result of a tragedy in nearby Devil's Lake.

Devil's Lake was named by Pottawattomi chief Meteau (or Mitteau) whose tribe lived in the area. His daugher, who was known as a good swimmer, drowned in the lake and her body was never recovered. Chief Meteau believed her body was taken away by evil spirits.

Place Name

The town was given the name after a township in Somerset, New York.

Place Name

William Cowhan named the town after a cement company was founded here around 1900.

Place Name

Aaron Goodwin, one of the original founders, named the township after the French Emperor, Napoleon Bonaparte, he greatly admired.

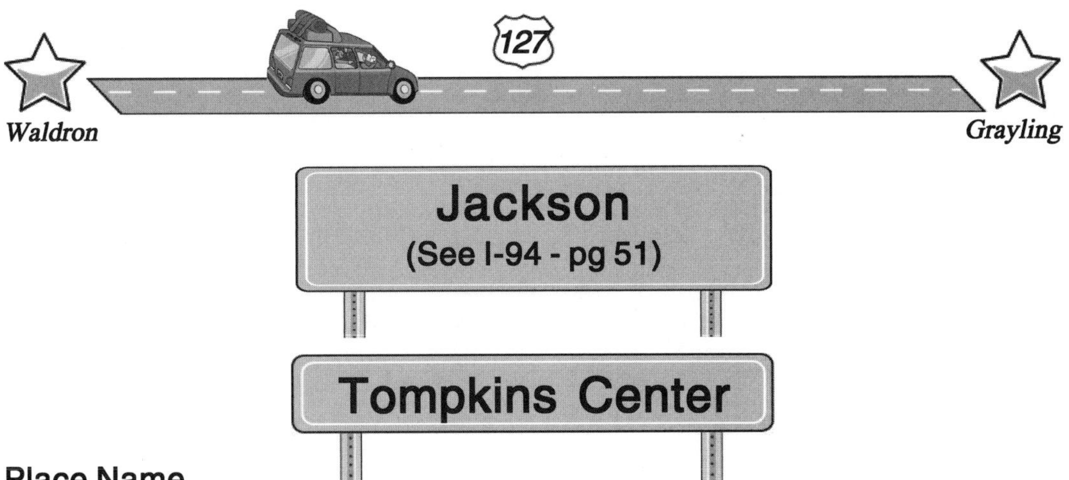

Place Name

The areas first settler Richard Townley named the township after a city in New York State which was named in honor of former New York Governor Daniel Tompkins. Tompkins was also United State's vice president under James Monroe from 1817 to 1825. He was elected to Congress but resigned to serve on the New York supreme court.

Place Name

This small town was settled by Elijah Woodward in 1836. Its original name was Meekerville for Benjamin Meeker, one of the area's most famous pioneers. Dr. A.J. Cornell renamed the town after a prominent family in his home state of New York.

Place Name

Known as the Garden of Eden, the township was given the name because of the fertility of the soil throughout the area.

Place Name

Lewis Lacey was the first settler here in 1836. He built a sawmill. The next year it was Ephraim Danforth who arrived to become the first postmaster. The town was then known as Mason Center, named after Stevens T. Mason, the first popularly elected governor of Michigan. It became the county seat in 1840 and the name was changed to simply "Mason" in 1842.

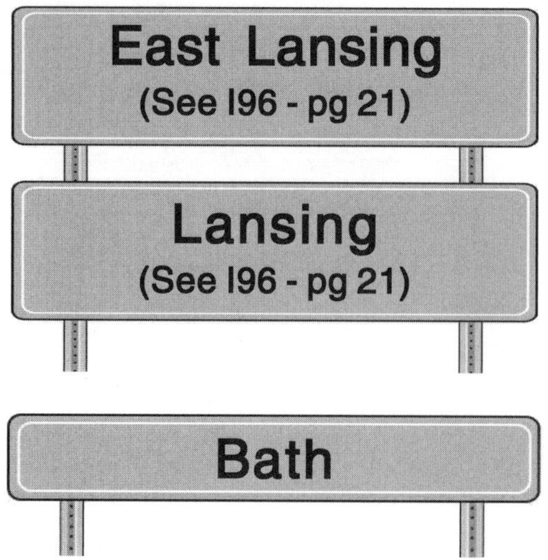

Bath

Place Name

Founder Ira Cushman and his family came to the area from Canada, naming their new home after Bath, England.

General Trivia

Bath was home to Andrew Kehoe, the school board treasurer for the town in 1927. In May of that year, Kehoe killed his wife and then went on to use dynamite to kill himself, thirty-eight students and teachers, several bystanders, and the school's superintendent. At that time, the incident was the state's worst mass murder, Kehoe had killed forty-five people in all.

Named for DeWitt Clinton, the Governor of New York at the time when the town was platted.

General Trivia

It was near the town of De Witt that the highway department installed the first sign in metric measurement in the state. It was located on northbound U.S. 27 and showed the distance in both miles and kilometers.

Prominent People

Philip Orin Parmalee, noted early aviator, lived a tragically brief but venturesome life. Born in 1887 in Matherton, Michigan. Parmalee grew up in nearby St. Johns, Clinton County, (12 miles north of De Witt) where he developed a keen interest in mechanical devices. This led him to join the Ohio flying school run by Wilbur and Orville Wright.

After training he went on to become a famous flier for the Wright Exhibition Team. Fascinated with aircraft, Parmalee was the first pilot to transport merchandise, drop live test bombs from a plane and search from the air for criminals.

(Historical marker located at the Capital City Airport terminal)

* * * *

Nicknamed "Skyman," Parmalee held world endurance, speed, and altitude records, and performed at flying exhibitions. During one such flight on June 1, 1912, in North Yakima, Washington, Parmalee's plane crashed and he was killed, ending a promising career dedicated to the then perilous adventure of flying. He was buried in East Plains Cemetery in Clinton County.

By constant experimentation with their primitive planes, Parmalee and other early fliers contributed to the science of aviation which was the forerunner of today's sophisticated and safe air travel.

(Historical marker located at the Capital City Airport terminal)

Place Name

The town is named for John Swegles, one of four state officials who examined the proposed Detroit and Milwaukee Railroad line. Swegles used his authority to purchase the land the townsite would be built on. Baptist Minister, Reverend C.A. Lamb would later add the Saint to the name of the town.

Place Name

Edward Stark gave this village the name Eureka, Greek for "I have found it" because he felt they found a nice place for doing business.

Place Name

Grand Rapids resident, George Campau built a trading post on a tract of land he purchased near the rapids of the Maple River.

Place Name

Name was given to the township where the state road bridge crosses the Maple River.

Place Name

The town which was platted by Joseph Foster and Burton Bradley was named after Pompeii, Italy.

Place Name

Ithaca, named after Ithaca, New York has been known for being located in a strong farming region. Nearby oil drilling has benefited the town as well.

Place Name

Alma was founded in the year 1853 by General Rallph Ely and three companions. Originally known as Elyton, the town was expanded by Mr. Gargett and renamed for his daughter, Alma.

Local Landmark

On October 26, 1886, the Presbyterian Synod of Michigan accepted an offer by Ammi W. Wright of Alma of thirty acres of land, containing two buildings, and a gift of $50,000 from Alexander Folsom of Bay City, for the purpose of establishing Alma College. The Synod had resolved: "We will, with God's help, establish and endow a college within our bounds." A charter was granted by the state of Michigan, April 15, 1887. Classes began September 12, 1887. In the first year there were 95 students and nine faculty members. Here the Presbyterian Church has fostered the pursuit of learning to the glory of God and to the dignity of men.

(Historical marker located on West Superior Street)

In 1975, France owned and operated an oil refinery company in Alma.

Oil refining and sugar beets have been some of the industries associated with the town.

General Trivia

A ghost was said to reside in the Tau Kappa Epsilon fraternity house at Alma College. The ghost was believed to have been a former member of the fraternity that died in a canoeing accident many years ago.

Prominent People

In 1922, Rayburn Wright, a jazz trombone player and director at New York City's Radio City Music Hall was born in Alma.

Place Name

General Charles Gratiot, for whom the county was named, was a native of St. Louis, Missouri; which gives the city its name.

Place Name

The original location of the townsite was a few miles down the road. Located on a higher ground and in an area that was heavily forested gives the town its name. However, when the improved roadway relocated, so did the town. The new location was neither hilly or wooded, but the village kept its name never-the-less.

Historical Significance

Isabella County is rich in both Cultural and Natural history. The land that was inhabited by the Chippewa Indian Tribe and had its first permanent white settlers during the mid 1800s. The area was rich with white pines that were harvested and milled, making lumber the first industry in the county.

In 1893, the city of Mount Pleasant became home to Central Michigan University. Over the years, the university has added to the enrichment of the community in many ways including education, sporting events, the arts and many other community services. During the 1920s, oil was discovered, which set the foundation for the industry that the city of Mount Pleasant would be built on.

The town's name refers to the pleasant location located on the scenic Chippewa River which flows by the area.

Today, the community has come full circle; the Saginaw Chippewa Indian Tribe is helping to bring new growth to the area not only with their casinos and resorts but also with cultural centers. The tribe also hosts the "Little Elk's Retreat Pow Wow" each August with traditional Native American crafts, food, dress, dancing and singing competitions and performances.

Local Landmark

The Chippewa Valley Audubon Club, formed in 1951, has been instrumental in preserving and restoring natural viewing areas in the county. The 40-acre "Florence Maxwell Wildlife Sanctuary" is open to the public from dawn to dusk and offers visitors a peaceful surrounding to explore nature.

Mount Pleasant citizen John Buckley became the first person to paddle a canoe alone across all five Great Lakes during the summer of 1984.

Prominent People

The last American soldier to die in the Vietnam Conflict was from Mount Pleasant. Lt. Col. William Nolde was a 22-yr. career Army officer. He died when an enemy artillery shell exploded in his bunker at An Loc. Eleven hours later, a cease-fire ended the role of American soldiers in Vietnam.

Place Name

Town is named for Mount Pleasant attorney John Leaton, who was engaged in real estate and lumbering operations throughout the county.

Place Name

When Cornelius Bogan built his general store here, the area was known as Halfway because of its location midway between Mount Pleasant and Clare. James Bush, later gave land to the Ann Arbor railroad for their depot and platted the village which was named for his wife, Rose Bush.

Historical Significance

This settlement started as a station on the Pere Marquette Railroad.

Place Name

The town of Farwell was founded around 1870 when the new railway passed through the area. However the town takes its name after Samuel Farwell, who had an interest in the road.

Place Name

The town of Clare is located in Clare County. The county was originally named Kaykakee, (Pigeon Hawk) after a chief who signed the Treaty of 1826. It was renamed after a county in Ireland.

Place Name

The city name was selected for the ninth president of the United States, William Henry Harrison, and also for Harrison Carey, one of the first surveyors of the area.

Place Name

The town is named for Netherland immigrant Wynand Modders who came to the area to raise his family and stayed.

Place Name

The town of Prudenville, founded by John Pruden, has been known for being in the middle of a strong farming region.

Place Name

Originally known as Muskegan Lake when it was surveyed by William Burt in 1849. In 1908, John Brink changed it to Red Lake. However, around 1952 the name was changed to that of the town, which honors the state geologist, Douglass Houghton.

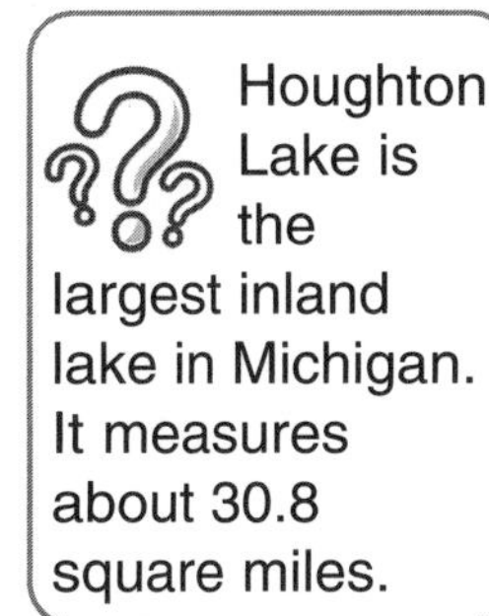

Houghton Lake is the largest inland lake in Michigan. It measures about 30.8 square miles.

General Trivia

In March of 1972, Ralph Bower found U.S. 27 to be quite useful. Poor weather at nearby airports made landing in those locations hazardous, so Mr. Bower landed his single-engine Cessna airplane on the northbound part of the highway.

Place Name

This town was named for topographer, Sylvester Higgins.

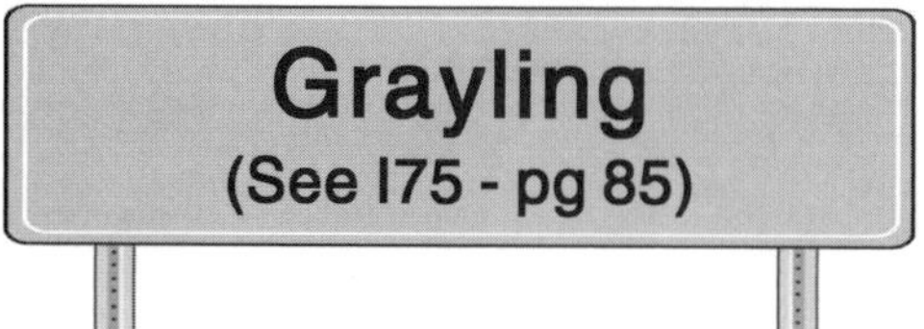

HIGHWAY
46

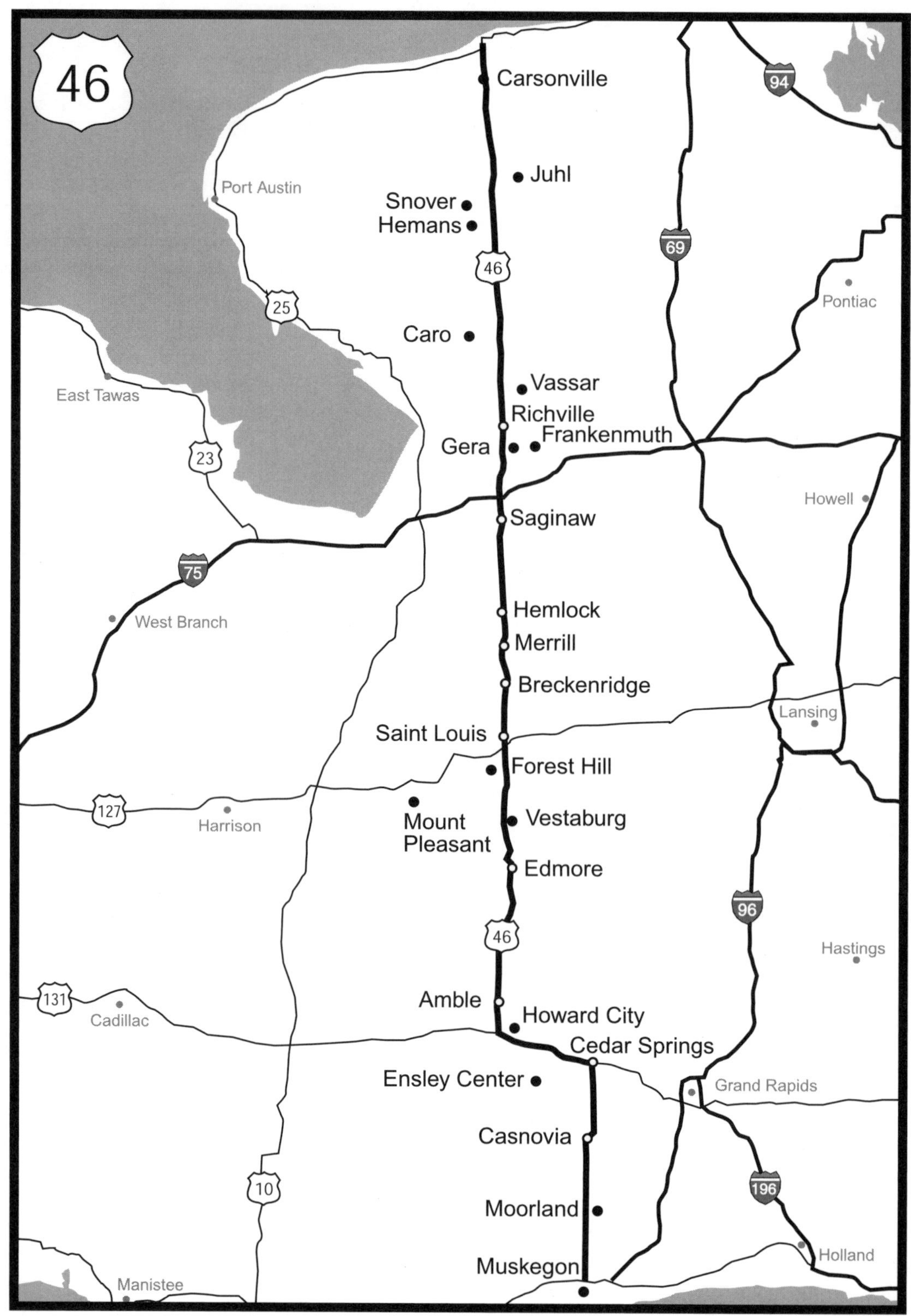
46
Carsonville
94
Juhl
Port Austin
Snover
Hemans
69
46
Pontiac
25
Caro
Vassar
East Tawas
Richville
Frankenmuth
Gera
23
Howell
Saginaw
75
Hemlock
West Branch
Merrill
Breckenridge
Lansing
Saint Louis
Forest Hill
127
Harrison
Mount
Pleasant
Vestaburg
Edmore
96
46
Hastings
131
Amble
Cadillac
Howard City
Cedar Springs
Ensley Center
Grand Rapids
Casnovia
10
196
Moorland
Holland
Muskegon
Manistee

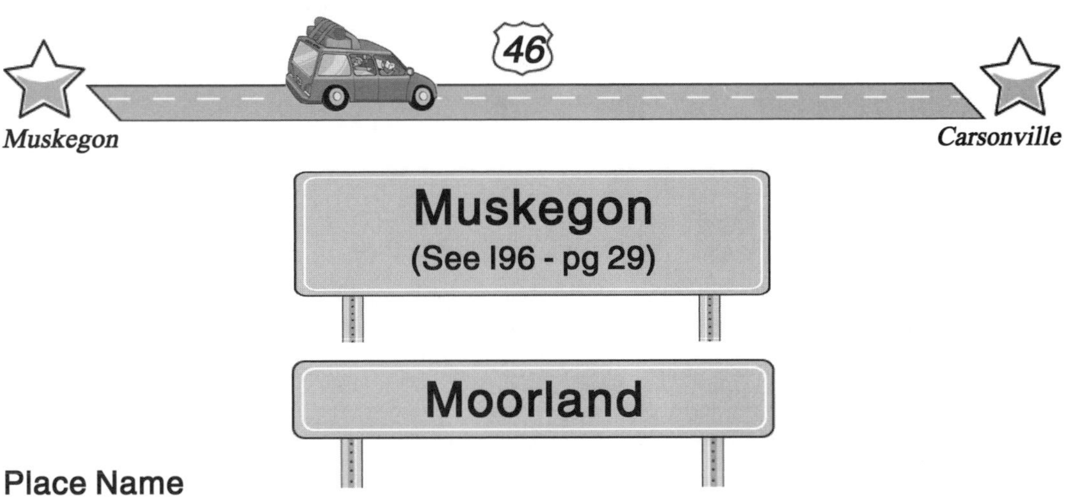

Place Name

Town received its name because it was originally swampland.

Place Name

The town's name comes from the Latin word casa, meaning home, and nova, meaning new, for the settlers new home.

Place Name

The town's name honors Reverend Ole Amble, pastor of the Danish Lutheran Church.

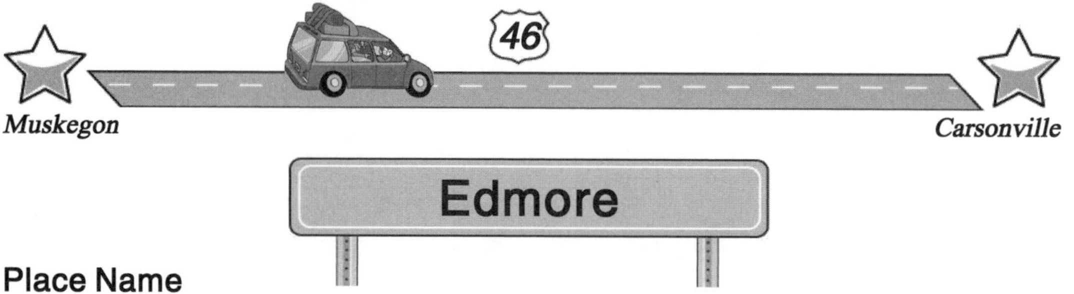

Edmore

Place Name

Edwin Moore, for whom the town is named, was the principal real estate man who founded and platted the village.

Place Name

George O'Donnell founded the village he named after his wife, Vesta Burgess O'Donnell.

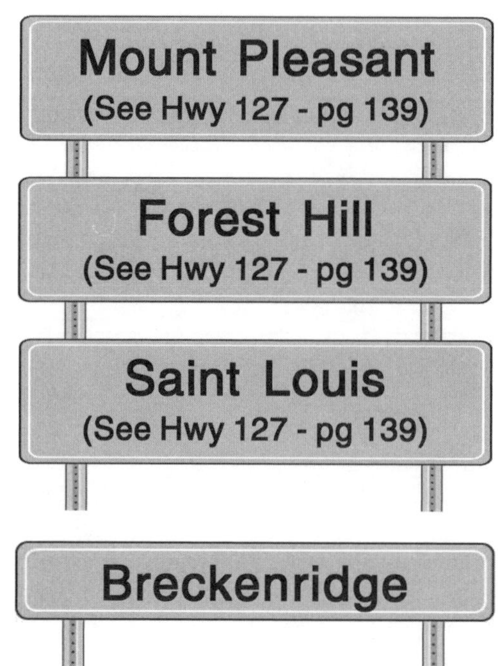

Breckenridge

Place Name

Village was named in honor of John C. Breckenridge. Breckenridge was born near Lexington, Kentucky. He studied law at Transylvania University and after graduating he set up as a lawyer. Breckenridge was elected to the House of Representatives in 1851 and served as vice-president of the United States (1857-61).

The Democratic Party that met in Charleston in April, 1860, were deeply divided. Most delegates from the Deep South argued that the Congress had no power to legislate over slavery in their territory. The Northerners disagreed and won the vote. As a result the Southerners walked out of the convention and another meeting was held in Baltimore. Again the Southerners walked out over the issue of slavery. With only the Northern delegates left,

Stephen A. Douglas won the nomination.

Southern delegates now held another meeting in Richmond and Breckenridge was selected as their candidate. The situation was further complicated by the formation of the Constitutional Union Party and the nomination of John Bell of Tennessee.

Abraham Lincoln won the presidential election with 1,866,462 votes (18 free states) and beat Stephen A. Douglas (1,375,157 - 1 slave state), Breckenridge (847,953 - 13 slave states) and John Bell (589,581 - 3 slave states). Between election day in November, 1860 and inauguration the following March, seven states seceded from the Union: South Carolina, Mississippi, Florida, Alabama, Georgia, Louisiana and Texas.

Representatives from these seven states quickly established a new political organization, the Confederate States of America. On February 8th they adopted a constitution and within ten days had elected Jefferson Davis as its president with Breckenridge as Secretary of War.

Place Name

The town was named for N.W. Merrill, the railroadman who had befriended the villagers when the area was swept by a forest fire in 1881.

Place Name

Town is named for the vast amount of hemlock trees that grew in the area.

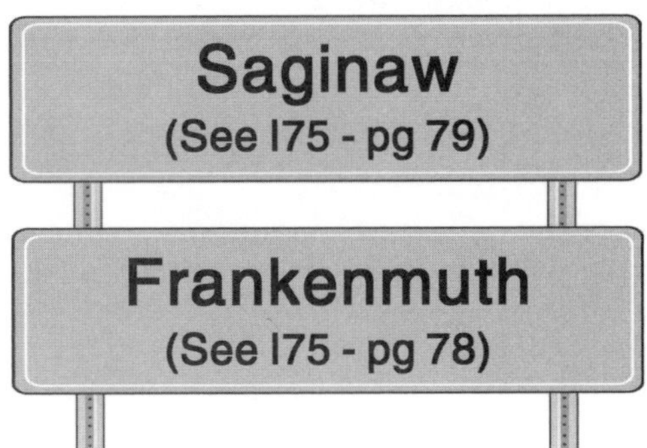

Saginaw
(See I75 - pg 79)
Frankenmuth
(See I75 - pg 78)

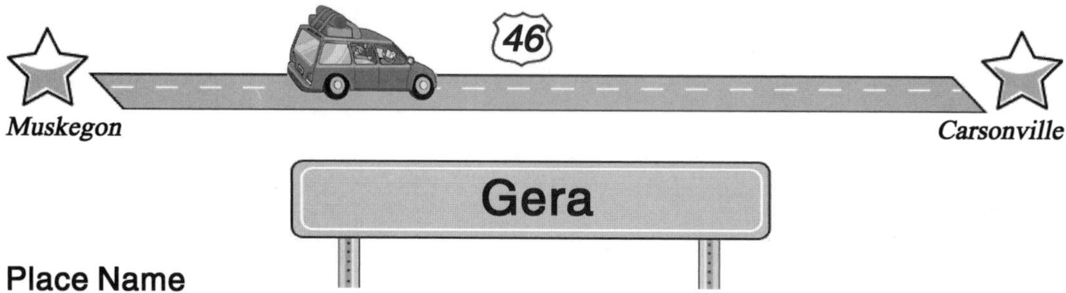

Place Name

This village began as a railroad depot on the Michigan Central Railroad and given the name Gera, after a town in Germany.

Place Name

Lutheran Pastor Loehe organized and led a group here to the area they called Frankenhilf, combining Franconia, a district of Bavaria, and hilf, the German word for assistance. The railroad conductors had difficulty with the name and called it Richville, in reference to the areas fine farmland.

Place Name

Townsend North suggested the name of James Edmund's wife's uncle, Matthew Vassar because Vassar loaned the money to start the village. Vasser was the founder of Vassar College in Poughkeepsie, New York.

Industry

The declining lumber industry had cleared thousands of acres of land suitable for the cultivation of sugar beets.

In 1897 farmers were encouraged further to grow this new crop when the state legislature offered a bounty to producers of one cent for each pound of sugar made from Michigan beets. Soon numerous beet sugar factories appeared. Many of them were in the Saginaw Valley area where both climate and soil were satisfactory for growing sugar beets.

One of the companies started in this era was the Peninsular Sugar Refining Company at Caro. Organized in 1898, it was first called the Caro Sugar Company. Today it is the oldest beet sugar factory still operating in Michigan.

The Peninsular Sugar Refining Company owes its success in part to the willingness of area farmers to grow sugar beets.

> The beet sugar industry in Michigan began growing rapidly in the late nineteenth century.

A German firm built the factory in 1899 on land donated by the community. A newspaper, the Tuscola County Advertiser, publicized the venture and Charles Montague, a local businessman, raised capital for it.

Farmers hauled tons of beets to the Caro factory in horse-drawn wooden-wheeled wagons and sleighs. In October of 1899, the company embarked on its first season of beet sugar production.

In 1906 Peninsular Sugar merged with several other companies to form the Michigan Sugar Company. With Charlie Sieland as superintendent, the Caro factory became known as a training ground for sugar craftsmen. Today Caro's modern automated equipment is housed in the original factory.

(Historical marker located on South Almer Street)

General Trivia

Edward Cole of Mayville won the Grand National Championship for Christmas tree growers and as a result, selected the 19 1/2 foot concolor fir used by President Ford and the First Lady in the 'Blue Room' of the White House in 1974.

Place Name

The town was named in honor of Michigan historian Lawton Hemans. Hemans served as a state representative, ran for governor twice and authored a book about Stevens T. Mason, Michigan's first governor.

Place Name

This village was named for U.S. Representative Horace Snover, the republican who represented the district in congress from 1895 to 1898.

Place Name

Town was founded and named for Jens Juhl, a Danish immigrant who came to the area with his wife and six children.

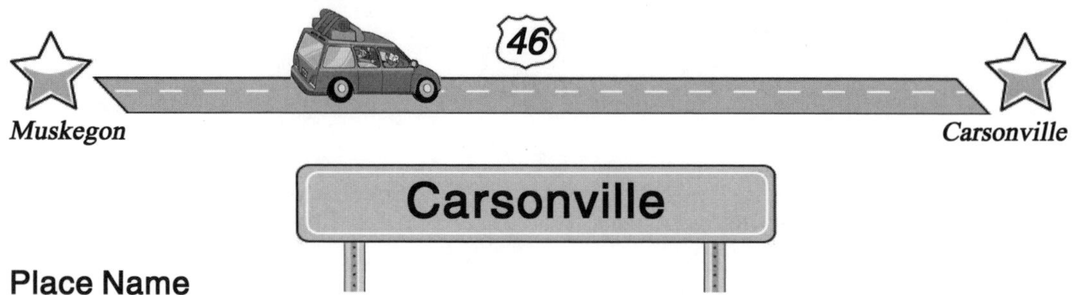

Place Name

Carsonville received its name after Arthur Carson, who built a store and grain elevator in the area.

HIGHWAY
41

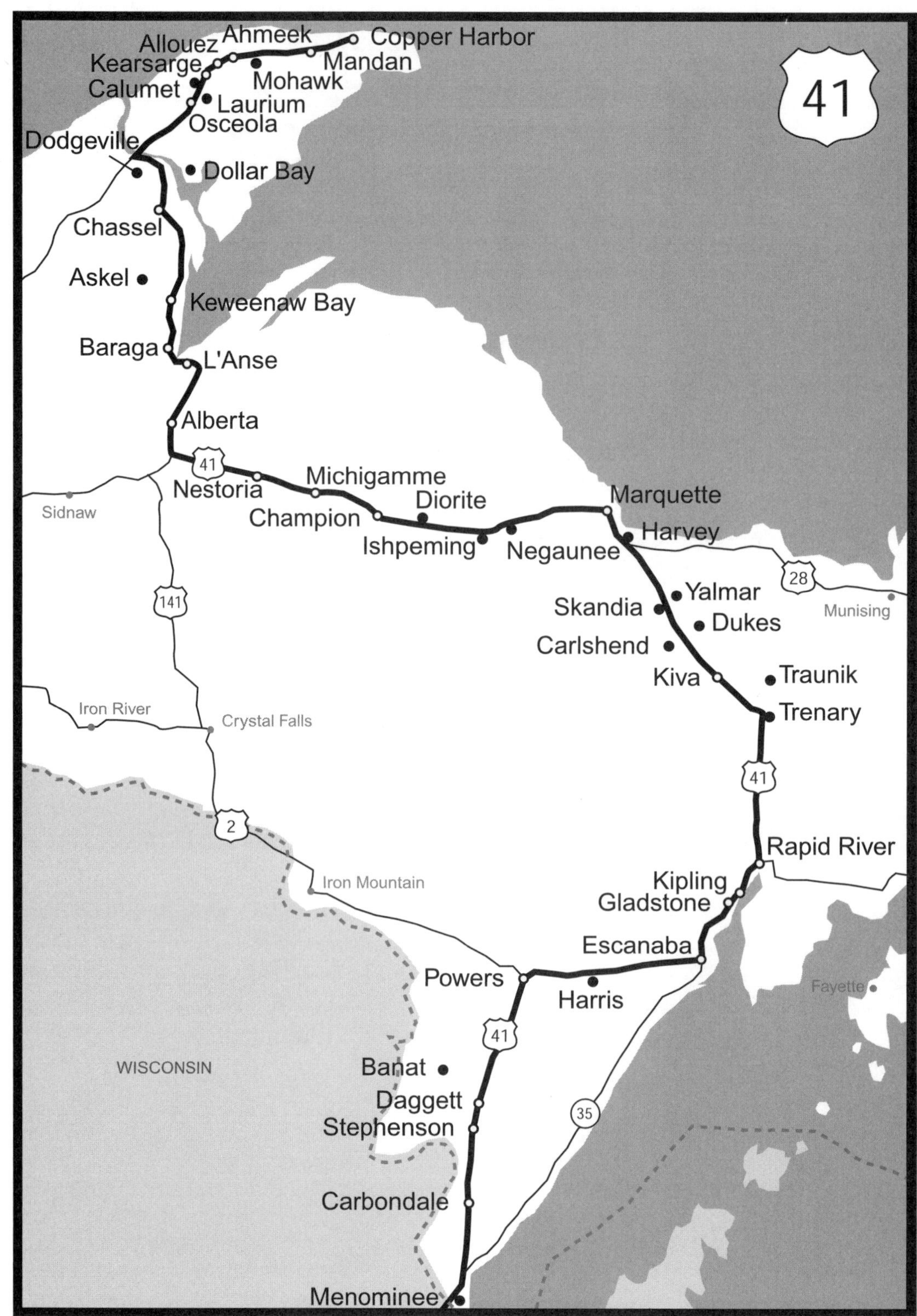
Copper Harbor
Ahmeek
Allouez
Mandan
Kearsarge
Mohawk
Calumet
Laurium
Osceola
Dodgeville
Dollar Bay
Chassel
Askel
Keweenaw Bay
Baraga
L'Anse
Alberta
41
Michigamme
Nestoria
Diorite
Champion
Marquette
Ishpeming
Negaunee
Harvey
Sidnaw
28
Yalmar
Skandia
Munising
Dukes
Carlshend
141
Kiva
Traunik
Trenary
Iron River
Crystal Falls
41
2
Rapid River
Iron Mountain
Kipling
Gladstone
Escanaba
Powers
Harris
Fayette
41
WISCONSIN
Banat
Daggett
35
Stephenson
Carbondale
Menominee

Place Name

The city's name comes from the Native American word for "rice men". This was the name given to people who harvested the wild rice that grew along the river.

Historical Significance

The federal government had obtained the rest of the Upper Peninsula from the Menominee Indian tribe by treaty in 1836.

The Indians used to fish with great dipping nets. The fish were so plentiful that the Indians could just scoop them out of the water. Hundreds of barrels of fish were prepared and packed each year. One fish story has it that two fishermen netted 4,200 pounds of smelt in less than five hours.

The first trading post was built here in 1796. Forty years later, Farnsworth & Brush built the area's first sawmill. By the 1890s, Menominee was the largest shipper of pine lumber in the world. It also ranked as the second most important lumber producing region in the country. The wood was so plentiful that the docks were jammed with shipments ready to go out. The railroad had reached here in 1871.

Agriculture replaced lumbering around 1917. Michigan's first agriculture school was established here in Menominee County. The county today is a leader in dairy products, especially cheesemaking.

Place Name

This settlement began with the Menomonie Furnace Company charcoal kilns (hence the name).

Place Name

It was named for Samuel Stephenson, a town founder who became the district's congressman.

Historical Significance

In 1870 a commission was given to the Chicago & Northwestern Railway. They had to build a line from Menominee to Escanaba. They had one year to finish it. The length to be covered was sixty miles. In order to meet the deadline, construction had to start at both ends simultaneously. Hopefully, the two crews would meet in the middle -- somewhere around Powers.

This settlement on the Menominee River was given a station on the new line in 1872. That brought in new settlers, many from Menominee. They were attracted by the abundance of timber to be found here.

The settlement grew from a few timber shacks into a real little town. The name was changed from Number 22 to Waucedah. On January 10, 1876, it became Stephenson.

Place Name

The village was founded in 1876 by Thomas Faulkner. He came here to run a farm for the Holmes & Son Lumber Company. Faulkner married Clara Daggett, who opened the first post office in the kitchen of their home in 1880. The town was named for her father, who lived in Elmira, New York.

Place Name

The village was settled by Austro-Hungarians, who came to the area mostly from St. Louis, Missouri. Never-the-less they named their new home after the district of Banat in Austro-Hungary from which their ancestors came.

Place Name

Edward Powers was a civil engineer with the Chicago & Northwestern Railroad. In 1872 he started buying land here and named the town after himself. The founder remained active in Powers' development.

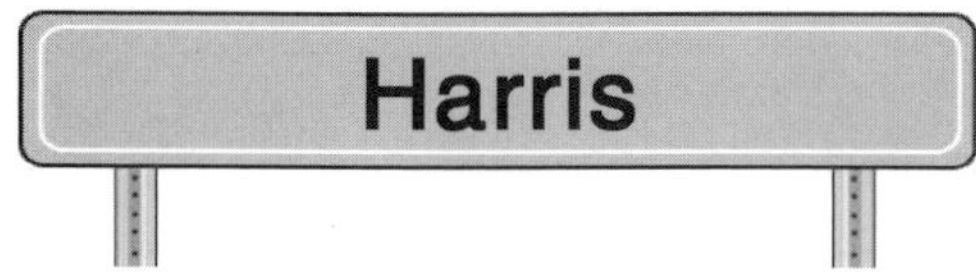

Place Name

Town is named for lumberman Michael Harris, who later served as a member of the legislature from this district.

Escanaba

Place Name

The first settlement here was called Sandy Point, because it sat on one. The point extended out into the Little Bay de Noc. It should have kept its original name, because things got confusing here for awhile. The village was given a post office in December of 1853 and named Esconawba. In June of 1864, the name was changed to Flat Rock, then back to Esconawba on the same day. No one is quite sure why. On June 1, 1875, the name was changed again to Escanaba, the Chippewa word for flat rock.

Historical Significance

Escanaba was born because of the lumber boom. It had a natural, deep harbor which made it a wonderful location for shipping. When the forests had given out, the iron companies came.

The Chicago and Northwestern Railroad started operations here in 1863 and they built the city's first ore dock. Millions of tons of ore were shipped from here annually.

> This town's name had already been given to the river here. It flows over a bed of flat rocks, and inspired the "rushing Esconawba" in Henry Longfellow's poem about Hiawatha.

Local Landmark

The Sand Point Lighthouse was built in 1868. For many years it was operated by the U.S. Coast Guard. After it was deactivated, the local historical society acquired the building. They have restored it and furnished it in turn-of-the-century style.

* * * *

Heading east to Manistique, it is obvious that not all of the trees in Michigan were removed. This is the Hiawatha National Forest. Covering 879,000 acres, the forest is divided into two sections and borders on three of the Great Lakes -- Huron, Michigan and Superior.

It is the forest made legendary by Longfellow in his poem "Song of Hiawatha": "From the forests and the prairies, from the great lakes of the Northland, from the land of the Ojibways, from the land of the Dacoutahs, from the mountains, moors and fen-lands, where the heron, the Shuh-shuh-gah, feeds among the reeds and rushes."

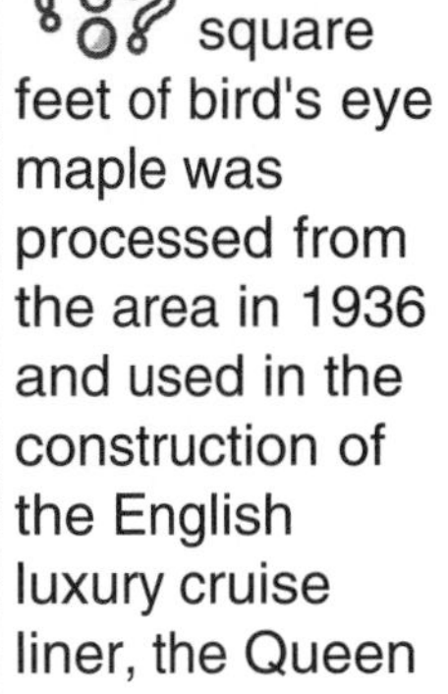

> Approx. 100,000 square feet of bird's eye maple was processed from the area in 1936 and used in the construction of the English luxury cruise liner, the Queen Mary.

Gladstone

Place Name

It started out as a township called Minnewasca, the Sioux word for "white water." It acquired the easier name of Gladstone, for British Prime Minister William Gladstone, when it was incorporated in 1889.

Hoegh Pet Casket Company is the largest pet casket manufacturing company in the world.

Industry

The Hoegh Pet Casket Company showroom appears as if a pet funeral is taking place. There's a casket, floral arrangements, candles and velvet paintings of sad, large-eyed puppies. Displays include the different sizes of pet caskets, as well as other amenities available. Outside there's a model pet cemetery. However, no pets are actually buried on the premises. In 2002, over 35,000 caskets and burial shells were sold. Plus a total of close to 6000 cremation urns.

Place Name

Fred Underwood, the general agent for the Soo Line, named the station here for the English poet, Rudyard Kipling.

Place Name

Town was given the name of the Rapid River which has a series of rapids from its headwaters to its mouth.

Place Name

The town grew around the sawmill of Levi Trenary.

Place Name

Not to be confused with the Brosnian city of Travnik, it was named for the native Slovene village of many of the settlers. Travnik is a word meaning meadow.

Place Name

Kiva is an abbreviation of the first postmaster name, which was Sigrid Kivimaki.

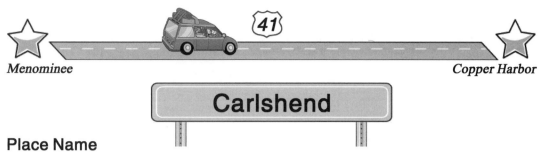

Place Name

When Karl Petros Janssen, known locally as Carl Peter Johnson, became postmaster of the town, he sent in the name as Carlslund, meaning Carl's land, but when it came back it was recorded as Carlshend.

Place Name

Scandinavian settlers called their town, Lehtola, (meaning a copse or grove) a popular name for a number of villages in Finland. When the post office was established it was changed to Dukes.

Geological

The Dukes Experimental Forest was established in 1926. A small amount of white pine and elm were logged during the early 1900s. The remaining forest is essentially old growth today. In 1974, a Research Natural Area (233 acres) was established within the Dukes Experimental Forest boundaries.

The Experimental Forest is on a ground moraine deposited by an advance of the Green Bay lobe as it moved southward from the Lake Superior basin. Dominant soils are the well-drained Munising sandy loam, somewhat poorly drained Skanee sandy loam, poorly drained Angelica sandy loam, and Linwood muck.

The uplands are dominated by old growth northern hardwoods and hemlock-hardwoods. Hemlock dominates the somewhat poorly drained soils and cedar-spruce and hardwood-conifers dominate the poorly drained soils and muck. Most forests are old growth.

Place Name

This village began as a station on the Munising Railroad and its name means Little Scandivania.

Place Name

This town was settled and named for Hjalmer Bahrman. Hjalmer and his family operated a farm in the area, shortly after the Civil War.

Note: the Hj is pronounced Y.

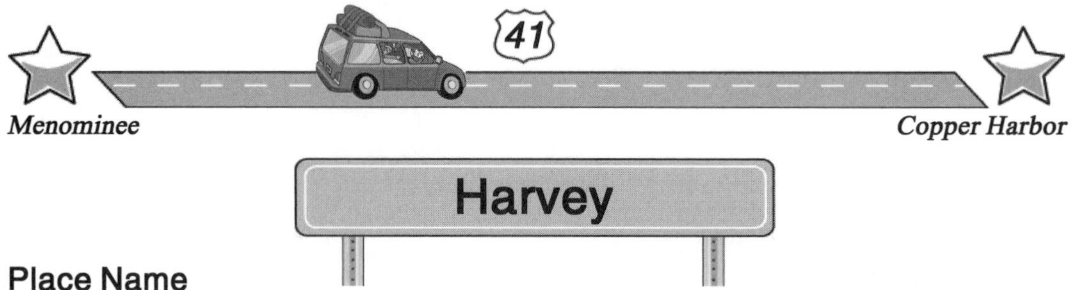

Place Name

Charles Harvey founded the village that began as the site of the North Iron Company blast furnace.

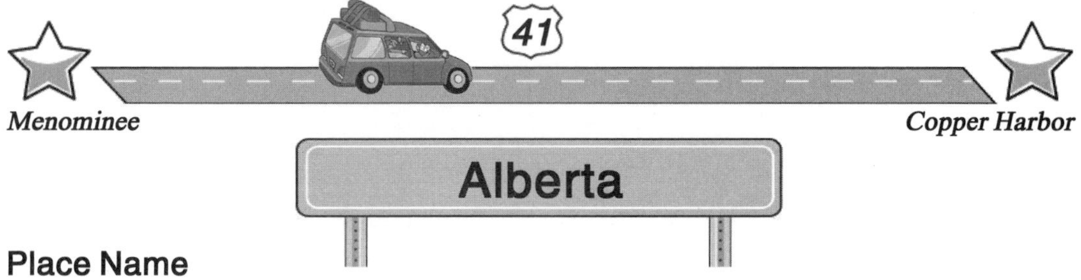

Place Name

This town was named after a daughter of one of Henry Ford's top executives. It is believed that Ford had the intention of building a plant in the region in the spring of 1936 and therefore began to build his "model" lumber town including homes, schools, churches, etc. However within seven years he closed the operation.

Place Name

This town began as a Native American mission, founded by French Jesuit Rene Menard. Later becoming a Methodist mission site. On the completion of the Marquette, Houghton & Ontonagon Railroad the town was founded to service the heavy mining and lumbering going on there. It was given the French name for the bay.

Local Landmark

On the stretch of US 41 between L'Anse and Baraga, is a 35-foot statue rising some 60 feet above the bluff overlooking Keweenaw Bay, honoring, Frederic Baraga. Baraga covered an estimated 700 miles of his journey each winter serving his churches on snowshoes.

Weighing four tons the giant copper figure of the bishop features a seven-foot-tall cross, along with his famous snowshoes measure 26 feet. It floats on a cloud of stainless steel supported by five laminated wood beams and teepees that signify the five Catholic missions the Bishop established in the region after coming to the Upper Great Lakes region from his Slovenian homeland.

Father Frederic Baraga was known as the Snowshoe Priest.

Place Name

The town grew around the Holy Name mission started by Reverend Frederic Baraga for the Native Americans in the area.

Place Name

This town was started by Reverend Frederic Baraga as a Native American mission he named for the Assiniboin chief whom he had converted and remained close friends with.

Michigan's Crown refers to the prime lumbering country with almost 17 million-plus acres covering 30 percent of the western Upper Peninsula.

Place Name

President U.S. Grant issued a land patent to Frank Laffrenire in May of 1875. The name of the town is the same as the nearby Keweenaw Bay which comes from the Native American word, Kewawenon, meaning portage.

General Trivia

In this region the whitest hard maple and rare birds-eye maple can be found. Both trees are rare, but the birds-eye maple is among the rarest and most expensive wood in the world because tiny knots give the sandy wood an abundance of swirls and circles in its grain.

Planting birds-eye maple seeds doesn't necessarily guarantee a birds-eye tree will grow. It is a growth "defect" and so it is genetic in origin. It results because of the grain deviation, which in turn gives the high contrast in color and reflectivity.

Place Name

Five Finnish woodcutters and their families filed land claim in the area they would settle. The town was given the Finnish name for a step, suggested by the topography of the place.

Place Name

This town was founded and named for a French farmer, John Cassell.

Place Name

This village started with the opening of the Dodge Copper Mine in 1901.

Place Name

The town was given the name in honor of Douglass Houghton, a pioneer state geologist.

Place Name

Named for John Hancock, one of the signers of the Declaration of Independence.

Jacobsville

Place Name

The first settler in this area was George Craig, Sr., who arrived in the mid-nineteenth century. However, the unincorporated community of Jacobsville did not spring into being until 1884, when John H. Jacobs of Marquette opened his sandstone quarries in the vicinity.

Stone was shipped from quarries in the area for such projects as the first Waldorf-Astoria in New York.

Historical Significance

The quarries provided high quality red stone for buildings throughout North America and abroad from 1884 to 1919. During this time, some 800,000 tons of stone were shipped.

The community, populated mostly by Finns, reached its peak about 1897, when it had eight hundred inhabitants.

(Historical marker west of Jacobsville)

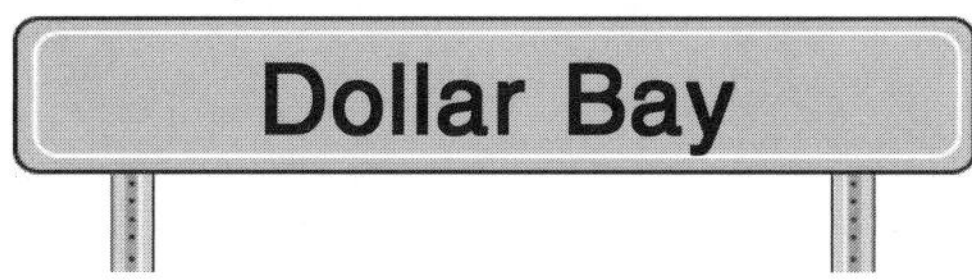

Industry

Horner Flooring has been producing hardwood flooring longer than anyone. In fact Horner began producing hardwood flooring the same year James Naismith invented basketball, 1891.

Horner floors are sold around the world and have become the national and international standard in competition basketball floors. Their Pro-King Portable is used each year for the NBA All-Star Game and NCAA Championship Playoffs, and by professional and national teams around the world. As well as for the 1984 Summer Olympic Games in Los Angeles.

Place Name

Edward Hurlbut discovered the Osceola copper mine and organized the successful Osceola Consolidated Mining Company which developed the surrounding area.

Place Name

The Laurium Mining Company platted the original village to establish copper mining. The name was taken from Laureium, a famed silver mining site in Attica, a district of ancient Greece.

Prominent People

From his deathbed, Notre Dame famed halfback George Gipp, from Lauriam, told his coach Knute Rockne, that "When things are wrong and the breaks are beating the boys, tell them to go in there with all they've got and win one just for the Gipper!"

It was to be eight years before Rockne asked a beleaguered Notre Dame team to make good of the Gipper's deathbed request.

> Coach Knute Rockne asked a beleaguered Notre Dame team to make good of the George Gipp's deathbed request, "win one just for the Gipper!"

Knute Rockne was desperate. His 1928 team, decimated by injuries, already had lost two of its first six games. Three powerful teams - Army, Carnegie Tech and Southern California loomed on the schedule before the season (the worst in Rockne's illustrious coaching career) would mercifully draw to a close. Rockne knew that if his Ramblers could upend Army - winner of six straight games - in Yankee Stadium, a losing record could be averted.

The week of the game he quietly told his neighbours that Notre Dame might not be able to win on talent, but Notre Dame would win on emotion and spirit. He began slowly - telling the team about George Gipp, a Notre Dame player who had died during his senior season eight years ago. Although none of the players had known Gipp personally, each and every one of them had heard of his exploits. They knew Gipp had been the greatest player of his time. Rockne who had been at Gipp's bedside, repeated the young athlete's last wish.

After falling behind 6-0 in the third period, Notre Dame scored two touchdowns and held off a last-chance rally by the Cadets for a 12-6 win. Jack Chevigny tied the score at 6-6 with a one-yard plunge. As he picked himself up in the end zone, he jumped up and shouted : "That's one for the Gipper". The emotional Chevigny was helping Notre Dame drive towards its final and winning score in the last quarter when he was injured. Rockne was forced to take him out and replace Chevigny with Bill Drew. Reerve Johnny O'Brien, a willowy hurdler for the track team, took Johnny Colrick's place at left end. The

Irish were 32 yards away from the goal line.

Left halfback Butch Niemiec took the ball, looked downfield to O'Brien and flung a wobbly pass over an Army defender. O'Brien hauled the ball in on the 10-yard line, squeezed past two tacklers and dove into the end zone for the winning touchdown. As O'Brien scored, the Notre Dame bench erupted in whoops and hollars. The injured Chevigny cried on the sidelines, "That's one for the Gipper too".

This legend of the gridiron was immortalized in the Warner Brothers, Knute Rochne - All American which starred Pat O'Brien as Rochne and the future President Ronald Reagan as the Gipper.

Place Name

The town started as a village for officers and employees of the Calumet & Hecla Mining Company.

Historical Significance

On December 24, 1913, area copper miners had been on strike for five months. The miners were fighting for better pay, shortened work days, safer working conditions and union recognition. That day, during a yuletide party for the striking miners and their families, someone yelled, "Fire!" Although there was no fire, seventy-three people died while attempting to escape down a stairwell that had doors that opened inward. Over half of those who died were children between the ages of six and ten. The perpetrator of the tragedy was never identified. The strike ended in April 1914.

(Historical marker located at corner of Seventh and Elm streets)

> ??? Calumet was the clay stone bowl of the Indian peace pipe.

Place Name

Town was named for the U.S.S. Kearsarge by a former naval officer who became an employee of the Calumet & Hecla Consolidated Copper Company.

The master amygdaloid lode was successfully mined by various companies from 1882 until it closed in 1925 due to its depletion.

Place Name

Founded by the Allouez Mining Company when they opened a copper mine in 1859. It was named for Claude Jean Allouez, an early Jesuit missionary.

Place Name

Ahmeek is the Chippewa word for beaver.

Place Name

The town and Mohawk Mining Company were named for the Native American tribe.

Place Name

The Keweenaw Copper Company began exploring the area with diamond drill, followed by shaft sinking. The mine location was called Mandan, some believed for, "that man Dan," referring to the Scottish-Irsh miner from Canada, Daniel Spencer.

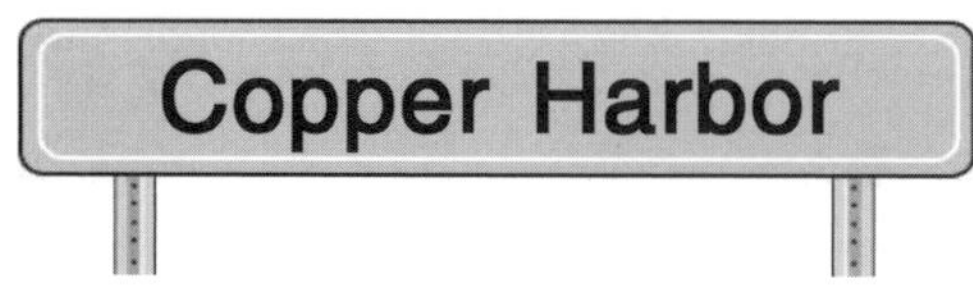

Place Name

The towns name is French for grey beast which was said to have been seen on the shore, although some believe it is actually derived from the shape of the bay, or the shore, or even the crest of the hills.

Copper Harbor

Place Name

The name of the town is in reference to the county's copper deposits that brought on a rush of prospectors to the area.

HIGHWAY
31

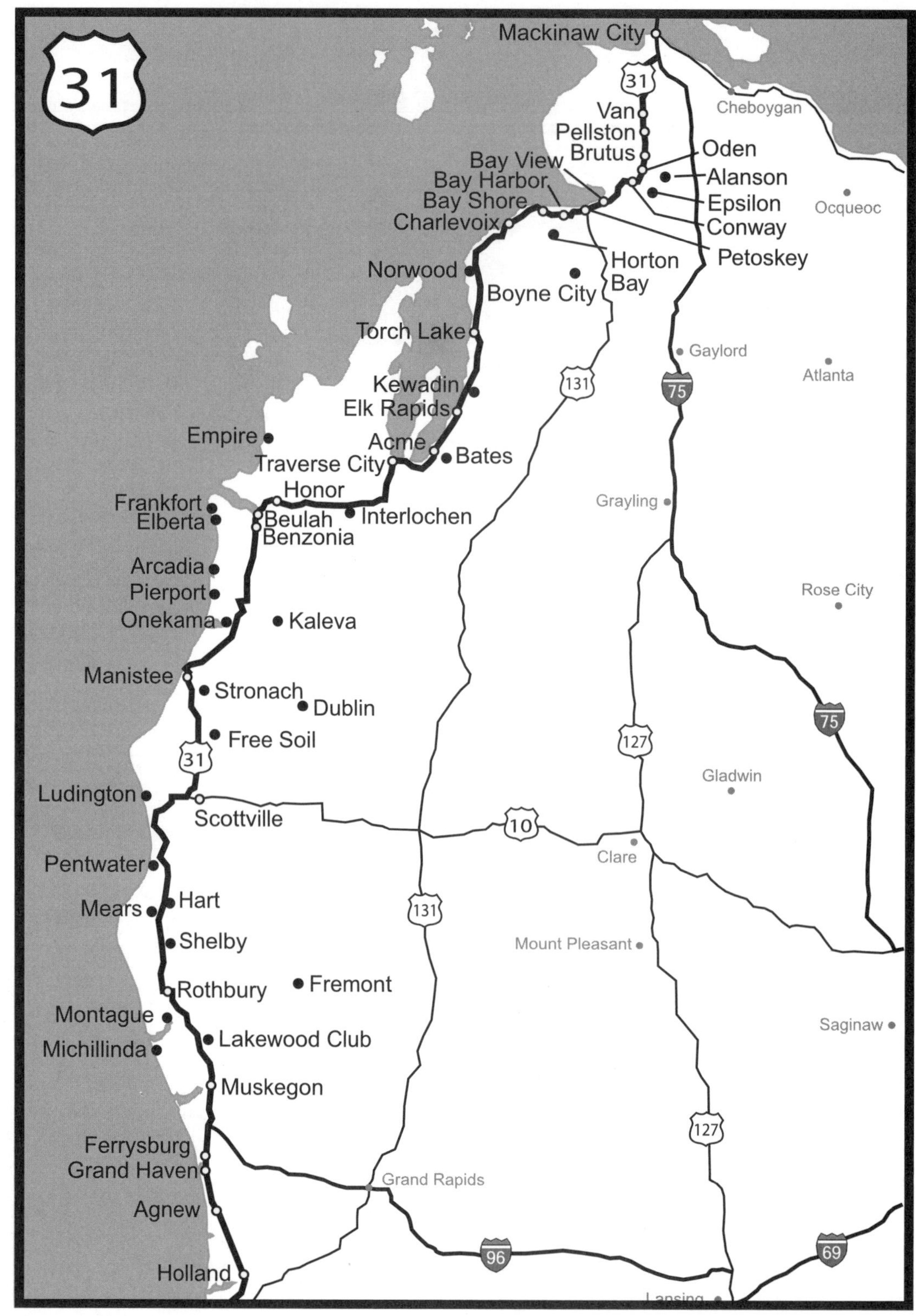
31
Mackinaw City
Van
Pellston
Brutus
Cheboygan
Oden
Alanson
Epsilon
Conway
Petoskey
Ocqueoc
Bay View
Bay Harbor
Bay Shore
Charlevoix
Horton Bay
Norwood
Boyne City
Torch Lake
Gaylord
Atlanta
131
75
Kewadin
Elk Rapids
Empire
Acme
Bates
Traverse City
Honor
Frankfort
Elberta
Beulah
Benzonia
Interlochen
Grayling
Arcadia
Pierport
Onekama
Kaleva
Rose City
Manistee
Stronach
Dublin
Free Soil
127
Gladwin
Ludington
Scottville
10
Clare
Pentwater
Hart
Mears
Shelby
Mount Pleasant
Rothbury
Fremont
Montague
Michillinda
Lakewood Club
Saginaw
Muskegon
Ferrysburg
Grand Haven
Grand Rapids
Agnew
96
69
Holland

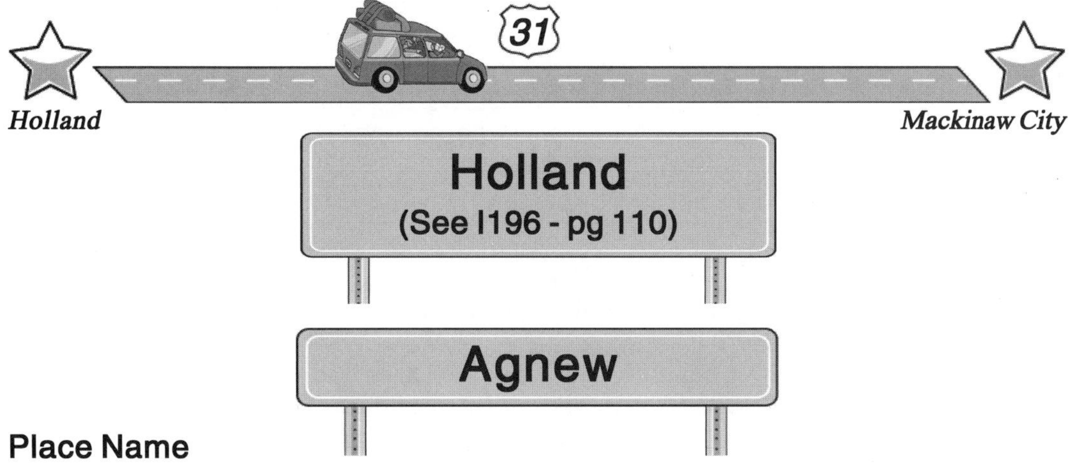

(See I196 - pg 110)

Place Name

Name for a Mr. Agnew, a Chicago and Western Michigan railroad executive.

Grand Haven

Place Name

The town was named Grand Haven in 1835 because it sits at the mouth of the Grand River.

Historical Significance

The Indians were the first to find this a beautiful area to live in. Ottawa, Chippewa and Pottawatomie all had fishing villages here.

French and British fur trappers came next and set up successful trading posts with the Native Americans.

The Grand River, which comes through here, is a water highway between Lakes Huron and Michigan. That made the spot ideal for fur trading and, later, for the lumber industry.

Ships were built here to get the cargo out. And commercial fishing also became an important part of the economy.

Rix Robinson built a trading post here. Along with Rev. William Ferry, Robert Stuart and Nathan White, Robinson formed the New Haven Company to develop the area.

After the trees and the fish were gone, the developers of Grand Haven turned to tourism. There were mineral waters here, and beautiful, peaceful white beaches. Today's economy is diverse, but tourism is still important.

Geologists swear it's true! This is one of the few places on the planet where the sand actually sings! When walked on, the sand emits a musical whistle.

Local Landmark

On Dewey Hill in Grand Haven is another musical phenomenon. An unusual fountain was created in 1962. It combines light, water and music and has a repertoire of billions of musical variations. It took 20,000 feet of wiring to make it work. The base of the fountain is nearly as long as a football field and about half as wide. The lighting equals 125,000 watts -- enough power to light a town of 1,000 people. The music and lights are synchonized to the movement of the water, which sprays up to 125 feet.

* * * *

Due to the strength of storms off the Great Lakes, many of Michigan's lighthouses sit on piers. Two of the most striking mark the entrance to the Grand River in Grand Haven.

The Grand Haven South Pier Inner Light and the Grand Haven South Pierhead Light stand several hundred feet on a long stone pier.

The older Inner Light was built in 1895. The fifty-one-foot steel cylinder is topped by a small lantern.

The pierhead light is a short, squat building that originally served as the fog-signal building. It was moved to its current location and turned into a lighthouse when the pier was extended in 1905. It is lit by a tiny lantern on the roof. Its wooden structure has been covered in iron to protect it from Lake Michigan's fierce storms.

Neal Ball has the distinction of the first unassisted triple play in Major League Baseball History.

Prominent People

National League baseball player Neal Ball is a Grand Haven native. The right-handed Cleveland infielder executed the major leagues' first unassisted triple play, catching a liner, doubling one Red Sox runner off second, and tagging another from first. He also hit an inside-the-park homer that inning.

Place Name

Founder Colonel William Montague Ferry named the town after his father, Reverend William Ferry; the founder of Grand Haven.

Place Name

This resort community received its name by suggestion from David Forbes, Sr. Forbes said many of the people came from MICHigan, ILLinois and parts of INDiana.

Lakewood Club

Place Name

This town was founded in 1912 by the Mayo brothers which was named by the lot owners association for its wooded location on Fox Lake.

Place Name

The town was founded by George Dowling, Joseph Heald, Peter Dalton and William Montague Ferry, for whom it was named.

Local Landmark

Erected on the shores of White Lake, is the world's largest weathervane. Built by employees of Whitehall Products, the weathervane stands 48 feet tall, with a 26 foot long arrow that will point into the wind with the slightest breeze. The schooner ornament was chosen to symbolize the lumbering and shipping heritage of the area.

Former President Ronald Reagon purchased a weathervane for his ranch in California.

Industry

Whitehall Products manufacturing plant, the world's largest manufacturer of weathervanes with over 50 different styles, is located just a few short blocks from here.

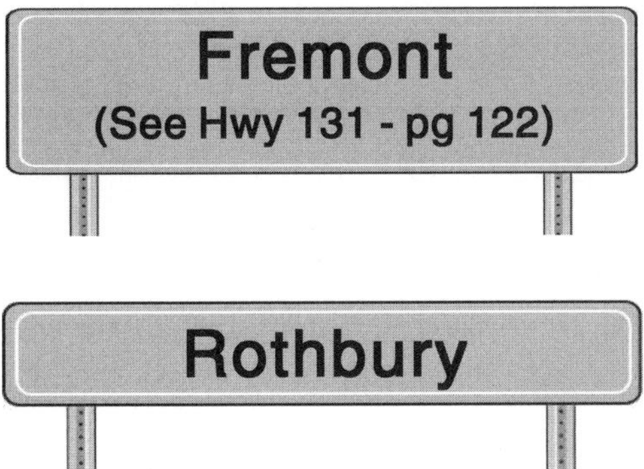

Place Name

The town became known as Greenwood, when Nelson Green, the first settler here in 1865, gave the Chicago & Northwestern Railroad right of way over his property.

There was already a city by that name in Michigan, so the name was changed to Rothbury in 1879 after the post office station.

Place Name

Shelby's original and more picturesque name was Churchill's Corners. It was named that in 1866 after Walter Churchill, the town's first postmaster.

When the village was incorporated in 1885, it became Shelby. The name was in honor of General Isaac Shelby, who led the Kentucky Rangers and recovered Detroit from the British during the War of 1812.

General Trivia

Shelby sits in the middle of a rich fruit belt. It is especially known for its apples.

* * * *

Shelby used to be a great place to watch migrating passenger pigeons as they flew over the area each year. Unfortunately in one year alone over 700,000 birds were hunted which led to their extinction.

The Shelby Gem Factory is one of the world's largest manufacturer of man-made gemstones.

Industry

Man-made or synthetic gemstones are formed when heat and pressure is applied to minerals over time in a laboratory. Synthetic gemstones are by no means "fake" gemstones; rather, they are man-made gemstones with the same chemical and crystal structure as natural gemstones. In addition, natural gemstones often have inclusions, or imperfections in the stone, while synthetic gemstones such as diamonds, rubies and sapphires are typically free from inclusions.

Place Name

This self-named village was founded by Charles Mears, a local mill owner and early settler of Pentwater.

Local Landmark

Charles Mills State Park was created from land once owned by Mears. His daughter donated the land to the state of Michigan in 1923.

* * * *

Thousands of visitors come here each year to visit the Silver Lake Sand Dunes. They extend one-and-one-half miles wide and are three miles long. They cover about 1,875 acres.

Marram or dune grass helps to hold the dunes in place. The underground stems of the grass reach down to the water table and then grow back upward to form new plants. Other dune vegetation includes sand reed grass, bluestem, bearberry, and hairy puccoon, which has yellow flowers.

Among the trees in the dune area are jack and white pine, juniper, wild cherry, birch and poplar. With the shifting of the sand, many of the trees have been buried. Only their tops show, making them look more like bushes.

The dunes shift a few inches east each year and will eventually completely fill in Silver Lake.

Place Name

Charles Mears founded the town when he built a sawmill here in 1856. The first name was Middlesex, which was changed to Pentwater the next year when it was incorporated as a village. Some believe the name refers to the smallness of the outlet of Pentwater Lake causes pent-up water. Still others say it was from the corruption of paint water, refering to the dark color of the water.

Place Name

James Ludington was the man who invested in the town that would eventually be named for him. He purchased the timber and built the sawmill here in the 1860s.

Historical Significance

Ludington grew throughout the lumber boom. The economy was made even stronger by the discovery of salt. In the late 1890s, Ludington became part of an intricate network of ferry boats, which were used for transporting lumber and cars.

> The last remaining car ferry on Lake Michigan, the S.S. Badger, runs today between Ludington and Manitowoc, Wisconsin.

* * * *

At least twenty-nine people died when one of the Ludington carferry fleet, the 350 foot S.S. Pere Marquette 18 sank in Lake Michigan twenty miles off the Wisconsin coast on September 9, 1910.

About midlake a crewman discovered the ship was taking on water. The captain set a direct course for Wisconsin and sent a distress signal by wireless. He and the crew battled for four hours to save the boat but she sank suddenly. All of the officers and many of the crew and passengers perished, among them the first wireless operator to die in active service on the Great Lakes.

The S.S. Pere Marquette 17, aided by other ships who also heeded the wireless message for help, rescued more than thirty survivors but lost two of her own crew. The exact cause of this disaster remains a mystery.

(Historical marker located in Stearns Park)

Local Landmark

Big Sable Point is 112 feet tall and reigns over the lakeshore. The Big Sable Light was originally a brick conical structure. However, around the turn of the century, it began to crumble. The lighthouse was encased in steel plates, which give it an unusual ribbed appearance. The solution to the problem worked and the lighthouse still stands solid today, after one hundred years.

> One of the most stunning lighthouses on Lake Michigan is Big Sable Point.

The light was automated in 1968 and is part of Ludington State Park. In 1989, the tower was painted white with a broad black band around its middle to make it stand out during the day time. With its setting among shifting sand dunes, the Big Sable Point Lighthouse is one of the most scenic in the country.

* * * *

Another interesting lighthouse in the area is the Ludington North Breakwater Light. It was built in 1924 and marks the entrance to Pere Marquette Harbor. It is a three-story pyramid-shaped tower and rests off center on a large, black concrete base.

The light was being worked on in August of 1994 when it suddenly settled six inches to one side. At the present time there are no plans to repair the "leaning light of Ludington."

* * * *

The Great Lakes Visitor Center is housed in Ludington State Park. The Center interprets both the geological and human history of the Great Lakes. It also identifies the many creatures found in the park.

Guests at the center can enjoy exhibits, audio-visual presentations, a gift shop and interpretive programming. Kids of all ages especially enjoy an exhibit called "Night Visitors." This hands-on experience features mounted nocturnal animals that are common to the area.

One entire wall is covered with a satellite map of the Great Lakes. There are also three-dimensional depth maps of each lake.

Prominent People

Father Jacques Marquette, the great Jesuit missionary and explorer, died and was buried by two French companions somewhere along the Lake Michigan shore on May 18, 1675. He had been returning to his mission at St. Ignace which he had left in 1673 to go exploring in the Mississippi country.

The exact location of his death has long been a subject of controversy. A spot close to the southeast slope of this hill, near the ancient outlet of the Pere Marquette River, corresponds with the death site as located by early French accounts and maps and a constant tradition of the past. Marquette's remains were reburied at St. Ignace in 1677.

(Historical marker located on South Lakeshore Drive)

General Trivia

Beginning in 1875, the Flint and Pere Marquette Railroad shuttled produce, passengers and freight in wooden steamers between Ludington and ports in Wisconsin.

In 1892 railroad car ferry service began on the lakes, eliminating the need to unload and load the cars before and after crossing the lake.

Five years later, the Pere Marquette, the first steel railroad car ferry on the Great Lakes, sailed from Ludington. The Pere Marquette could carry thirty fully loaded freight cars.

By 1930, nine boats made up the Ludington fleet.

During the peak season of 1955, the ferries carried 205,000 passengers, 71,000 automobiles, and 141,000 freight cars in nearly 7,000 crossings.

* * * *

S.S. Badger is one of fourteen ships that served in the Ludington railroad car ferry fleet. Badger and its sister ship S.S. Spartan, where built in 1952 by the Christy Corporation of Sturgeon Bay, Wisconsin, for the Chesapeake & Ohio Railroad (C & 0). Named for the athletic teams of the University of Wisconsin and Michigan State University, the boats were a vital commercial link between the two states. The ferries joined the fleet begun in 1897 by the Flint and Pere Marquette Railroad.

Car ferry traffic peaked in the 1950s, then declined steadily. In 1983 the C & 0 sold off the last of its fleet, including Badger, and Spartan. Badger, newly renovated in 1992, resumed automobile, truck freight and passenger service between Ludington and Manitowac.

(Historical marker located on South Williams Street)

Place Name

In 1882, Hiram Scott and Charles Blain platted the village. According to legend, the men determined the name of the village with the toss of a coin. Scott won the toss and named the village Scottville. Charles Blain named the streets, the first of which were Blain, Crowley, State and Main.

(Historical marker located on South Main)

Place Name

This lumbering settlement named the town after the anti-slavery party known as the Free Soil which was organized in Buffalo, New York.

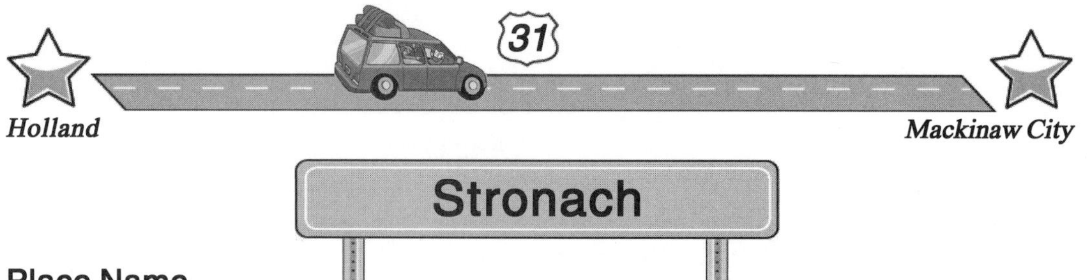

Stronach

Place Name

Named for the founders of the Stronach Lumber Company, John and Adam Stronach.

Manistee was given an Indian name referring to the sound of the winds through the forest.

Historical Significance

French and English fur traders came through this area in the 1790s. Official settlement had to wait until 1841, when John Joseph and Adam Stronach built a sawmill here. Its name means "spirit of the woods" and it is appropriate for a town that once supported 100 logging companies.

The forest around here was vast. And its location, where the Manistee River flows into Lake Michigan, made it ideal for shipping the timber.

A fire destroyed the growing city in 1871, but its citizens quickly rebuilt it.

One of its citizens, Charles Reitz, reinvested in the area in 1881 after he had successfully drilled for salt.

Local Landmark

Manistee is known for both the quality and the number of its well-preserved Victorian buildings. Its architecture and its spectacular setting between Manistee Lake and Lake Michigan make it a natural draw for tourists. The combination has also earned Manistee the title of "Victorian Port City".

The city also has one of only four "catwalks" remaining in Michigan. Manistee's Historic North Pier and Catwalk date to 1855. It is located at 5th Avenue Beach and is one of the most photographed and painted sites in Michigan.

* * * *

The Huron-Manistee National Forests are a prime example of how to renew the environment. They were created out of lumbered wastelands and abandoned farms. Approximately 964,413 acres of lands are included in the forests, which are actually two separate areas.

The Huron Forest is located in the northeastern part of the lower peninsula. It is sixty miles wide and ranges from twelve to thirty miles long north to south.

The Manistee Forest is located in western Michigan. It covers an area forty miles wide east to west and seventy-five miles long. The forests were "combined" in 1945 for administrative purposes.

Geological

Just twelve miles southwest of Manistee is the 3,450-acre Nordhouse Dunes Wilderness. It is the only National Forest Wilderness that includes Great Lakes sand dunes. Although small for a designated wilderness, the Nordhouse Dunes has many unique features. Well over a mile of undeveloped Lake Michigan shoreline and parallel dunes lie within the area.

The dunes are relatively new, geologically speaking, with none of them more than 13,000 years old. Throughout time, the water level of the Great Lakes has gone up and down. The high was about 640 feet. As the water receded, winds would move the exposed sandy lake bed and shift them into dunes.

As long as there was a supply of sand, the dunes continued to build. Most come from the Nipissing period, meaning that they are between 3,500 to 4,000 years old. They stand about 140 feet.

Some vegetation is scattered amongst the dunes and many are covered by dune grass.

A great variety of wildlife makes their home here -- from white-tailed deer to coyote, fox, porcupine and, of course, many species of waterfowl and songbirds.

Prominent People

Actor James Earl Jones grew up near Manistee in the nearby small town of Dublin. Jones took acting lessons at an early age to control his stutter. It appeared to work as he has since starred in many films after graduating from The University of Michigan. His first time acting was at the Ramsdell Theater in Manistee, Michigan.

Over a 40-year period, beginning with the Stanley Kubrick classic: Dr. Strangelove or: How I Learned to Stop Worrying and Love the Bomb (1964).

Jones provided the thunderous voice (uncredited) of the anti-hero, Darth Vader, in the 'Star Wars' film trilogy.

James Earl Jones is the commanding voice that says "This is CNN."

Place Name

Adam Stronach started a settlement here in 1845. He built a lumber mill on the channel between Portage Lake and Lake Michigan. The small town of Onekama sits on beautiful Portage Lake. Its name comes for the Indian word for portage, "Oneka-ma-engh". Shortened to Onekama, it was chosen for the town when it got a post office in 1871.

Place Name

The town's name is derived from that of the national Finnish epic, Kalevala.The Kalevala marked an important turning-point for Finnish-language culture and caused a stir abroad as well. It brought a small, unknown people to the attention of other Europeans, and bolstered the Finns' self-confidence and faith in the possibilities of a Finnish language and culture. The Kalevala began to be called the Finnish national epic.

Local Landmark

Each figure of the totem pole is from the epic poem, The Kalevala. Vainamoinen portrayed at the base of the totem pole, symbolized power and knowledge. He taught that good triumphs over evil, especially in Kaleva, "the land of the good". The Moon and Sun represented day and night, and the cycle that brought each year. The duck is the Messenger that helps Vainamoinen discover his true powers. The Wolf symbolized war and the harshness of survival in Arctic Finland. The Owl, Reindeer and Bear represented animals, which the Finns treasured and respected.

* * * *

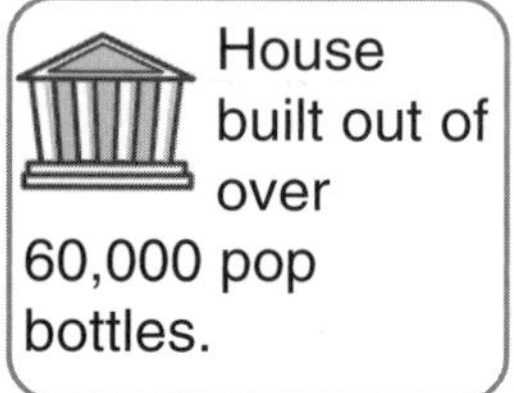

House built out of over 60,000 pop bottles.

John J. Makinen, Sr., (1871 - 1942) built this house out of pop bottles, most of which came from his business, the Northwestern Bottling Works. The bottles were laid on their sides with the bottom ends to the exterior. A native of Finland, Makinen moved to the area in 1903. He completed the house in 1941, but died before his family moved into it.

(Historical marker located on Wuoksi Avenue)

General Trivia

The movie entitled "Car 99" was based on the Kaleva bank robbery which happened on January 5, 1933. It was a national event because it resulted in the first two way radio manhunt in history.

Place Name

The Turnersport Pier Company built their pier along the shore of Lake Michigan here as a place to ship wood. Originally called Turnersport after the company, then Perry's Port for Charles Perry a local property owner, it was eventually renamed Pierport.

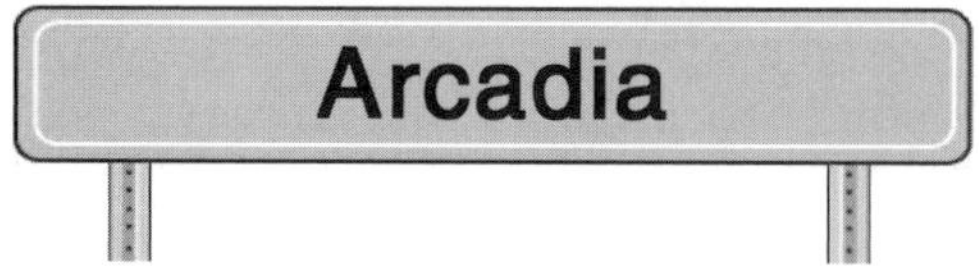

Prominent People

Early aviatrix Harriet Quimby (1875-1912), was inspired to learn to fly when she covered the October 1910 Belmont international aviation meet for Leslie's Illustrated Weekly newspaper in New York. She authored drama reviews, travel pieces and eventually wrote about her own adventures as a pilot.

On August 1, 1911, Quimby received the first aviation license granted to an American woman. With this success came immense popularity.

On April 16, 1912, seeking additional recognition, she became the first woman to fly solo over the English Channel. Her achievement was overshadowed in the press, however, by reports of the sinking of Titanic.

(Historical marker on Erdmann Road)

Note: On July 1, 1912, Quimby and a passenger died when her plane plunged into Dorchester Bay during a meet at Squantam, Massachusetts.

Place Name

The name is an interesting derivation of what started as the French name for the local river. They called it Aux Bec Scies. "Bec Scie" referred to the once-plentiful sawbill duck. Sailors traveling through here corrupted the name to the Betsie River, which later became known as the Benzie.

Local Landmark

Point Betsie Light was built in 1858 just north of Frankfort, and is said to be Michigan's most photographed lighthouse.

The tower is only 37 feet. However, it is a very important light because it marks the point where ships begin their turn toward the Manitou Passage.

Just south of the light, which was automated in the 1980s, are seventy-one undeveloped acres of sand dunes, known as the Point Betsie Dunes Preserve.

Benzonia gave America one of its best-known historians, Bruce Catton.

Prominent People

Bruce Catton grew up fascinated by the town's Civil War Memorial. He is considered one of the premier experts on the subject and has written thirteen books on the Civil War. A Stillness at Appomattox won Catton the Pulitzer Prize.

Place Name

The name of the town comes from a large freestone peach called the Elberta peach with a sweet, succulent flesh and red-blushed, yellow skin. This superior quality peach is good both for eating out of hand and for cooking.

Note: Freestone is a term used to describe fruit that has a pit to which the flesh does not cling.

Historical Significance

On May 18, 1675, Father Jacques Marquette, the great Jesuit missionary and explorer, died and was buried by two French companions somewhere along the Lake Michigan shore of the lower peninsula.

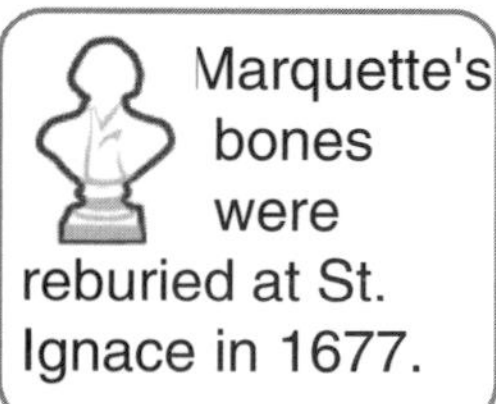

Marquette's bones were reburied at St. Ignace in 1677.

Marquette had been returning to his mission at St. Ignace which he had left in 1873 to go on an exploring trip to the Mississippi and the Illinois country.

The exact location of Marquette's death has long been a subject of controversy. Evidence presented in the 1960s indicates that this site, near the natural outlet of the Betsie River, at the northeast corner of a hill which was here until 1900, is the Marquette death site and that the Betsie is the Riviere du Pere Marquette of early French accounts and maps.

Place Name

Town named by Reverend Charles Bailey after the bible verse, "You shall no more be termed Forsaken and your land shall no more be termed Desolate; but you shall be called My Delight in Her, and your land Beulah, that is Married", found in Isaiah 62, verse 4.

General Trivia

In 1973 the world's largest recorded coho, weighing over thirty-nine pounds, was taken at a state weir.

Since 1870 several unsuccessful attempts have been made to establish Pacific salmon in the Great Lakes.

In 1966 the Department of Conservation released coho fingerlings, hatchery-reared from eggs given by the state of Oregon. They migrated to Lake Michigan and fed on its enormous alewife population. Augmented by subsequent annual plantings, the coho became firmly established. By 1970 the sport fishery catch reached ten million pounds.

Other species of Pacific salmon - the chinook and kokanee - were also successfully introduced to the Great Lakes area in the late 1960s.

To complete their life cycle the salmon return to their home stream to spawn and then die. Millions of salmon are now planted each year.

(Historical marker located on US 31)

Place Name

This village on the Platte River was founded in 1895 by the building of the Guelph Patent Cask Company and was named for the baby daughter of its general manager, J. A. Gifford.

Place Name

The post office which opened the same winter (in 1865) that the schooner Empire became icebound in the harbor, adopted the ship's name as a result.

Place Name

Interlochen is German for "between two lakes". It refers to the town's location between Duck and Green Lakes. The more interesting names for those two lakes are Lake Wahbenakes, meaning water lingers, and Lake Wahbekanetta, meaning water lingers again.

Local Landmark

Although it may seem a surprising place for it, Interlochen is home to one of the country's cultural treasures. The Interlochen Center for the Arts has long been considered the premier site for young artists to develop their talents. Musicians, dancers, actors, visual artists and writers -- all have the opportunity to learn and grow through the programs offered here.

Every summer the Interlochen Arts Camp provides intensive training to talented students from around the world. The programs at the Center have expanded through the years.

Interlochen Public Radio is one of the best-subscribed public stations in the country.

The Interlochen Arts Festival presents more than 750 art events each year. Students, faculty and nationally-renowned artists are featured in a variety of concerts and exhibits.

> Among a few of the famous alums are actresses Linda Hunt and Meredith Baxter and TV journalist Mike Wallace.

The Interlochen Center sits on a 1,200 acre campus of glacial lakes and pines. There are 451 buildings on the site. Interlochen employs 1,000 people during the summer and 280 year 'round. Over a quarter of a million guests visit the campus each year. The Center has an annual operating budget of $20 million.

Interlochen's 67,000 alumni include more than ten per cent of the members of the country's major sympony orchestras.

* * * *

Interlochen State Park was Michigan's first, established by the state legislature in 1917. The state paid $60,000 for the land. The name was originally "Pine Park" and was created to preserve the 200-acre virgin pine stand for future generations.

Place Name

Grand Traverse Bay is split into East and West sections by the Old Mission Peninsula. At the base of both sections of the Bay sits Traverse City.

The area was first settled in the 1850s by William Boardman near the mouth of the river that was later named for him.

Many of the original settlers came from a town in Slovenia called Travnik. The name for their new home was based on the old.

Historical Significance

The location of Traverse City on Lake Michigan made it a logical place to build sawmills for the logging industry. Boardman and his son built one, but they were bought out by Perry Hannah. It is Hannah who really started development here and is considered the town's founding father.

Industry

In the 1890s, as the town was expanding, the remains of old orchards were discovered. Today Traverse City is one of the top cherry producing centers in the country. Cherry orchards are abundant and an incredible sight to see when they bloom in May.

Every July Traverse City hosts the National Cherry Festival, an event which dates back seventy years. There are air shows, all kinds of races, sporting events, and the fabulous Cherry Royale Parade, one of the longest in Michigan. Oh, yes, there are also pie-eating contests -- cherry pie, of course.

Note: The Hawkins Bakery hand-delivered a special dessert (a three-foot-diameter, 42 pound cherry pie) to President Calvin Coolidge and his wife while they were enjoying a dinner party at the president's summer white house in the Adirondack Mountains of New York.

One of the finest collections of Inuit Eskimo Art is found at The Dennos Museum Center.

Local Landmark

The northern tip of Old Mission Peninsula is marked by the Old Mission Lighthouse. It was built in 1870 and sits right on the 45th parallel, putting it half-way between the North Pole and the equator.

Prominent People

Actor David Wayne was born in Traverse City. His father was an insurance executive; his mother died when he was four. Wayne won fame and one of the first Tony Awards for acting as Og the leprechaun in the original productions of "Finian's Rainbow." His Broadway stardom led to a busy decade in front of the movie camera, including Adam's Rib, as the songwriter neighbor who flirts with Katharine Hepburn.

Place Name

This town was named after the secretary of the Traverse City Railroad Company, Thomas Bates, who was said to have been responsible for having the road go through here in 1891.

Historical Significance

Acme was founded by L.S. Hoxie, a native of Saratoga County, New York in 1864.

Local Landmark

The Music House is dedicated to bringing back the joyous sounds of mechanical music machines. The large collection of rare antique automated musical instruments are authentically restored pieces displayed in historic turn-of-the-century farm buildings in period settings.

Most everyone is familiar with the typical player piano that grandma used to have in her parlor. Less familiar and far more complex were the "reproducing" pianos. These instruments were typically grand pianos fitted with a mechanism that was not only capable of playing the correct notes, but also controlled the exact degree to which each key was struck. The rolls for the "reproducing" piano were "hand played" by some of the world's greatest musicians with special holes which controlled how hard or soft each key was played to re-create the exact sound of the original performance.

The Music House also has several different examples of pipe organs. From a late 18th century organ clock to the great Belgian Dance Organ.

Place Name

Abram Wadsworth, the Connecticut-born founder who built the first cabin in the area, which was incidently the first white man's home in the county, named the village after finding a pair of elk horns in the sand at the mouth of the river.

Industry

During the 1870s the Elk Rapid furnace was one of the nation's greatest producers of charcoal iron.

Elk Rapid furnace, forty-seven feet high and twelve feet in diameter, was begun in 1872 and produced the first blast of iron on June 24, 1873.

The local logging firm of Dexter and Noble constructed the furnace, locating it in Elk Rapids to utilize the vast stands of hardwood timber which surrounded the town. The hardwood was converted to charcoal to fire the furnace, and iron ore was imported form the Upper Peninsula by freighter.

Once the town's major employer, the furnace closed during World War I when the nearby forests were depleted, and cheaper smelting processes were developed.

(Historical marker located on Ames Street)

Place Name

Charles Avery acquired patents on property here in 1856, which was occupied primarily by Native Americans until 1876. Known as Indian Town the name was changed to Kewadin after a local Indian Chief.

Place Name

Captain John W. Brown built a log house and barn here about 1858 and the settlement which later became known as Brownstown. Brown sold out to Wilcox & Newell in 1864. Two years later Torch Lake Township (the Indian name was Waswagonlink, or lake of torches, from the fishing lights they used on the lake) was organized. Major Cicero Newell, the first postmaster dropped the name Brownstown, taking the name Torch Lake.

Famous cartoonist Jay Norwood Darling was born in Norwood Michigan, in 1876.

Place Name

This town gets its name from its location in the Michigan northwood.

Prominent People

Jay Norwood Darling spent much of his youth in Sioux City, Iowa where he began his cartooning career with the Sioux City Journal in 1900. After joining the Des Moines Register as a cartoonist in 1906, he began signing his cartoons with the nickname Ding - derived by combining the first initial of his last name with the last three letters.

A top-ranking political cartoonist syndicated in 130 daily newspapers, Darling reached an audience of many millions with cartoons noted for their wit and political satire. He was awarded Pulitzer prizes in 1923 and 1942, and in 1934 was named the best cartoonist by the country's leading editors.

President Franklin Roosevelt asked Darling to head the U.S. Biological Survey in 1934, the forerunner of the U.S Fish and Wildlife Service. He initiated the Federal Duck Stamp Program, which uses the proceeds from the sale of duck hunting stamps to purchase wetlands for waterfowl habitat.

For many years, Darling had a winter home in Florida on Captiva Island. Through the efforts of his island neighbors and the J.N. Ding Darling Foundation, a refuge was created on Sanibel Island and named in his honor.

> ??? Jay Norwood Darling drew the first Duck Stamp.

Place Name

Charlevoix was named for the Jesuit missionary, Pierre F.C.X. Charlevoix.

Historical Significance

It was first settled by a colony of fishermen in 1852. Later a large dock was built on Lake Michigan and Charlevoix became a popular resort.

* * * *

In 1847, before Charlevoix was even settled, a religious community was formed on nearby Beaver Island. It was led by James Strang, one of the first elders of the Mormon Church. Strang was elected "King of the Kingdom of St. James" in 1850 and he ruled as a dictator. His supporters even got him elected to the state legislature. However, not all of his followers were happy with his methods. Two of them assassinated Strang and the colony disbanded.

Local Landmark

One of the town's most notable features is part of U.S. 31. The Charlevoix Memorial Bridge crosses the Pine River Channel, which connects Round Lake with Lake Michigan. In the summertime, the bridge opens on the hour and half-hour to allow boats to pass through. Pleasure boats and huge freighters all come in and out of the port.

The Charlevoix bridge is one of only two bascule bridges in the state of Michigan. It took two years to build the current bridge, which opened to traffic in June of 1949. The bridge measures 111 feet overall with a 90-foot clear span above the water. Clearance from the water varies with the water level.

It was officially dedicated to honor the men of Charlevoix and the surrounding area who had given their lives during World War II.

> ??? A bascule bridge opens at the middle, with each half hinged at the end.

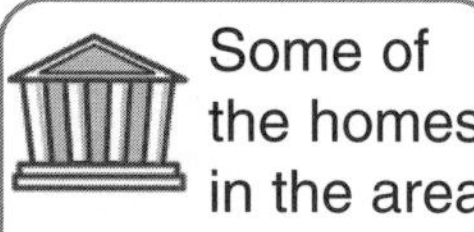

Some of the homes in the area are known as mushroom homes, due to the curved rooftops that look like a mushroom cap.

Prominent People

If you notice unusual buildings in Charlevoix, they were probably built by Earl Young. In the early 1920s he started creating homes with the exterior walls made of huge boulders dug up around the area.

Young did not have any formal architectural training, but over a period of 40 years built about 30 homes, most along Park Avenue, in Boulder Park and on Round Lake. He also built the Weathervane Restaurant on Pine River Channel, the Weathervane Terrace and the Lodge motel.

General Trivia

After President Ronald Reagan first tried Tom's Mom's Cookies, he liked them so much that the company sent 15 dozen of their chocolate-chunk specialty each week to the White House.

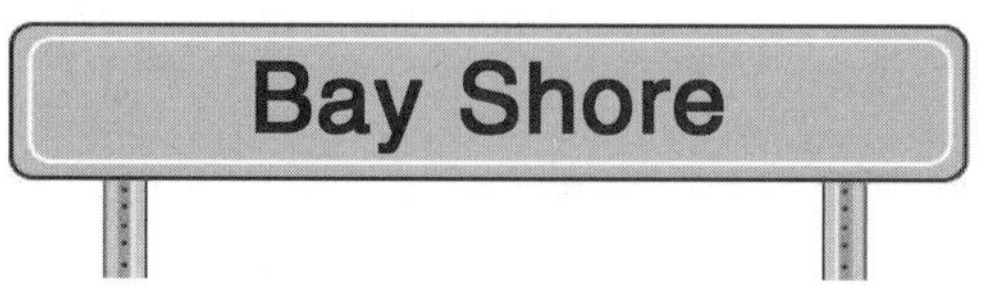

Place Name

Bayshore was given its name for its location on Little Traverse Bay.

Ernest Hemingway was married here in 1921.

General Trivia

Young Ernest Hemingway frequently came here to fish and camp on "The Point." This area is the setting for several of his famous "Nick Adams" short stories.

(Historical marker located at corner of Lake Street and Boyne City Road)

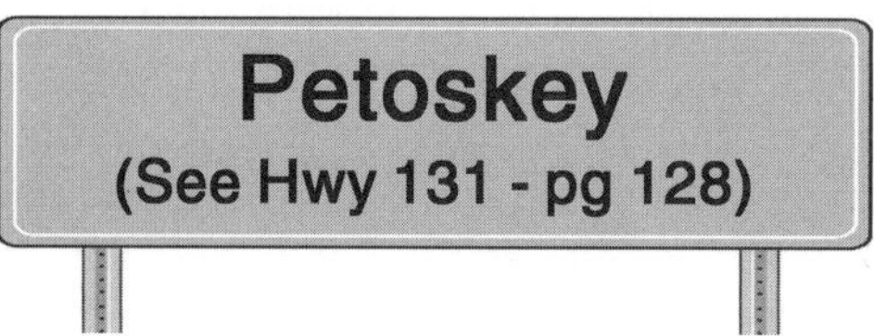

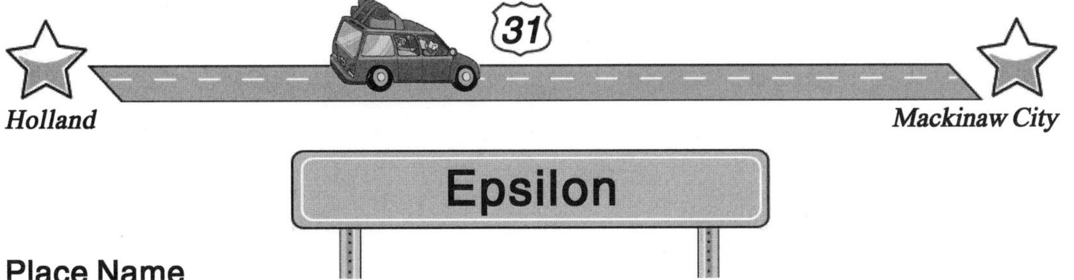

Place Name

Epsilon, like many Michigan post offices such as Alpha, Delta and Sigma, were named for letters of the Greek alphabet.

Place Name

Named for its view of Little Traverse Bay.

Historical Significance

The Methodist Church founded Bay View in 1875. It was originally intended as a summer retreat because of its lakeside location. The climate was healthful; railroad and steamer lines were close, so it was a good place to get away to. But Bay View was more than just a place to relax. In addition to its religious ties, there were programs on science and literature. In fact, Bay View became sort of a movement. The Bay View Reading Circle was a popular endeavor from 1892 to 1921. Study groups were located across the country.

Today Sunday vesper services are still an important part of the Bay View program. But guests are also treated to concerts by the Conservatory of Music and plays performed by the Bay View Theater Arts Department.

People who came here to speak included Helen Keller, William Jennings Bryan and Booker T. Washington.

Local Landmark

A feature that has earned Bay View acclaim is its delightful Victorian architecture. The community's 440 cottages have been designated a National Historic Landmark. Many of the cottages are occupied by descendants of the founding families.

Place Name

This town was named in honor of Conway Dodge, of the famous auto family who donated the first church and school.

General Trivia

At one time Michigan was a favorite nesting ground for the passenger pigeons. Vast quantities of beechnuts and other food attracted them. Each spring immense flocks arrived, literally darkening the skies hours at a time as they flew over. Here at Crooked Lake a nesting in 1878 covered ninety square miles. Millions of birds were killed, packed in barrels, and shipped from Petosky. Such wanton slaughter helped to make the pigeon extinct by 1914. The conservationist's voice was heard too late.

(Historical marker located at the State of Michigan fish hatchery on US 31)

Place Name

Village named for Alanson Clark, an office of the Grand Rapids and Indiana Railroad.

Place Name

Brutus is the name of the town in New York where Ephraim Meech, the areas first settler came from.

Place Name

Pellston was named after William Pells. A native of Poughkeepsie, New York, Pells purchased 1300 acres in the area, building a store and hotel in the town that would be named for him.

Van

Place Name

Van is named for lumbermen, Albert Van Every and his brothers.

HIGHWAY
28

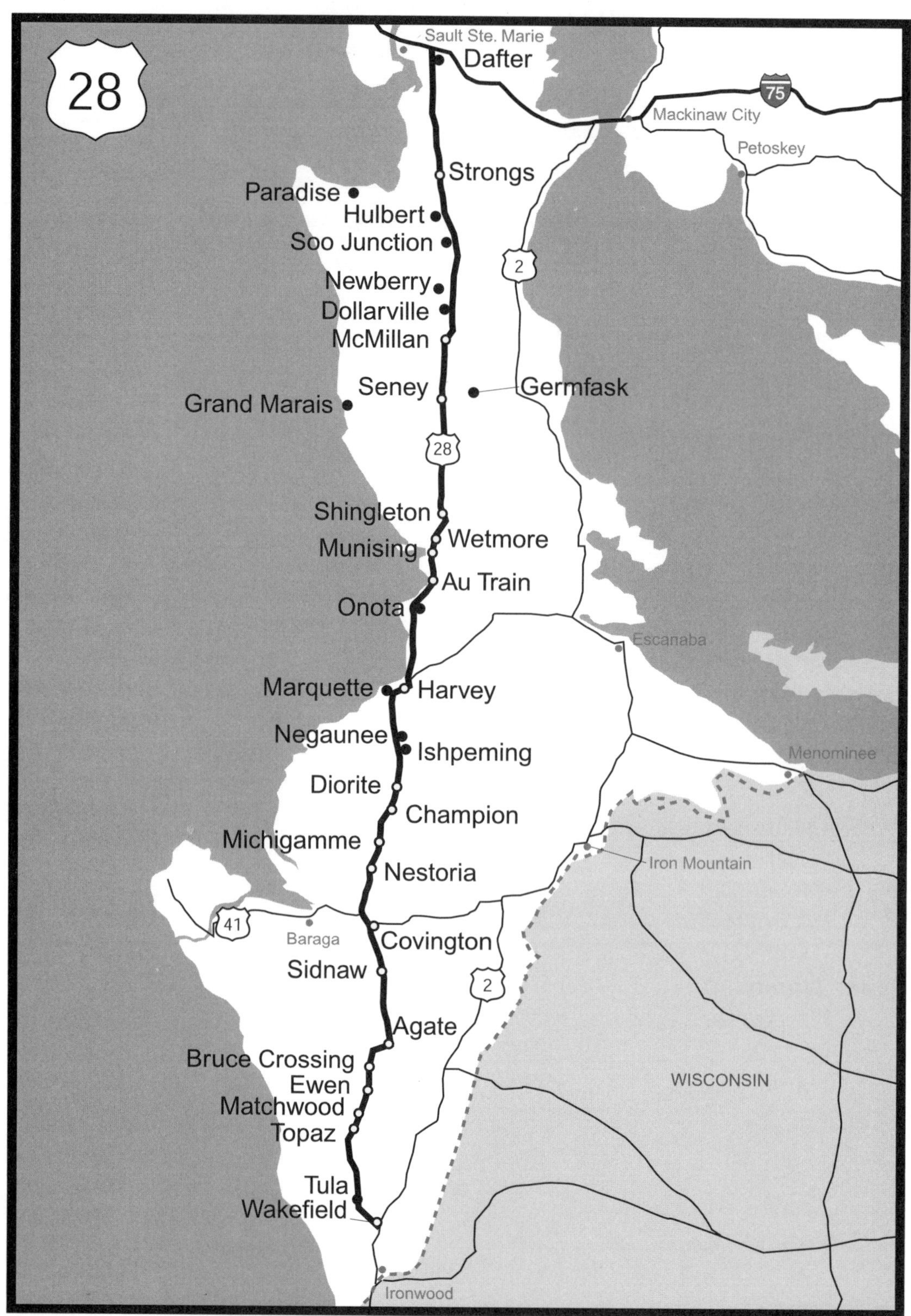
28
Sault Ste. Marie
Dafter
75
Mackinaw City
Petoskey
Strongs
Paradise
Hulbert
Soo Junction
2
Newberry
Dollarville
McMillan
Seney
Germfask
Grand Marais
28
Shingleton
Wetmore
Munising
Au Train
Onota
Escanaba
Marquette
Harvey
Negaunee
Ishpeming
Menominee
Diorite
Champion
Michigamme
Iron Mountain
Nestoria
41
Baraga
Covington
Sidnaw
2
Agate
Bruce Crossing
Ewen
Matchwood
Topaz
WISCONSIN
Tula
Wakefield
Ironwood

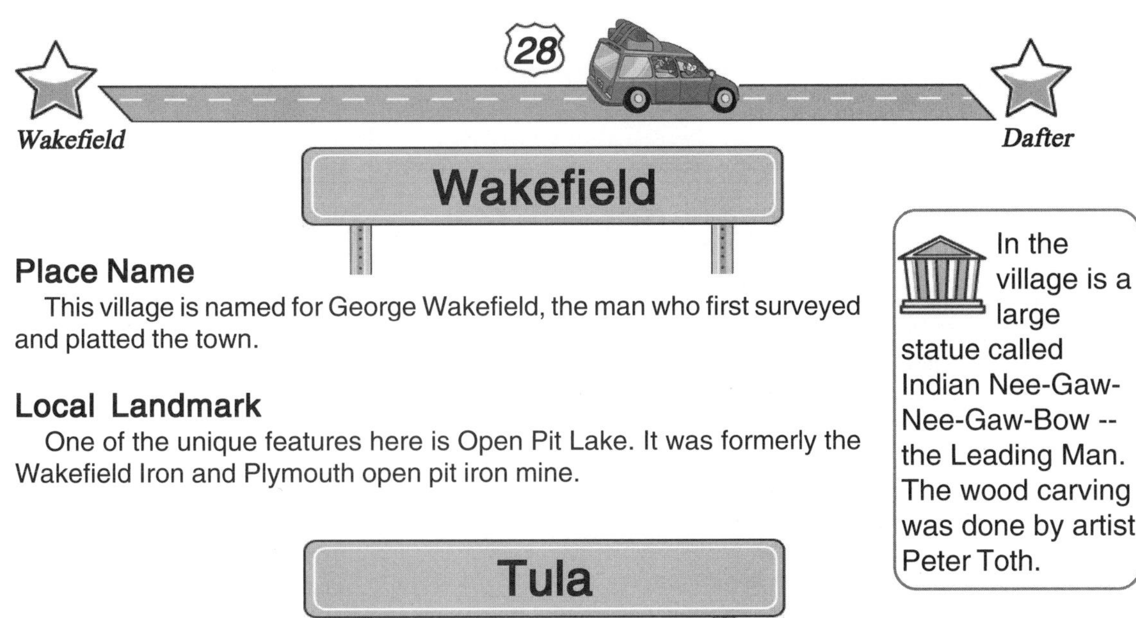

Place Name

This village is named for George Wakefield, the man who first surveyed and platted the town.

Local Landmark

One of the unique features here is Open Pit Lake. It was formerly the Wakefield Iron and Plymouth open pit iron mine.

> In the village is a large statue called Indian Nee-Gaw-Nee-Gaw-Bow -- the Leading Man. The wood carving was done by artist Peter Toth.

Tula

Place Name

The village is named for a Russian village approximately 20 miles south of Moscow.

Place Name

The village was named after the semiprecious stone, the topaz. Topaz is a very hard gemstone but it can be split with a single blow, a trait it shares with diamond. The Egyptians said that topaz was colored with the golden glow of the mighty sun god Ra. This made topaz a very powerful amulet that protected the faithful against harm.

Place Name

The Diamond Match Company which owned most of the pine in the area, established the village to accommodate and supply their logging camps.

Local Landmark

Ontonagon County sent an amazing 36,000 board feet of timber to the 1893 World's Fair in Chicago. A replica of the "Load of Logs" which was hauled by a single team is located in Ewen.

Place Name

The town was built primarily around the location of August Neuman's sawmill. Donald Bruce established a store in the vicinty of where the Duluth, South Shore and Atlantic Railroad crossed the old Military Road. When the post office was established it was called Bruce's Crossing, with the apostrophes later omitted.

Place Name

This town started as a Duluth, South Shore & Atlantic Railroad spur in the mining district. The name was given from the translucent quartz, the agate.

Place Name

This town was founded by lumbering firms harvesting white pine. It was given the Native American name meaning "a small hill by a creek."

Place Name

Originally settled by French Canadians, the town was named after their first postmaster, John Lyons, hometown of Covington, Kentucky. Others believe that a committee selected to chose a new name for the town, gathered around a stove with the maker's name from Covington, Kentucky stamped on it.

Nestoria

Place Name

The Nester Lumber Company was logging here when the Duluth, South Shore & Atlantic Railroad built a depot in the area which was named Nestonia. The name was later changed slightly to Nestoria.

Place Name

When Jacob Houghton discovered the Michigamme Mine, the first log cabins, used by the engineers were being built on the shores of Lake Michigamme (meaning Great Lake).

Place Name

The village name was given due to the proximity of the Champion Mine which opened in 1867 by the Champion Iron Company.

Place Name

This town was given the name of the geological word for igneous rock when the village was established as the site of the American Bostin Mine.

Ishpeming

Place Name

The town of Ishpeming was first settled in 1854. It was originally called "The Lake Superior Location". That name was a bit unwieldy for a town, so it became Ishpeming in 1862.

The name, of course, comes from an Indian word and means "high place" or "heaven".

Historical Significance

At one time Ishpeming was the "boom-town" of the U.P. The iron ore industry had helped the town develop into a cultural center, with its own opera house and dozens of upscale stores.

Local Landmark

The Republic Mine, just outside of Ishpeming, is Michigan's only open pit mine that offers free public viewings. It is owned by the Cleveland Cliffs Iron Company and is currently inactive. Visitors can stand on an observation deck and look into a pit that is 600 feet deep, with a pit surface area of 250 acres. The total area of the mine is four square miles.

At its peak production, 2.7 million tons of specular hematite pellets were shipped from the Republic Mine.

Seeing the immense size gives people an appreciation for what it took to get the ore out and also make the operation profitable. This is especially true when you think that this hole was once a 200-foot-high cliff that rose from the banks of the Michigamme River.

The mine provided low grade, surface deposits of ore which supplied the country's steel mills. The ore went by rail to Marquette and Escanaba. It was then shipped by ore boat throughout the Great Lakes.

* * * *

The National Ski Hall of Fame and Museum was first established here in 1953. It was designed to highlight the history of skiing in the United States in its various forms. The facility is organized as a "Walk Through Ski History." Visitors can see how the sport has evolved and grown over the years.

On the main floor is the National Ski Hall of Fame. The top athletes and developers of the sport are honored here with individual plaques which feature photographs and brief biographical sketches. The collection of U.S. National ski trophies is also on display. Among the historic artifiacts in the museum are a 4,000-year-old ski and pole recovered from a Swedish peat bog and a diorama of the legendary Birkebeiners. The development of skis, poles, and bindings is explained.

On the second floor are exhibits about ski clothing and ski lifts. A highlight for many visitors is the section about the 10th Mountain Ski Troops who served in Europe during World War II.

Glenn Seaborg discovered radioisotopes used to treat millions of cancer patients.

Prominent People

Chemist Glenn Seaborg was born in Ishpeming. While at the University of Chicago Seaborg and a group of scientist worked on the early stages of developing the atomic bomb discovering the element (plutonium) that makes bombs explode. Seabord won a Nobel Prize before he was 40.

General Trivia

The movie "Anatomy of a Murder" was based on the best-selling novel by Ishpeming defense attorney and author John Voelker. The courtroom drama is a true story of his experience successfully defending an Army Lieutenant charged with shooting a bartender in Big Bay. The film was directed and produced by Otto Preminger and starred Jimmy Stewart and Lee Remick.

Negaunee comes from the Chippewa word for pioneer.

Historical Significance

Negaunee is where iron ore was first discovered in the Lake Superior region. An Indian chief was the first to lead explorers to ore beds in the area. It is natural, then, that Negaunee was the first mining city in the Marquette Range.

Local Landmark

Michigan's iron industry is depicted at the Iron Industry Museum in Negaunee. The facility sits in the forested ravines of the Iron Range. It overlooks both the Carp River and the site of the first iron forge in the area. The museum tells the story of Michigan's three iron ranges and the people who worked them. And it goes back in time to explain the geologic origins of the iron. The effect of the industry today on the nation, the mining firms, and the people and cities of the U.P. is also explored. In addition to covering the story of Michigan's $48 billion iron mining and smelting industry, it also features the logging and copper industries.

Historical Significance

It was first settled in 1849 as a shipping center. The original town was begun where the lower harbor sits today. A.R. Harlow and Peter White developed the site and Harlow originally named it Worcester, in honor of his home town in Massachusetts.

A group from the Cleveland Mine, led by Robert Graveraet, built a dock here in a record-setting three-and-a-half days. There was one minor flaw in their design, however. They had used wood cleared from the area and it wasn't strong enough to hold the dock in place. It went down even more quickly than it had gone up!

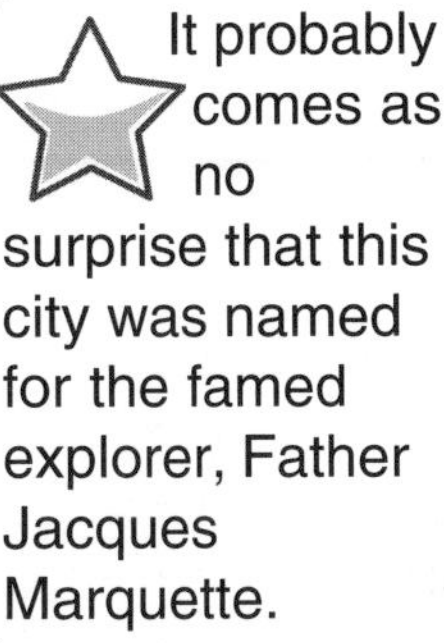

It probably comes as no surprise that this city was named for the famed explorer, Father Jacques Marquette.

Iron ore had been discovered here just a year earlier. That expedition of surveyors was led by William Burt and Dr. Jacob Houghton in September of 1844. Indians had previously informed two Marquette residents, P.B. Barbeau and J.P. Pendill, about the ore, but nothing came of that.

Once the ore was discovered, a plank road was built from Marquette to the mines. In 1855 the Iron Mountain Railroad was completed. It provided a way to ship the ore from the mines to the furnaces in the lower Great Lakes.

The production of iron ore and charcoal pig iron increased until 1873. Marquette County was then providing more than a quarter of all the iron produced in the United States.

The region's mining industry suffered a near collapse in the 1950s. But a means was found to improve the lower grades of ore by pelletizing.

Two open pit mines operated in the Marquette area, the Empire and Tilden mines.

Local Landmark

Three to nine million tons of iron ore were shipped annually from the Upper Harbor Presque Isle Ore Dock. It is located next to the Marquette Marina near Presque Isle Park.

The Duluth, South Shore & Atlantic Railway Co. Ore Dock No. 6 is 969 feet long to the fender on the outer end. It stands majestically above Marquette's Ellwood Mattson Lower Harbor Park.

The ore dock was built in 1926 to replace a timber structure. There are 150 pockets on the dock with individual storage capacities of 5,940 cubic feet -- or seven 50 ton cars of ore. It is 85 feet, 7 inches to the top of the deck. Each chute is 36 feet long and 7 feet, 2-1/2 inches wide. The weight of each is 4-1/2 net tons.

* * * *

The Marquette Maritime Museum recounts the fascinating maritime history of the city and Lake Superior. The Old Water Works Building, which is on the National Register of Historic Places, houses the museum. Its mission is to promote a greater understanding of the relationship between man and these incredible lakes he has tried to master. Among the displays are historic boats and marine hardware.

* * * *

Marquette is rich in lighthouse history as well. The Marquette Harbor Lighthouse can be seen from the downtown harborfront. It sits high atop a massive rock and is considered one of the most picturesque lighthouses on Lake Superior. The scene is reminiscent of a castle on a lake. The light and its attached quarters rest on a stone bluff and its bright-red color dominates the landscape.

Nearby is Stannard Rock Lighthouse and it is said to be one of the most desolate and dangerous lights on the Great Lakes. The Stannard Light towers 102 feet above the water. What makes it so dangerous is its location -- fifty miles off shore, where strong winds and storms off Lake Superior can move in quickly.

One November a maintenance crew had gone out to work on the light. They had been there for several weeks and were almost done when a storm moved in. Lake ice was pushed up against the lighthouse by the strength of the storm. The light became covered in 12 feet of ice by the time the storm ended. The men were running out of food and it took them two days to chop the ice away and escape the light.

* * * *

In 1985 Marquette was honored when the United States Olympic Committee designated Northern Michigan University as the site of the country's third Olympic Training Center. The others are in Lake Placid, New York and Colorado Springs.

Four years later the USOC redesignated the university as the nation's only United States Olympic Education Center. The focus of this center is the resident athlete training program. Here athletes can actively train for the Olympic Games, while still taking classes at the university or at Marquette High School. Most athletes in the program have been ranked in the top ten percent of their sport by the USOC.

The Olympic Education Center in Marquette has resident athlete training programs in biathlon, boxing, cross country skiing, luge and speed skating.

General Trivia

President Theodore Roosevelt used a local Marquette newspaper in 1913 for libel after the editor ran an article stating the former president was

habitually drunk. Roosevelt attended the hearing in person, and produced a number of character witnesses that testified on his behalf that attested to his temperance. Roosevelt won the court battle where by the jury awarded him six cents in damages, and a public apology from the editor.

The 1959 picture, "Anatomy of a Murder" was shot entirely in the area and is suppose to be the first movie to be filmed on location in Michigan.

Place Name

Charles Harvey founded the village that began as the site of the North Iron Company blast furnace.

Place Name

Originally a Native American fishing site, it was given the name Onota, meaning the place where the fisherman lived.

Place Name

The river carried so much sand into the lake here as to form a shoal over which the voyageurs would drag (trainerant, in French) their canoes to make a short cut. Old maps called the area Train River, with the Au added later.

Place Name

Julius Thorson of Munising bought swamp land where he built a factory to make gift articles. With the holiday trade in mind, he named the place Christmas. A fire in June, 1940, wiped out the place and ended the endeavor, but the area retains the name.

Place Name

The name Munising comes from the Chippewa Indian word for "Place of the Great Island."

Le lac superieur the French called it, meaning only that geographically it lay above Lake Huron.

Historical Significance

In size however, Lake Superior stands above all other fresh water lakes in the world. The intrepid Frenchman Brule discovered it around 1622. During the 1650s and 1660s French fur traders such as Radisson and Groseilliers, and Jesuits, such as Fathers Allouez and Menard explored this great inland sea. Within 250 years, fur-laden canoes had given way to huge boats carrying ore and grain to the world.

(Historical marker located in Scotts Falls Roadside Park
11 miles west of Munising)

* * * *

The Chippewas had a village here at the mouth of the Anna River in 1820. White men came here in 1850, but the first real town in the area was nearby AuTrain. It had thirty homes, a blacksmith shop, a sawmill, the bay furnace, and a government-owned lighthouse.

Capt. Taylor ran an excursion boat named the City of Munising. In 1894 Timothy Nestor took a ride on that boat to Munising Bay. He explored the area and hired men to start work on what became the city of Munising.

Local Landmark

It is still a small town. Its spectacular location and surrounding countryside make Munising one of the most picturesque cities in the midwest. People come to enjoy sites such as the many waterfalls in the area. Wagner Falls, Memorial Falls, Horseshoe Falls and Alger Falls are just a few to be found here.

* * * *

A passenger ferry travels between Munising and Grand Island National Recreation Area several times a day during the summer. The trip takes just ten minutes. The island is a 13,000-acre nature preserve. Visitors can hike, comb the beaches, mountain-bike and camp in an area roughly the size of Manhattan. A large iron company once owned the island. All but forty acres of it was purchased by the Hiawatha National Forest in 1989. There are close to fifty miles of hiking trails on the island.

* * * *

Because of Munising's location on the south shore of Lake Superior, it is to be expected that the area would be dotted with lighthouses. The Grand Island East Channel Lighthouse was built of hand-cut timber in 1867.

It was abandoned years ago and had been in danger of collapse. The owner of the property and other private citizens repaired the light's stone foundation and secured the tower with cables. The Grand Island Light was replaced by the Munising Range Lighthouse.

* * * *

One of the Great Lakes' most popular and unique scuba diving areas is here at Munising. The Alger Underwater Diving Preserve was the first established in Michigan. Divers can explore sea caves, intact shipwrecks, and even underwater interpretive trails. Some of the wrecked ships lie as deep as 110 feet in the water, while parts of some can be seen at the surface. Probably the most famous ship here is the Superior. The steamer sank in 1856 and is just ten to twenty feet down.

The caves offer exceptional shallow water diving. They are made of underwater sandstone cliffs created when the stone has been eroded by waves. Underwater visibility at the Alger Preserve is considered outstanding. It is not uncommon for divers in one hundred feet of water to be able to see up to thirty feet around them.

There are many other unusual aspects to this diver's dream. An underwater "museum" is located among the dock ruins off shore. Underwater signs depict maritime artifacts. There's also the Cathedral Caves, Miner's Castle, Ferry Dock Landing Drop-Off, and Pancake Rocks. Divers can see unique rock formations, a variety of large fish, and multicolored rocks in an amazing reflection of light.

* * * *

Mineral-stained sandstone cliffs rise two hundred feet above Lake Superior at Pictured Rocks National Lakeshore. This was the first such site to receive the national lakeshore designation. The park is made up of 40,000 acres along forty-two miles of Lake Superior shoreline.

The Chippewa Indians camped here in the summer and believed that the gods of thunder and lightning lived in the caves.

The cliffs are magnificent in shades of brown, tan and green. The colors come from the iron, manganese, limonite and copper found in the water. The shapes of the cliffs are caused by the constant battering of wind, ice and waves. And the shapes have given certain rocks their names -- Battleship Rock, Indian Head, Lover's Leap, the Color Caves, Rainbow Cave, and Chapel Rock are just a few to be found here.

> Thinking the rock formations looked like an evil face, they called it Nanitoucksinago, which meant "likeness of an evil spirit."

* * * *

A very different, but equally spectacular part of the shoreline here, is known as Grand Sable Banks. Sand dunes as high as 200 feet and sand-and-pebble beaches stretch along the shore for twelve miles.

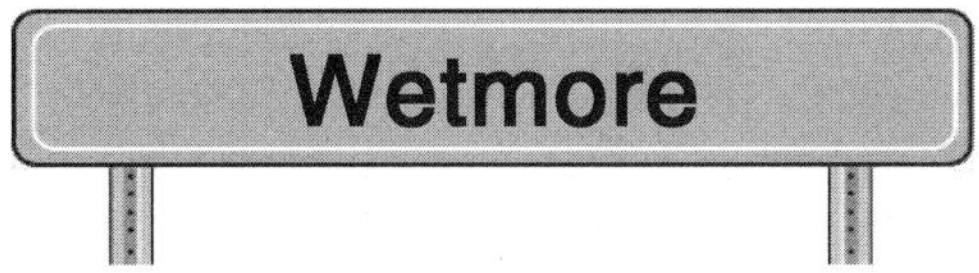

Place Name

William Wetmore came to the area to cut off hardwood for charcoal. He also built a kiln and general store. After he retired the village was named for him.

Shingleton

Place Name

Starting as a station stop on the Detroit, Mackinaw & Marquette Railroad it was named Jeromeville for the first born governor of Michigan, David Jerome. When the post office was established, the name was changed to Shingleton, referencing the site of the shingle mill.

Michigan's only snowshoe business is the culmination of a traditional concept developed over the years by Native Americans living in the northern reaches of this continent.

Industry

Located along the picturesque shore of Lake Superior, Iverson Snowshoe Company is a family-owned business dedicated to craftsmanship and value. Generations of satisfied customers including the U.S. Forest Service, Michigan Department of Natural Resources and backpackers throughout the country have made Iverson Snowshoes the hallmark in snowshoeing since the late 1950s.

Over the centuries, improvements were made to the snowshoe to accommodate various geographic conditions, but the snowshoe remained basically unchanged until Clarence Iverson led to the adoption of nylon-reinforced neoprene as an alternative to traditional rawhide lacing which has proven to be the most comfortable, durable, and best-performing snowshoe available.

Grand Marais

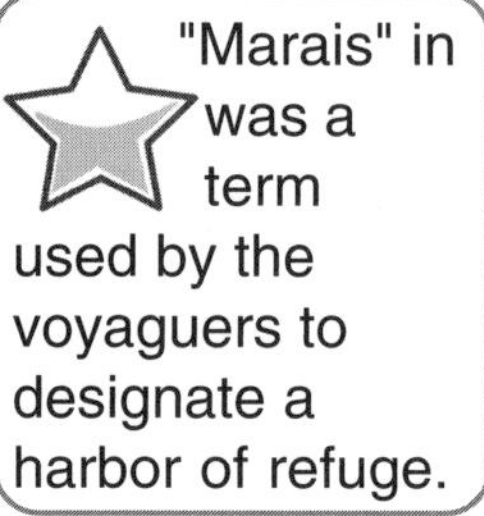

"Marais" in was a term used by the voyaguers to designate a harbor of refuge.

Place Name

Grand Marais, which is among Michigan's oldest place names, received its name from French explorers, missionaries and traders who passed here in the 1600s.

Historical Significance

In the 1800s Lewis Cass, Henry Schoolcraft and Douglass Houghton also found the sheltering harbor a welcome stopping place.

Grand Marais's permanent settlement dates from the 1860s with the establishment of fishing and lumbering. At the turn of the century Grand Marais was a boom town served by a railroad from the south. Its mills turned out millions of board feet annually. Lumbering declined around 1910, and Grand Marais became almost a ghost town, but the fishing industry continued.

Many shipping disasters have occurred at or near the harbor of refuge, which has been served by the Coast Guard since 1899. In 1942 the first radar station in Michigan was built in Grand Marais. Fishing, lumbering and tourism now give Grand Marais its livelihood.

<u>(Historical marker located in Bay Shore Park)</u>

Place Name

Dr. W.W. French suggested the name which was formed using the initial of the eight founding settlers surnames; John Grant, Matthew Edge, George Robinson, Thaddeus Mead, Dr. W.W. French, Ezekiel Ackley, Oscar Shepard and Hezekiah Knaggs.

Place Name

When this town was established, it was named after George Seney, a railroad director from New York.

Local Landmark

If it's wildlife you're looking for -- of the natural kind -- look no further than the Seney National Wildlife Refuge. An amazing diversity of wildlife species and habitat are found in this refuge, managed by the U.S. Fish and Wildlife Service. It was established in 1935 to help with both the protection and production of migratory birds and other wildlife. Marsh, swamp, bog, grasslands and forest are all found within its borders. And nearly two-thirds of the refuge is wetlands.

> Two hundred species of birds, twenty-six species of fish and fifty different mammals have all been recorded here.

* * * *

Another important natural site is the Huron Islands Wilderness Area. It is made up of 147 acres on eight remote islands in Lake Superior.

The bedrock of the islands is pink and gray granite and the islands are covered with trees, shrubs and herbaceous plants. Lichens and mosses have attached to exposed rock. The rocks rise to a height of 200 feet above the lake. The south side features steep cliffs. On the north side, the rock surfaces have been rounded by waves and glaciers.

The Coast Guard owns a historic lighthouse and its outbuildings which sits on one of the islands.

Place Name

Town is named for James Stoughton McMillan, an executive of the Duluth, South Shore & Atlantic Railroad, who later went on to be a U.S. Senator.

Place Name

This village developed around the mill and general store of the American Lumber Company. It was named for the general manager Robert Dollar who went on to make a fortune in shipping.

Place Name

Grant's Corner was founded as logging headquarters for the Vulcan Furnace Company in 1882. That same year the name was changed to Newberry in honor of the Detroit industrialist, Truman Newberry.

Local Landmark

Upper Tahquamenon Falls is more than 200 feet across and has a drop of nearly fifty feet. A flow of up to 50,000 gallons of water per minute has been measured cascading over the falls.

> The largest waterfalls east of the Mississippi is the Upper Tahquamenon Falls.

A series of five smaller falls, known as the Lower Falls, are four miles downstream. They may not be as high or as dramatic as the Upper Falls, but they are equally as beautiful.

The Tahquamenon drains an area of more than 820 square miles. It rises from springs north of McMillan and then meanders for 94 miles before emptying into Whitefish Bay.

The color of the water is amber, but that doesn't come from rust or muddiness. Tannin leached from cedar, spruce and hemlock trees in the swamps drains into the river. The water churned by the falls is extremely soft and results in a large amount of foam. This trademark of the Tahquamenon has been noted since the days of the voyageurs.

Place Name

The name indicates the location at the junction of the Soo branch and the St. Ignace branch of the old Duluth, South Shore and Atlantic Railroad, now known as the Soo Line.

Place Name

Francis Hulbert discovered this area when out cruising for timber for himself. Unfortunately he died before a village was established, which was accomplished by his son Richard Hulbert.

Place Name

Resort promotor Leon McGregor suggested the name from the abundance of fish and game, along with the beautiful country and shoreline.

General Trivia

A giant seventy-foot-tall, 22-foot-diameter blue spruce was used in a gigantic, five-ton, $15,000 Christmas display at Disney World in 1971.

Place Name

When Mr. Strong loaded logs on the Duluth, South Shore & Atlantic Railroad, the station here became known as Strongs Siding. A few years later, fifteen families came here to work in Eugene Turner's shingle mill and the community began to grow. The name Turner was suggested for the post office, but was declined with the recommendation that simply drop the word Siding and call it just Strongs.

Place Name

This lumber settlement was founded by George Stevens and originally called Stevensburgh after him. Later it was changed to Dafter. Probably after another one of the early settlers.

HIGHWAY
25

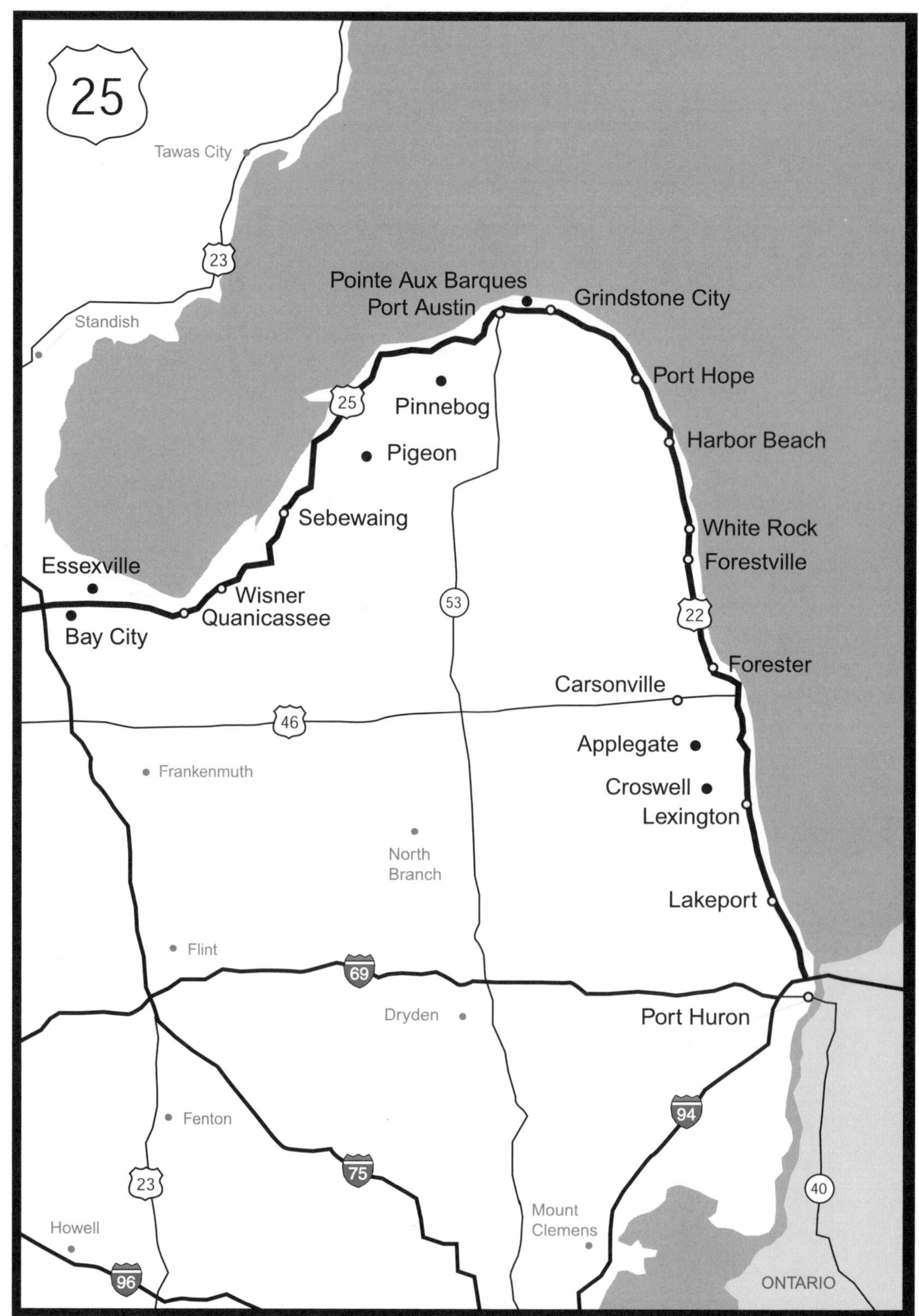
25
Tawas City
23
Standish
Pointe Aux Barques
Port Austin
Grindstone City
Port Hope
25
Pinnebog
Harbor Beach
Pigeon
Sebewaing
White Rock
Forestville
Essexville
Wisner
Quanicassee
53
22
Bay City
Forester
Carsonville
46
Applegate
Frankenmuth
Croswell
Lexington
North
Branch
Lakeport
Flint
69
Dryden
Port Huron
Fenton
94
75
23
40
Howell
Mount
Clemens
96
ONTARIO

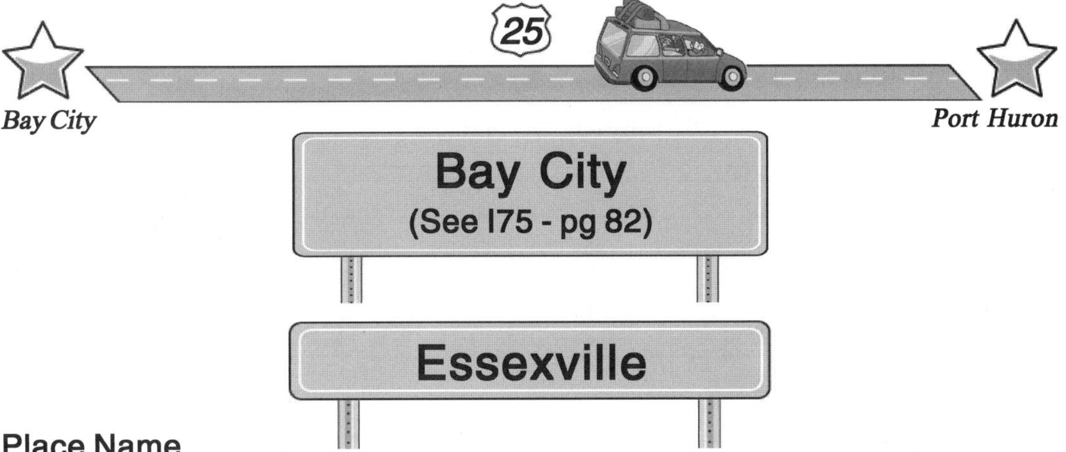

Place Name

The town is named after Ransom Essex, the areas first settler.

Industry

The first successful beet sugar factory in Michigan was built in 1898 by the Michigan Sugar Company on Woodside Avenue in Essexville. A year later the Bay City Sugar Company built a competing factory across the street. The two plants merged in 1903 with the original plant closing down shortly thereafter. The name of the merged company was Bay City-Michigan Sugar Company which was then shortened to Michigan Sugar Company. It operated continuously until 1929 and closed permanently in 1933. The company's early success sparked the construction of many other beet sugar plants. All were part of the drive which has made beet sugar vital to Michigan's economy.

<u>(Historical marker located on Woodside Avenue)</u>

The Monitor Sugar factory is the only beet sugar plant still in operation in Bay County.

Prominent People

Essexville barber, Terry McDermott won the gold medal in the 500-meter speed skating event at the 1964 Olympics in Innsbruck, Austria. Things were looking pretty bleak for the U.S. team competing against two time Gold Medalist, Evgeni Girshin of Russia. But McDermott was the first to cross the line. The U.S. team had their Gold Medal victory!

Terry McDermott clocked at 40.1 seconds -- set a new Olympic record!

Place Name

The town name is a Native American word meaning long tree.

Place Name

Moses Wisner was inaugurated as the governor of Michigan in 1859. Two years later when the town was organized they named it after him.

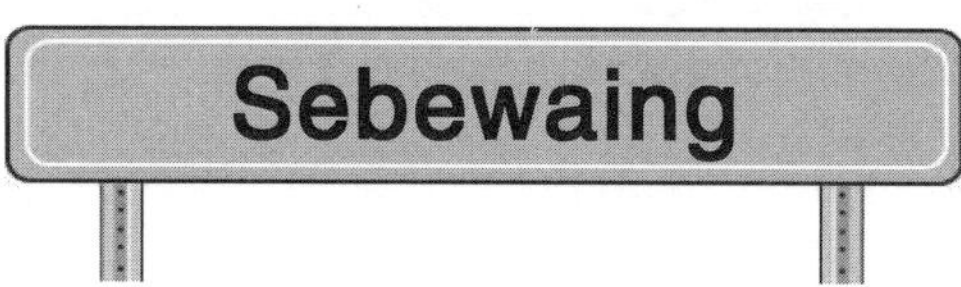

Place Name

Lutheran minister John Auch, came to the area looking for good farmland for a settlement; and to do missionary work among the Native Americans. The town was given the Native American word for crooked creek, which flowed nearby.

Place Name

The township was named for its location on the Pigeon River, which was named in reference to the large number of wild pigeons in the area.

Place Name

Originally called Pinnepog by the early settlers, a Chippewa word for partridge drum, was changed to Pinnebog when they found out another city by the same name was five miles north on Saginaw Bay. The revised spelling was suppose to be "a high sounding and dignified way of saying pine bog."

Place Name

Jeduthan Byrd, builder of a sawmill in the area, sold his lumbering firm to the Smith, Austin and Dwight company. Alfred Dwight, one of the proprietors built a large boat dock for himself and others; adding a street light on a pole for a lighthouse. This dock and surrounding area would be known as Austin's Dock, later renamed as Port Austin.

New York contractor Charles G. Learned helped build New York City's water-works system and the Erie Canal.

Local Landmark

Around 1837 Charles Learned and his brother-in-law purchased several thousand acres of pine land in Michigan's Thumb area. Two years later, Learned and his wife, Maria Raymond, came to Port Austin and bought a house and three acres. Learned's cutover pine land became a 2,000-acre farm where he prospered as an agriculturalist and dairy farmer. With profits from his lumbering and farming enterprises Learned enlarged and updated his house in the French Second Empire style.

In the 1860s Ohio congressman, later president, James A. Garfield, a family friend, was a frequent guest here.

(Historical marker located on Lake Street)

Place Name

Point aux Barques means point of ships and was given the name by French sailors who said the ragged rock formations gutting out into Lake Huron resembled boats moored along the shore.

Place Name

Captain Aaron Peer, along with James Dufty came to the area in 1834 to open a grindstone quarry.

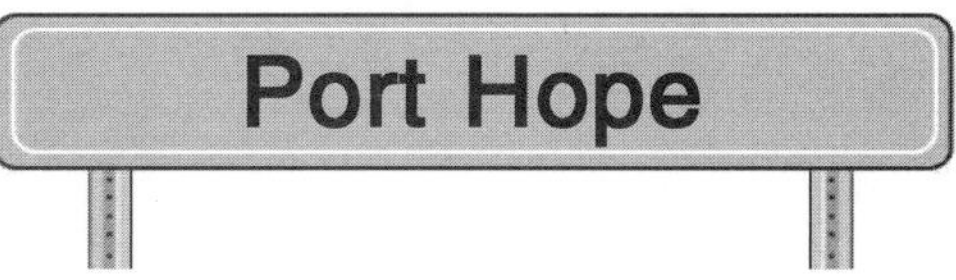

Place Name

Drifting in a small boat, Mr. Southard and Mr. Witcher succeeded in making it to land and responded by naming it Port Hope.

Place Name

The town, originally known as Sand Beach was given the name Harbor Beach as a means to rid outsiders of the impression that the area was nothing but sand.

Place Name

The town's name was given for the large white boulder in Lake Huron which marked the entrance to the area.

Place Name

Name was given because of the heavy timber in the area.

Place Name

Orginally spelled Forrester, the spelling was later shortened, was given in reference to being a lumbering center.

Place Name

Village named for Jesse Applegate, leader of the party which founded the Applegate Trail, the southern route of the Oregon Trail.

Place Name

Charles Croswell became the Governor of Michigan in 1877, the year the original town of Davisville changed its name.

Place Name

Named by Reuben Diamond, whose wife was a cousin of Ethan Allen who fought at Lexington.

Place Name

Local lumberman B.C. Farrand named the village Lakeport because of its closeness to Lake Huron.

HIGHWAY
23

23
Saint Ignace
Mackinaw City
Cheboygan
Grace
Alverno
Manitou Beach
Ocqueoc
Rogers City
Petoskey
Hagensville
Presque Isle
Posen
Alpena
31
Ossineke
Traverse City
Alcona
Grayling
Harrisville
23
131
Oscoda
39
Cadillac
Tawas City
127
Alabaster
Omer
Au Gres
Standish
10
Pinconning
Linwood
Kawkalin
Mount Pleasant
25
Bay City
Sandusky
Zilwaukee
46
Saginaw
Frankenmuth
Birch Run
Clio
Flint
Grand Rapids
Port Huron
23
96
Fenton
94
Lansing
Parshallville
Howell
Brighton
ONTARIO
Hell
Detroit
Hamburg
Battle Creek
94
Ann Arbor
Windsor
Ypsilanti
Saline
Kalamazoo
69
Milan
Deerfield
Dundee
Coldwater
Adrian
Samaria
Riga
Temperance
Lamberton
INDIANA
OHIO

Place Name

This township takes the name for its founder, John Lambert.

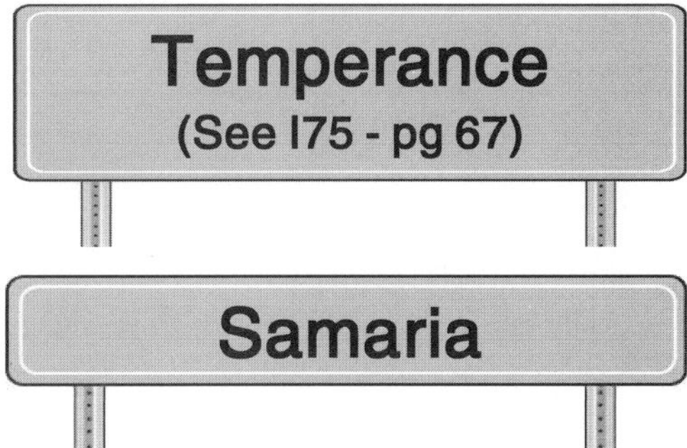

Place Name

When the Ann Arbor Railroad established a station in the area, and a township to soon follow, it was given the name for musically talented Samuel and Mary Weeks, whose home was a major gathering place.

Place Name

Reverend Kroenke suggested the name for this township after his college roommates hometown in Germany.

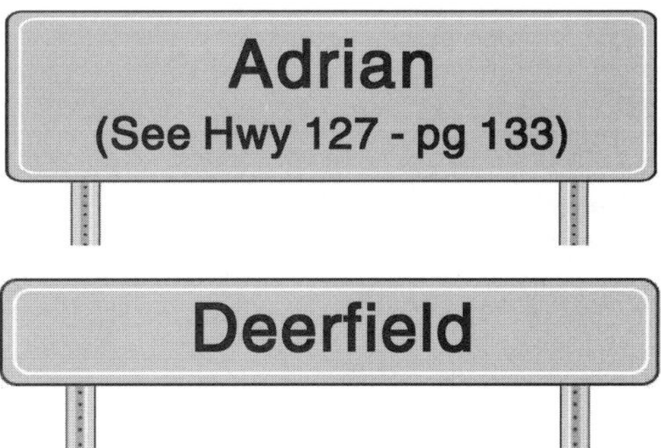

Place Name

The town was so named because of the abundance of deer in the area.

Prominent People

Amos Muzyad Jacobs, better known as entertainer Danny Thomas was born in Deerfield to Lebanese immigrants. The fifth of nine children he began his career as a singer for a Detroit radio station in 1934, later working his way into nightclubs and eventually on television. He starred in "Make Room for Daddy," and "The Danny Thomas Show."

Place Name

Dundee was named after the city of Alonzo Curtis (one of the areas first postmasters) ancestors in Scotland.

Place Name

When Henry Tolan built the first potash factory in the area, the town was named after him. When the post office was established it was changed from its present name of Farmersville to Milan.

Place Name

Named after the Saline River which runs through town and gets its name from the salt springs.

General Trivia

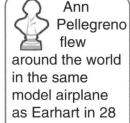

Ann Pellegreno flew around the world in the same model airplane as Earhart in 28 days.

On the thirteenth anniversary of Amelia Earhart's disappearance, thirty-year-old junior-high-school English teacher, Ann Pellegreno retraced the famed aviatrix's flight.

* * * *

In 1992, when Harry Brannon was digging a pond he discovered some of the oldest preserved mastodon tracks. Estimated around 10,000 years old, the location of some of the mastodon bones and 20 footprints are so clear that scientist can almost tell exactly where the huge dinosaur stumbled as they went through the area.

* * * *

Henry Ford once owned and operated "Weller's" Mill.

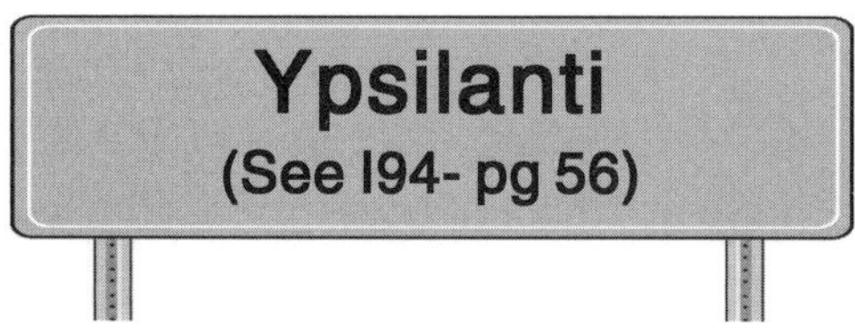

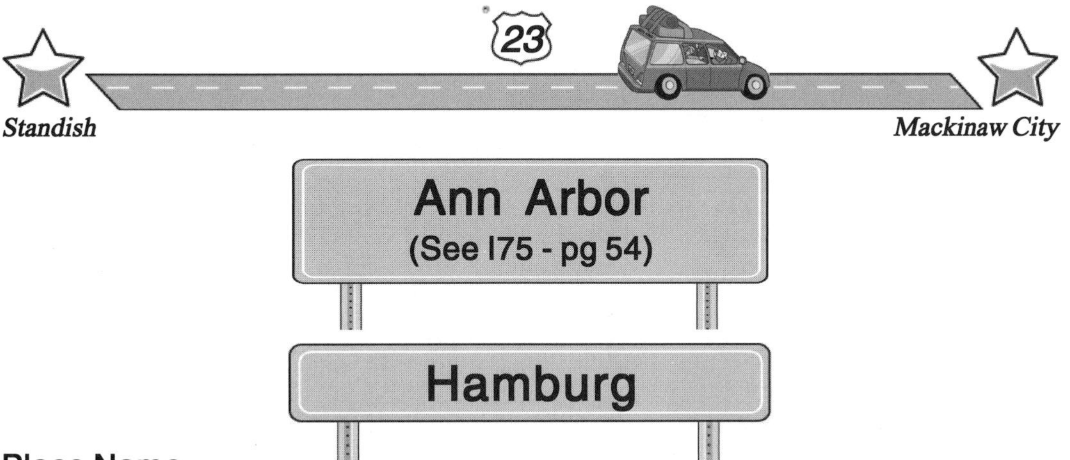

Place Name

Messrs Grisson purchased a large tract of land in the area where he built a grist mill, store and hotel. When the village was platted, a group of 19 men held a meeting to name the town. After a deadlock vote of 8 and 8 over naming the town Steuben or Knox, the men agreed to let Messrs Grisson name it. Grisson chose the name of his native city of Hamburg, Germany.

Place Name

Founded by New Yorkers, who came to the area via traveling through the Erie Canal, established numerous businesses in the area, including as a sawmill, flourmill and distillery. Local tradition says the name of the town is attributed to the description of the drunken brawling by the Native American's in the area.

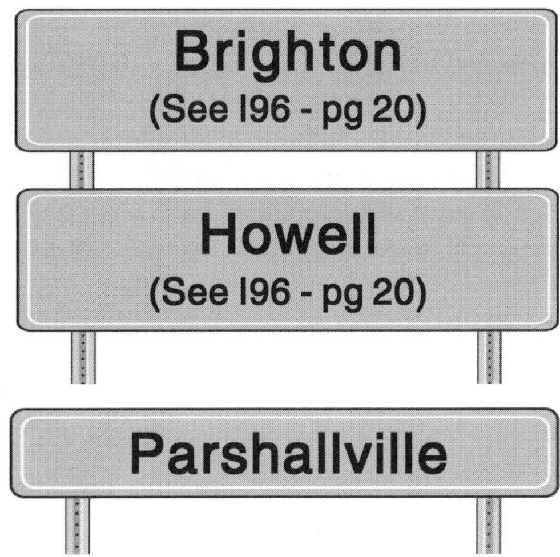

Place Name

The village is named for Isaac Parshall, who owned 400 acres of land in the area when it was established.

Town is named for a local lawyer William Fenton, who later became Michigan's lieutenant-governor in 1847.

General Trivia

Some people say that Fenton won a card game between Robert Leroy and Norman Rockwell, giving him the right to name the town. The town's main streets are named after the losers.

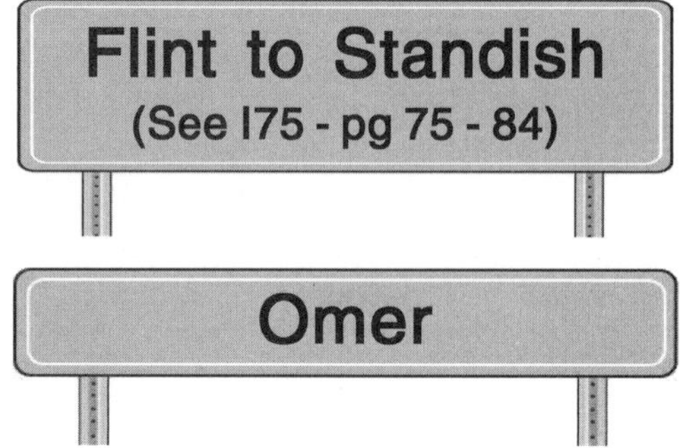

Place Name

George Carscallen and George Gorie, builders of a large sawmill on the Rifle River wanted to name their township Homer. After they found out there already was a Homer in the state, they shortened it to Omer.

The town was founded by workers building the Saginaw-Au Sable railroad, which reached here in 1862.

Place Name

Both the city and the river that runs through it are named for the gritty stones or "Au Gres" that were found here by the French explorers.

General Trivia

Called the "Perch Capital of Michigan", Au Gres is a favorite with fishermen.

Place Name

The town was named for the location where the first alabaster rock (gypsum) was bored in 1841. Note: The 1981 Guinness Book of World Records listed Alabaster as having the worlds largest gypsum quarry.

Place Name

Gideon O. Whittemore founded the town in 1854, when he gave up being a judge in Oakland County to build a sawmill here. The town, named after Otawas, a local Ottawa chief, became very important in the lumber boom and served as home for the historic Detroit & Mackinaw Railroad.

Local Landmark

Tawas Point Lighthouse sits at the northern point where Lake Huron enters Saginaw Bay. It was built in 1876 and is equipped with a Fresnel lens. The Fresnel lenses were made in Paris and are now considered both historic and artistic treasures.

The first lighthouse on this spot was built in 1853. However, the shifting sands had built up the shoreline so much that the light was almost a mile from the Lake.

Place Name

Michigan historian Henry Schoolcraft created the word Oscoda in the mid-1800s. It comes from two Indian words -- "ossin", which means stones, and "muskoda", which means prairie. Used together, the name denotes a pebbly prairie.

Local Landmark

More than half of the county is in the Huron National Forest and another quarter is in the Oscoda State Forest. There are no official communities. One rather rare resident of the area is the Kirtland Warbler. This small blue-gray bird winters in the Bahamas, but comes to the Huron National Forest to breed. The bird, is known for its singing.

Kirtland Warbler. comes to the Huron National Forest to breed -- the only place that it does so.

* * * *

The River Road Scenic Byway runs for twenty-two miles along the Au Sable River near Oscoda. It provides visitors with an amazing variety of experiences. Wildlife, such as spawning salmon and bald eagles, can be seen. Forests and reservoirs add to the scene.

The Lumbermen's Monument sits on a riverbank and looks out across the valley. This nine-foot high bronze statue of lumberjacks was erected "to perpetuate the memory of the pioneer lumbermen of Michigan through whose labors was made possible the development of the prairie states."

Another attraction is the unusual Stairway to Discovery, an interpretive trail that descends 260 steps to the river. It is the only such trail that is comprised solely of a staircase.

General Trivia

A major annual event in the area is the Weyerhauser Au Sable River Canoe Marathon. The canoeists start off from Grayling at dusk. Fourteen hours and 120 miles later, they arrive in Oscoda. The Marathon is the second leg in the North American Triple Crown and brings in visitors from around the world, both to participate and to watch. It is called "the toughest spectator sport in the world."

Place Name

Two fishing partners, Simeon Holden and Crosier Davison purchased the pine lands, along with the water power priviledge here when they developed Davison's Mill. Holden and Crosier sold their mill and surrounding land to Benjamin Harris. Harris along with his sons organized the township which would take their names.

Place Name

Canadian-born commercial fisherman William Hill settled this area known originally as The Cove. It was renamed after the county which Henry Rowe Schoolcraft called Alcona, after a Native American word meaning the beautiful plain.

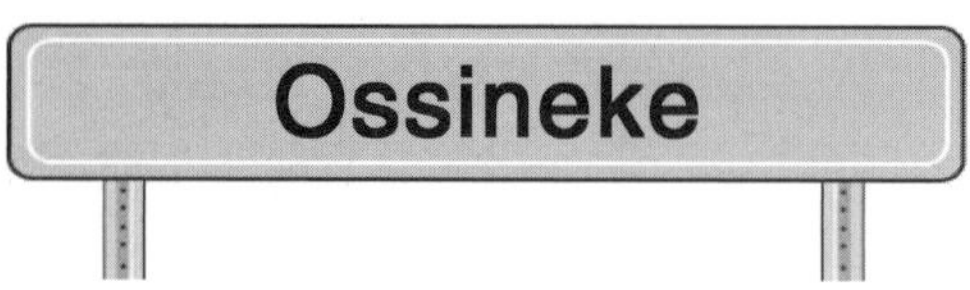

Place Name

Jonathan Burtch and Anson Eldred purchased the first government land here at the mouth of the Devil River where the Native American's called the site, Wawsineke. Later changed to Ossineke by the white settlers.

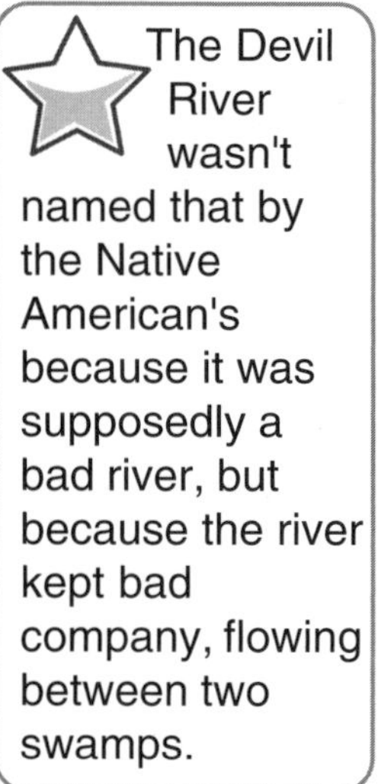

The Devil River wasn't named that by the Native American's because it was supposedly a bad river, but because the river kept bad company, flowing between two swamps.

Place Name

The town and county were named Alpena at the suggestion of Henry Rowe Schoolcraft, after the Indian word for partridge.

George N. Fletcher and three other men from the Detroit area first platted the village in 1856, calling it Fremont, after General John Fremont. But since there was already a city in Michigan with that name, its name was changed to Thunder Bay in reference to the nearby lake where Huron Indian chief, "An-a-ma-kee" or "Thunder" fished. Another theory is that the thunderous sound of the waves hitting the shore gave the place its name. Never-the-less, the name was later changed back to that of the County's.

Historical Significance

The first real settlers on the island were fishermen. They were very successful until eviction by the U.S. Government, which owned the island. Troops came from Fort Mackinac, declared the fishermen squatters, and told them they had to leave. This was due in part to the U.S. Revenue Service's attempts to halt the smuggling and sale of whiskey to the Indians.

Industry

Portland cement was first produced in the United States in 1871, in Michigan in 1896. Because of Alpena's location in the midst of immense limestone deposits, the Huron Portland Cement Company, founded at Detroit in 1907, chose this site for its plant. Cement production began here in 1908. Able management and skilled workmen made this the world's largest cement plant. From Thunder Bay, ships of the Huron fleet deliver cement to all parts of the Great Lakes region.

(Historical marker located on Ford Avenue)

Portland cement, so-called because it resembles in color stone from the Isle of Portland in the British Isles.

Local Landmark

Thunder Bay Island lies outside the north end of the bay. The piece of land is small, but it has played an important role in the history of the area, particularly the maritime history.

At least eighty shipwrecks took place here, which is one of the most significant concentrations of such disasters in the Great Lakes.

The Thunder Bay Underwater Preserve was established in 1981 and offers divers from around the world the unique opportunity to dive the wrecks. The Preserve also works to prevent people from looting the ships.

In a 288-square-mile area are the remains of the Montana, a steamer that burned and sank in 1914. It lies seventy feet below the surface. There's also the Oscra T. Flint, the Monohansett and the Lucinda Van Valkenburg among others. Most famous among the wrecks is the Grecian, which went down in 1906 in 110 feet of water. The 290-foot steamer makes a tremendous site for underwater photography, with the ship's steam engines of particular note. The wrecks are making Alpena a mecca for amateur and professional divers alike.

Mariners of the past called this area "Shipwreck Alley" because the shoals, fog, and storms caused many boats to miss the route around the island and on into Alpena.

Legend has it that the isolation drove one lightkeeper's wife mad and she haunts the place still, screaming from inside the lighthouse on windy nights.

Place Name

Presque Isle is French for "almost an island." The name was first given to the county, then adopted by the village.

Local Landmark

Lighthouses also play an important part in Presque Isle's history. The Old Presque Isle Lighthouse was built in 1840. It is only thirty feet tall, fairly short for a lighthouse. It marked the north end of Presque Isle Harbor, which served as a refuge for boats and provided wood for ships' boilers. Two range lights would guide boats through the harbor channel.

* * * *

One mile north is the New Presque Isle Lighthouse, which was built in 1871. It stands a grand 113 feet tall at the turning point into North Bay.

Place Name

Posen, like the nearby township of Polaski, was founded by a group of Polish immigrants who named their new home after the province of Boznan in Poland.

Place Name

Township was named and established around the (William) Hagen and (Wilson) Pines sawmill.

Place Name

William Rogers, Albert Molitor and Frederick Denny Larke came to the area to establish a lumber company. Molitor built a cabin, dock and mill on the shore owned by Rogers. The townsite which grew around the mill became known as Roger's Mill and later changed to Rogers City.

General Trivia

It is only right that Rogers City has become known as "The Nautical City". It is situated on one of the most natural and pristine sections of beautiful Lake Huron.

> Rogers City boasts the site of the largest limestone quarry in the world.

Local Landmark

Rogers City limestone quarry is more than three miles long and two miles wide. It makes sense then that Rogers City is also the site of the largest limestone processing plant in the world.

* * * *

Lake Huron is considered by many as the most dangerous of the Great Lakes. Some call it "the graveyard of ships". Its open north shore is famous for its hidden shoals and false bays.

Because of the increase in the amount of shipping here in the late 1800s, Forty Mile Point Lighthouse was built in Rogers City in 1896. This blinking sentinel for ships stands forty miles southeast of Old Mackinaw Point and the same distance northwest of Thunder Bay. Like many other lighthouses today, it has been deactivated from service.

* * * *

On October 19, 1905 fierce storms arose that threatened even the big steel-hulled ships. Smaller wooden ships were at even greater risk as the squalls swept across the Lakes. Twenty-seven ships didn't make it back home and over fifty lives were lost in that storm.

The "Fay", an 1871-freighter, was headed south with a wooden schooner-barge, the D.P. Rhodes, in tow. Both were loaded with coal and iron ore. The Fay's captain tried to protect his ship, cargo and crew by staying close to the shore. But the waves were too treacherous. The ship broke up on a sandbar. Today you can still see about 150 feet of her side. Metal rods and spikes hold her in place on the beach west of the lighthouse.

Place Name

Manitou is a Native American word for Great Spirit.

Place Name

Village named after the winding Ocqueoc River which was given the Native American wording meaning crooked waters.

Place Name

Grace was founded and takes its name from the Grace Lumber Company of Detroit which was established here in 1893.

Place Name

Town is named in honor of the patron of the parish, St. Francis of Assisi, who, while praying at Mount Alverno, received the stigmata.

Note, stigmata are wounds believed to duplicate the wounds of Christ's crucifixion that appear on the hands and feet, and sometimes on the side and head, of a person.

Place Name

Cheboygan means "Water of the Chippewas" and was once an Indian campground called Shabwegan.

Historical Significance

Jacob Simmons was the first white settler. He was a cooper from Mackinaw City and built a cabin here in 1844 to give him access to more business. The lumber industry caused the area to grow, with Cheboygan becoming a city in 1889. It became an important Great Lakes port.

* * * *

Cheboygan has its own Coast Guard station, where the Great Lakes largest icebreaker, the Coast Guard Cutter Mackinaw, is based. The Mackinaw breaks up ice flowes that would close shipping lanes at least six weeks earlier each winter.

Local Landmark

An important site related to navigation is the Cheboygan Crib Lighthouse.

A crib is a wooden box that is built as a base for an offshore lighthouse. It is filled with rocks and cement before being put at its permanent location. This crib was set offshore in Duncan Bay at the entrance to the Cheboygan River. However, the crib settled over time and the tower fell into the river. The light was recovered and placed on the end of the Cheboygan River's western pier by the citizens of the city.

* * * *

In the late 1800s a lock was built on Cheboygan's inland waterway, becoming a major link in Michigan's transportation system. Pleasure craft use the lock today to travel as far as Conway, twenty-five miles to the south.

* * * *

There are some buildings in Cheboygan that have an interesting history attached to them.

Marie Dressler, Annie Oakley and Mary Pickford were among stars of the past who appeared at the city's Opera House. It was built in 1877 and rebuilt eleven years later after a fire. Local entertainers still use the Opera House for its original purpose.

In 1882 a building was erected for use as the county jail and sheriff's residence. It served that role until 1969. Today it is the home of the Cheboygan County Historical Museum, with the parlor, school room, kitchen and bedroom restored to the period. On the grounds are a 19th-century log cabin and a building which houses logging and marine displays.

* * * *

The Colonial Path Parkway is an example of what can happen when people work together for a common cause. This 150-year-old forest contained stands of the largest old-growth oak south of the Straits. It was purchased by a sawmill in the 1980s and scheduled to be cut. Several environmental groups in the area bought the 282 acres and preserved it for future generations.

Industry

Today Cheboygan's major industries are paper production and tourism.

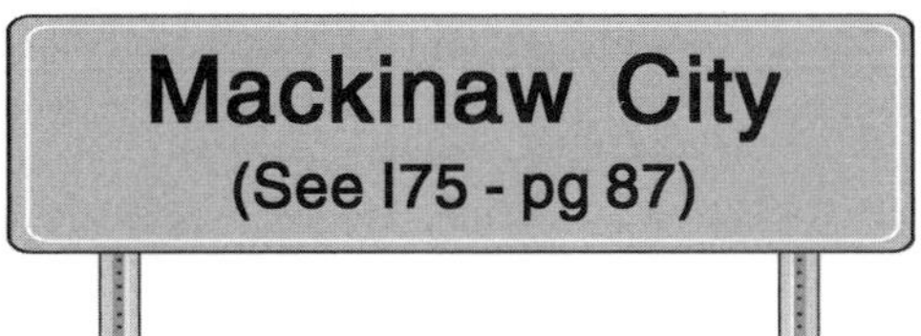

HIGHWAY
10

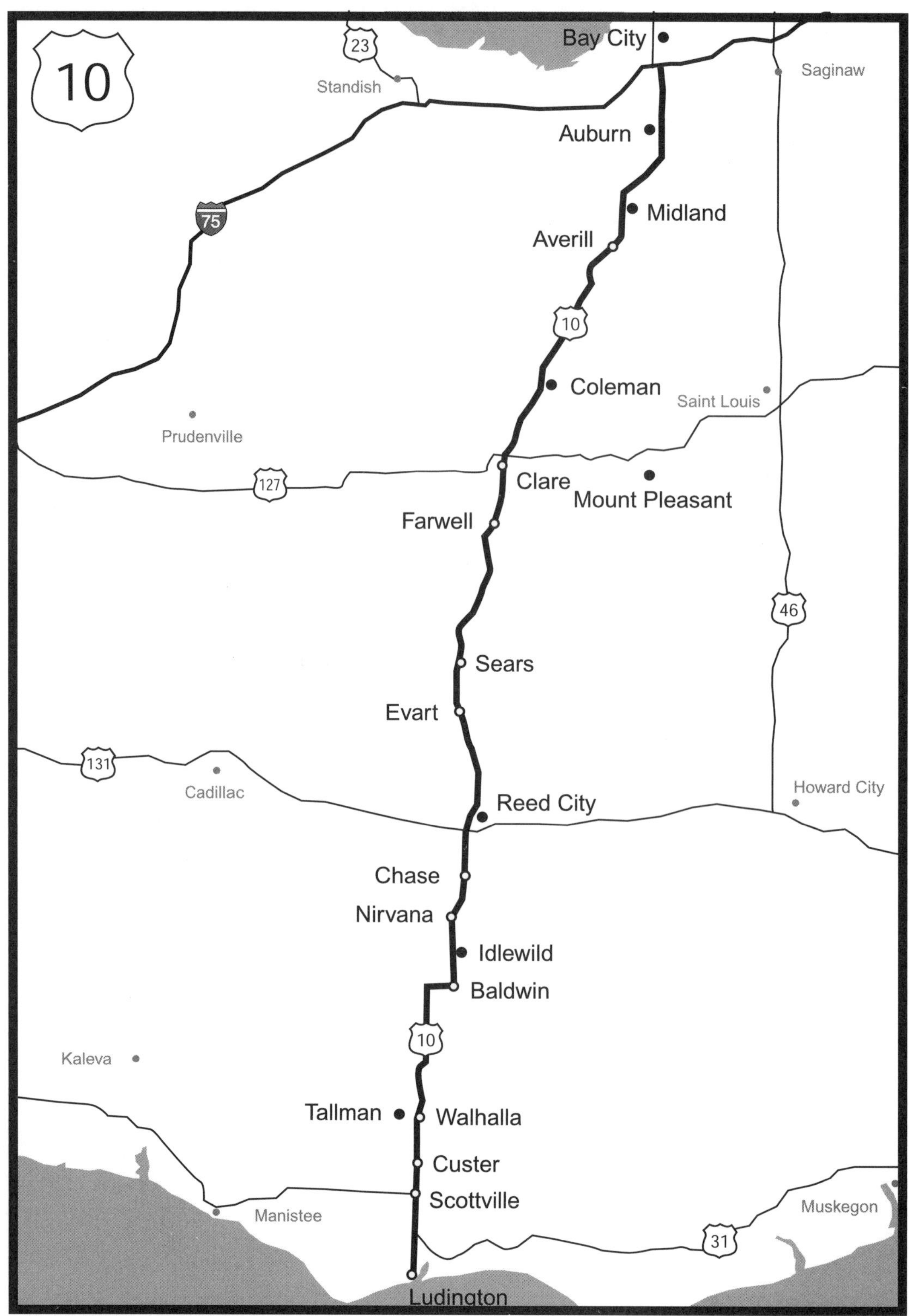
10
23
Standish
Bay City
Saginaw
Auburn
75
Midland
Averill
10
Coleman
Saint Louis
Prudenville
127
Clare
Mount Pleasant
Farwell
46
Sears
Evart
131
Cadillac
Reed City
Howard City
Chase
Nirvana
Idlewild
Baldwin
10
Kaleva
Tallman
Walhalla
Custer
Scottville
Manistee
Muskegon
31
Ludington

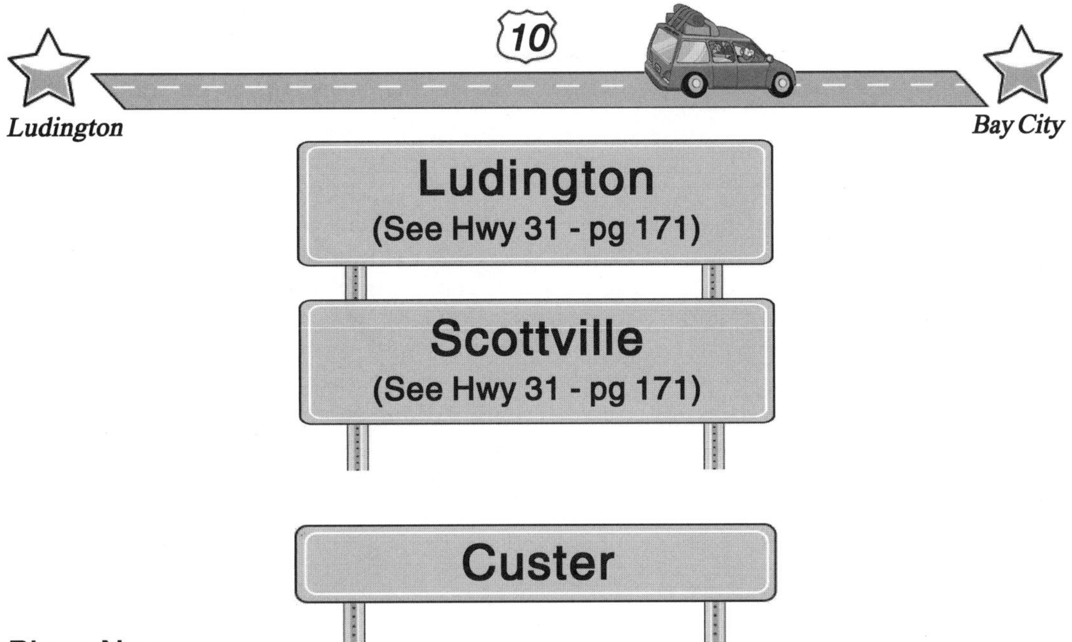

Place Name

It was named after General George A. Custer, of Custer's Last Stand fame, who lived from 1839 to 1876.

Place Name

Walhalla means the banquet hall of the gods.

Place Name

Horace Butters from the lumber firm of Butters, Peters & Company founded this village in 1879. The town, named after attorney H.C. Tallman, became a station on the Pere Marquette Railroad.

Baldwin

Place Name

Baldwin is the county seat of Lake County. The county was named because of its location on the water. The town named in honor of Henry Baldwin, the governor of Michigan at the time.

General Trivia

On April 11, 1884, the first recorded planting of brown trout (Salmo fario) in the United

States was made into the Pere Marquette River system by the Northville, Michigan Federal Fish Hatchery.

The trout eggs from which the planting of 4,900 fry was made had been obtained from Baron Friedrich Von Behr of Berlin, Germany, by Fred Mather, superintendent of the Cold Springs Harbor Federal Fish Hatchery at Long Island, New York.

Some brown trout eggs had been shipped to the United States and distributed to various fisheries in the country for observation in 1883, but the Northville station was the first to stock American waters with the fish. From this beginning, the species (known in Germany as Bachforelle) has become widely established throughout the United States.

(Historical marker located on Hwy M-37)

Prominent People

A gentleman by the name of Oberholzer moved to Lake County around the 1920s. Oberholzer quickly became known for the furniture he chiseled from the pines in the area. He was truly a woodworking master, sometimes sun-drying pieces for years before he used them. Oberholzer carved a table and drawers from a gigantic 700 pound pine tree stump. That piece would later be shown at the Shrine of Pines Museum, located in the town.

Place Name

This city in Lake County was named after one of the five lakes that are nearby.

Historical Significance

The first village was founded here in 1912 with only two year-round residents. Three years later a real estate company known as Branch, Anderson & Tyrell bought up the land, platted it, and sold the lots, thus beginning a village.

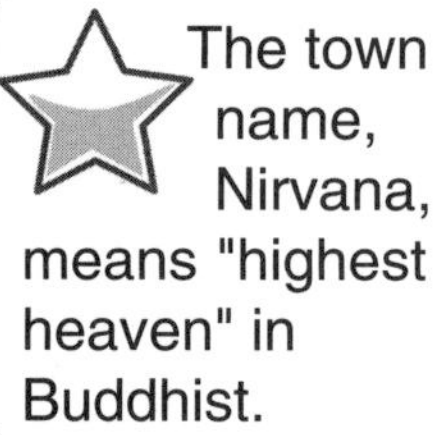

The town name, Nirvana, means "highest heaven" in Buddhist.

General Trivia

The town also had a hotel by the name of Indra House, named after Indra, the principal god in the Ayran-Vedic religion. This has led many to believe that Mr. Knight, the founder, was a believer or an admirer of Oriental religion systems.

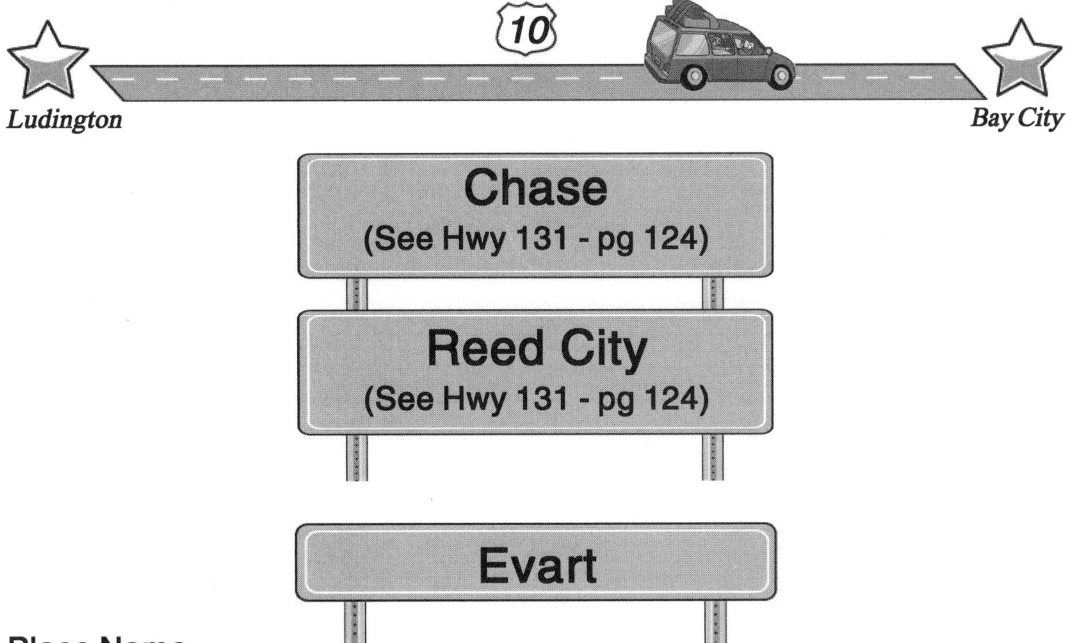

Place Name

Perry Oliver Everts purchased 80 acres in this area after serving with the Union Army during the Civil War. When the settlement was founded, it was named after him, but the name was misspelled at the founding fathers' meeting. The name stuck, mispelling and all.

Sears

Place Name

Orient was the first name for this village. After it became a town, it was renamed after an early surveyor that had worked with the Flint & Pere Marquette Railroad.

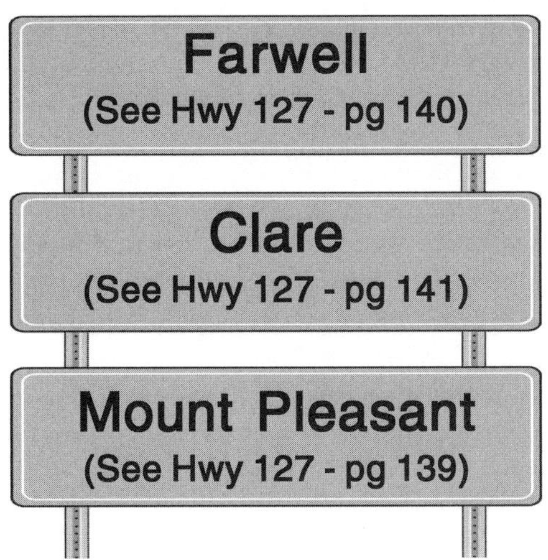

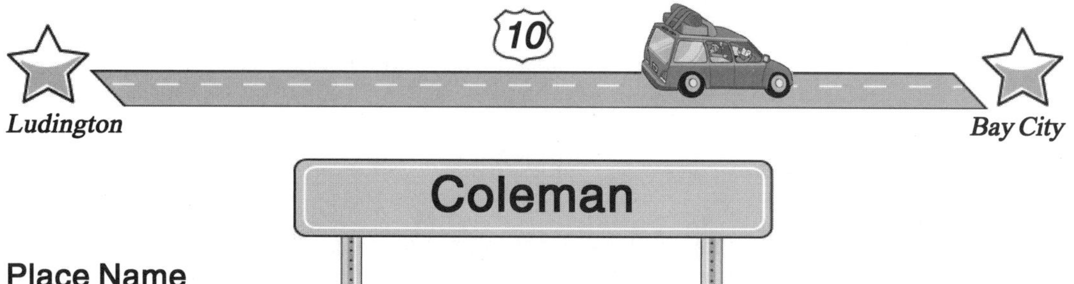

Place Name

Ammi Wright, purchased alot of government land here for speculation. Unfortunately for him, the area was not rapidly settled. After a few years, he sold 1,000 acres to Seymour Coleman who had 160 acres of it surveyed and platted to give to the Pere Marquette Railroad in return for the depot being located here. The depot was the start of the towns development which was named for Seymour Coleman.

Averill

The Red Keg saloon became known in Eugene Thwing's novel "The Man from Red Keg."

Place Name

Although the township is named after Averill Harrison, the areas first postmaster

Local Landmark

The town's claim to fame is a local saloon called the Red Keg.

Place Name

Serving as the county seat of Midland County, this community's first white settler was John A. Whitman. He made a clearing for his farm here in 1836. This community and the county got its name due to the fact that it's located near the center of the state.

Industry

Midland is home to Snow Machine Inc., the largest manufacturer and supplier of snowmaking equipment in the world. This company has placed its equipment in more than 100 American ski resorts and another 200 resorts elsewhere in the world. Snow Machines provided the 1984 Winter Olympics in Yugoslavia with 22 snowmaking machines.

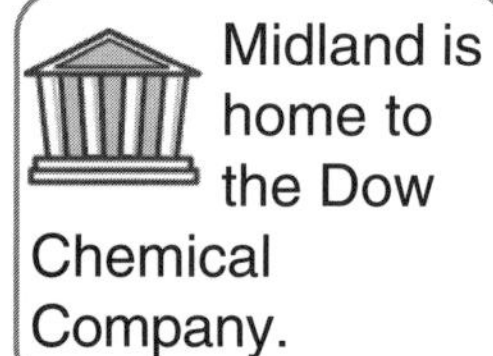

Midland is home to the Dow Chemical Company.

* * * *

Herbert Henry Dow, better known as "Crazy Dow" was the son of a Cleveland mechanic. As a teenager Dow invented the first egg incubator, but a customer stole his idea and he never made any money off it. Dow would soon make up for this missed opportunity at income.

In 1897, he founded a chemical company in Midland. The plant had a

few explosions from time to time, but Dow was eventually very successful. He discovered an ingredient used to make explosives during World War I. He also discovered that natural gas was full of bromine, which was used in medicines and film developing. Dow was named to the National Inventors' Hall of Fame in 1983. His company at one time supplied most of the world with aspirin. Today, Dow is still a world leader in chemicals.

Prominent People

Midland is home to famed architect, Alen Dow. Dow was named in 1983 as the first Architect Laureate of Michigan. He is the designer of the Ann Arbor City Hall, McMorran Auditorium and Sports Arena, and the Northwood Institute.

* * * *

Mary Sinclair of Midland led a fight against a proposed Consumers Power nuclear power plant in her city. She was named one of Ms. Magazine's 12 Women of the Year for 1985. Sinclair, who because of her crusade was a virtual outcast in her own home town at one time, was also profiled in the Wall Street Journal, appeared on the Today Show and 60 Minutes, and was named one of 10 Michiganians of the Year by the Detroit News.

* * * *

In 1981, Midland's former Rep. Louis Cramton was named by Governor William G. Milliken to serve as the first man on the Michigan Women's Commission. The fifteen member commission was first established back in 1968 and served to overcome discrimination in the workplace. The commission also recognized the accomplishments of women in the state of Michigan.

* * * *

Of note, the town's own Betty D. Engles has participated in the national Pillsbury Bake-off finals some six times. She has won $4,600 in cash, five mixers, five stoves, one microwave, one toaster oven and many all-expense paid trips! Now that's a cook!

Local Landmark

There is a three-way bridge located in Midland. This unique bridge spans the Tittabawassee and Chippewa rivers and connects three different shorelines. The three walkways meet in the middle where they form a hub of benches overlooking the merging rivers.

Place Name

The towns name comes from the Anglo-Irish poet Oliver Goldsmith who began his poem "The Deserted Village", "Sweet Auburn! lovliest village of the plain".

Bay City

(See I75 - pg 82)

HIGHWAY
2

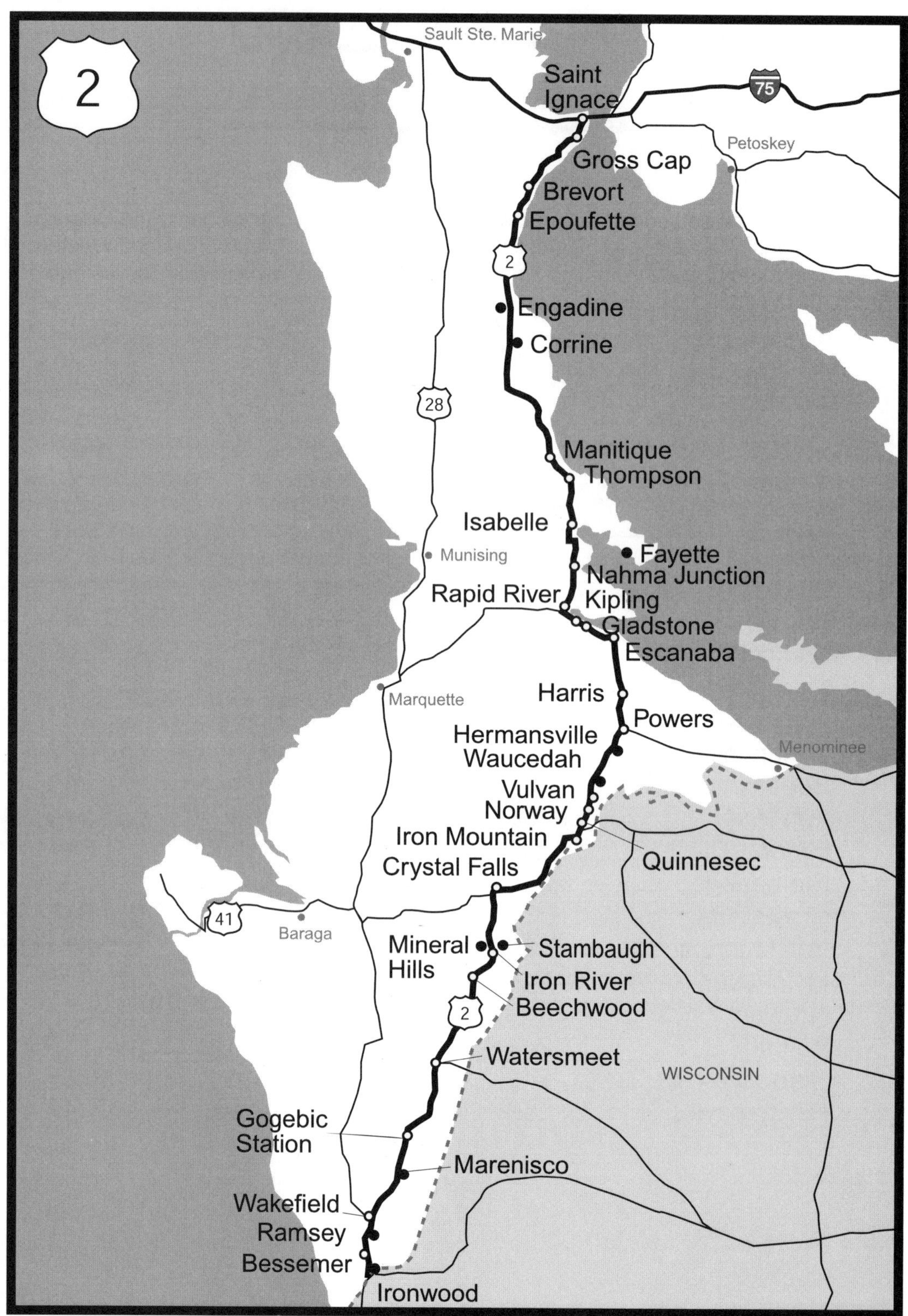

2
Sault Ste. Marie
Saint Ignace
75
Petoskey
Gross Cap
Brevort
Epoufette
2
Engadine
Corrine
28
Manitique
Thompson
Isabelle
Munising
Fayette
Nahma Junction
Rapid River
Kipling
Gladstone
Escanaba
Marquette
Harris
Powers
Hermansville
Waucedah
Menominee
Vulvan
Norway
Iron Mountain
Quinnesec
Crystal Falls
41
Baraga
Mineral Hills
Stambaugh
Iron River
Beechwood
2
Watersmeet
WISCONSIN
Gogebic Station
Marenisco
Wakefield
Ramsey
Bessemer
Ironwood

Place Name

Ironwood was first settled in 1885 and served as the commercial center of the Gogebic iron mining district. It was platted by employees of the Milwaukee, Lake Shore and Western Railroad. Its name honors a man who figured prominently in early mining deals. His name was James Wood and he bargained so well that he earned the nickname "Iron" Wood.

Historical Significance

The city's peak population was over 15,000. However, with the end of the iron mining, the population shrank to its present 8,000. Ironwood still serves its original purpose as the region's center for lumber and winter recreation.

Local Landmark

The Ottawa National Forest's headquarters are located in Ironwood. The forest covers one million acres, from Lake Superior's south shore to Wisconsin and the Nicolet National Forest. Five hundred lakes are found within its borders. The Forest's Superior Upland country is also interwoven with rivers. Waterfalls are found throughout the forest as rivers rush to Lake Superior. Elevations range from 600 feet at the Lake Superior shoreline to more than 1800 feet in the Sylvania Wilderness. The northern portions of the Forest offer the most dramatic views. In addition to the beauty of the rolling hills, lakes and rivers, the area is rich in wildlife. Deer, fox, coyotes, bald eagles, loons and songbirds are all found here.

* * * *

Skiers also flock to Ironwood to enjoy the many ski areas. Copper Peak Sky Flying Complex has a 17-story jump. From the top, jumpers can see Michigan, Wisconsin and Minnesota, as well as Canada. The longest jump recorded here is 505 feet.

At the site of an old copper mine is the largest ski jump in the Northern Hemisphere.

* * * *

The world's largest Native American statue is located in Ironwood. Hiawatha stands 52 feet tall with his hand extending out 26 feet in a gesture of peace.

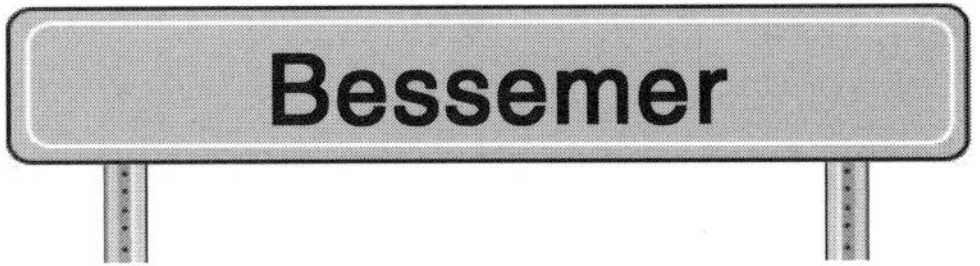

Place Name

Named for Sir Henry Bessemer, the English inventor of the process of manufacturing malleable iron and steel without fuel.

Historical Significance

Richard Lanford was a trapper and hunter from Rockland. He discovered iron ore in this

> For seventy-five years, from 1884 to 1958, over 245 million tons were shipped out of the county.

area under an overturned birch tree. His discovery in 1880 would become the Colby Mine. The Milwaukee, Lake Shore and Western Railroad reached the mine in 1884 and the railroad platted the village. F.H. Rhinelander, president of the railroad named the village for the man who invented the smelting process, Henry Bessemer.

* * * *

The Gogebic Iron Range was the last of the three great iron ore fields opened in the Upper Peninsula and northern Wisconsin. Beginning in 1848 with Dr. A. Randall, federal and state geologists had mapped the ore formations almost perfectly long before any ore was mined. One geologist, Raphael Pumpelly, on the basis of his studies in 1871, picked out lands for purchase, which years later became the sites of the wealthy Newport and Geneva Mines.

The first mine to go into production was the Colby. In 1884 it shipped 1,022 tons of ore in railroad flat cars to Milwaukee. By 1890 more than thirty mines had shipped ore from this range. Many quickly ran out of good ore and had to close. Others took their place as richer ore bodies were found. Virtually all mining here has been underground, as attested by many shafts and "cave-ins."

The soft hematite ores common on this range usually have been sent in ore cars to Ashland and Escanaba, there to be loaded in ore boats and taken to America's steel mills.

(Historical marker located at roadside park on US 2)

Local Landmark

Fifteen miles from Bessemer is Black River Harbor, one of only two harbors in the National Forest System. It sits at the mouth of the Black River, which flows through huge stands of pine, hemlock and hardwood trees. The river also features a series of scenic waterfalls, as it drops to meet Lake Superior. The Black River area was officially dedicated a National Scenic Byway on September 19, 1992.

Place Name

Ramsay was named for Sir William Ramsay, a Scotch chemist born in Glasgow, Scotland. He won his chief reputation for his discovery of rare gases. He was awarded the Nobel prize in chemistry. His discoveries are a major factor in the iron ore processes.

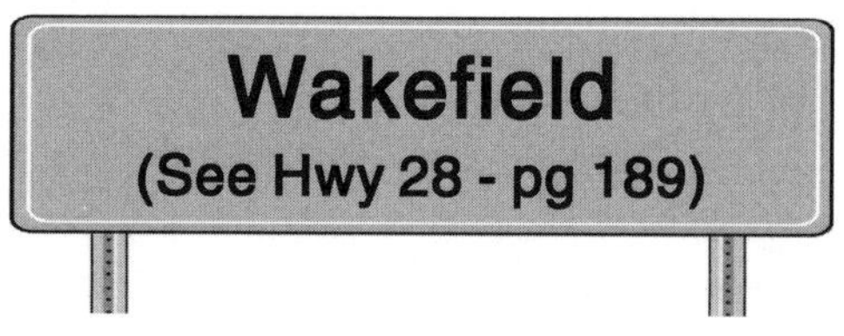

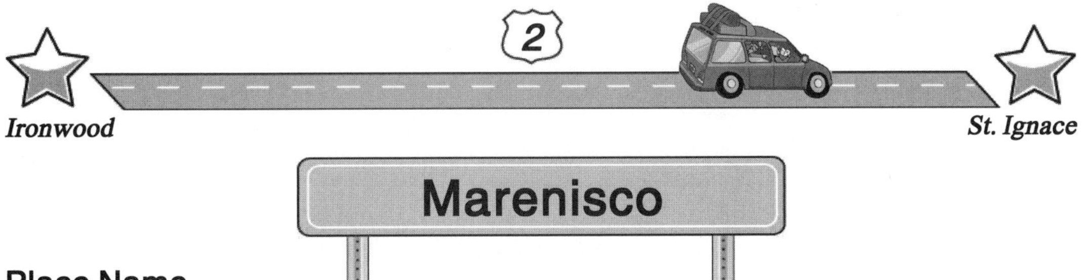

Place Name

Marenisco was named after Mary Enid Scott, wife of one of the early pioneers of the settlement and the wife of the founder. It will be noted that the first three letters in each name are used to spell "Marenisco."

Place Name

Town's name was derived from the Native American word agogebic. The Indians called the lake, "Abobebic," because in their native language the word meant, "A Body of Water Hanging on High." They knew that the lake had a high elevation, which was caused by the glaciers centuries ago. In other words, Lake Gogebic is 1,290.81 feet above sea level, but when the water reaches Lake Superior, the lake level is only 602 feet above sea level.

The exact definition of "Gogebic" will never be known, as it all depends on the interpreter. The popular meaning, used for the purpose of tourism is "Where Trout Rising Make Rings on the Water." Research by historians has not been able to determine how and when and why "Agogebic" was changed to "Gogebic." A satisfactory conclusion is that a printer either purposely or accidentally dropped the "A" during a printing job.

General Trivia

And this is truly a meeting of waters. The Ontanagon River flows north into Lake Superior; the Wisconsin River flows south, eventually into the Mississippi River; and the Paint River flows east to Lake Mchigan. In the area are 302 lakes and 241 miles of trout streams.

Native Americans gave this village its beautiful name, because it was the place where the waters of the Ontonagon River and Duck Creek meet.

* * * *

An oddity about Watersmeet is the "mystery light." It was first seen many years ago and can be spotted almost every night once darkness has come to the northern wilderness. There has never been a logical explanation for it. That has not stopped people from tromping through dense woods and up and down hills to spot the light. It seems to rise slowly out of the forest and hover low in the sky. The intervals might be a couple of minutes to over a quarter of an hour. People often describe it as a bright star that at first looks like a campfire ember. It reaches an intense reddish glow, becomes a haze, and then fades to a spark before it once again vanishes.

Some think the light is the spirit of a long dead mail carrier who was ambushed by Indians over a century ago. Others think it's the ghost of a train engineer killed in a railroad accident nearby. And there's one woman who thinks it is a mystical sign of religious significance.

Place Name

The town gets its name from the beech trees that were said to have been plentiful in the area.

Place Name

The profitable Nanaimo Mine gave the town its first name of Naniamo. With the quick growth of miners and homesteaders into the area, led Donald and Alexander MacKinnon to acquire the land. The bachelor brothers had J.A. Van Cleve plat the village they would call Iron River, after its location in the iron ore region.

Place Name

This town was named for the very productive iron bearing hills in the area.

Place Name

The land that makes up the town of Stambaugh were originally assigned by the U.S. to Elizabeth Slaten, as the widow of the War of 1812 veteran, Joshua Slaten. It was later named for John Stambaugh, the president of the Todd, Stambaugh Company from Youngstown, Ohio who had acquired the Iron River Mine.

Place Name

George Runkel, Samuel Hollister and William Morrison founded this village in 1880. It was Runkel who gave it its name. He was inspired by the crystal beauty of the falls on the Paint River, which runs nearby.

Local Landmark

Not far from Crystal Falls is the Iron County Museum Park complex. The former engine house for the Caspian Mine serves as the main museum building . Over one hundred exhibits can be found inside. There are mining dioramas, a miniature of a working mine, and the largest miniature logging display in the world. It measures eighty feet long and contains over 2,000 pieces.

Among the twenty buildings in the Museum Park are the 1890 Stager depot and log barns, a pioneer cabin, a two-story homestead log house, a sauna, a 1920 logging camp, and a sleigh barn.

The 1890 home of Carrie Jacobs-Bond is located in Crystal Falls. She was the composer of "I Love You Truly" and "Perfect Day".

* * * *

Fortune Pond (3/4 miles north of US 2 on New Bristol Rd., 2 miles west of Crystal Falls) is a wonderful example of the many mines that have been reclaimed by nature as she heals the scars of the minter's pick. Imagine the pumps that worked 24 hours a day to keep the open pits and tunnels dry. This mine produced 1,316,905 tons of iron ore from 1953 to 1958. It had one shaft with two drifts used to drain the 210 foot deep pit. The pit is 1,930 feet long by 750 feet wide. What was once a major mining operation now lends itself to a scuba divers and fisherman's paradise.

Place Name

The Civil War had ended and the Chapin brothers were looking for a new way of life. They bought a forty-acre tract here in Michigan's U.P. and opened the Chapin Mine nearby. It became one of the greatest iron mines in the world and gave birth to the town of Iron Mountain in 1879.

Historical Significance

The Chapin Mine sits on the Eastern Menominee Iron Ore Range. It was well over 6,000 feet wide and had depths from fifty to 150 feet. In a period of just over fifty years -- 1880 to 1932 -- over twenty-seven million tons of ore were brought out of this mine. The mine operated continuously during that time.

There was, however, a major problem in running the Chapin Mine. Part of the iron was under a cedar swamp, which made this mine the wettest on the Menominee Range. A commission was given to the E.P. Allis Company of Milwaukee in 1889 to design and build a pumping system. The company was a forerunner of Allis-Chalmers. Their solution was the Cornish pumping engine, named for the pumps that had drained the water out of Cornwall's tin mines.

The engine was put into operation west of the Chapin Mine's "D" shaft in January of 1893. It cost $250,000. The machine weighed 725 tons and could pump 3,400 gallons per minute or five million gallons every twenty-four hours. The Cornish Pump is now a National Historic Site, a National Historical Engineering Landmark, and a Michigan Historic Civil Engineering Landmark.

The Cornish Pump is an awesome structure. A steeple rises fifty-four feet from the engine's floor and it is powered by the nation's largest steam-driven pumping engine. The flywheel measures forty feet in diameter.

* * * *

Inventor John T. Jones of Iron Mountain recognized the economic potential of the low-grade iron ore of the Upper Peninsula. He developed a method for processing the ore and built an experimental furnace in 1908, named for his daughter Ardis, to test his theory. The furnace, a huge metal tube lined with firebrick, was placed on an incline and charged with ore. The whole device was rotated with an electric motor, with iron suitable for mill use discharged from the lower end of the tube. The experiment was plagued with financial and mechanical problems, and by the end of World War I the Ardis was dismantled, Jones moving to other mining endeavors. Elements of the Jones method were later incorporated into successful processing operations for low-grade iron ores.

(Historical marker located on the corner of Aragon and Antoine streets)

Local Landmark

The Iron Mountain Ski Jump was built in the 1930s and sits on Pine Mountain. Jumpers from around the world come here each February to challenge ski jump records. The international record of 459 feet, 140 meters, is still held here. The Giant Pine jump measures 123.5 meters, with the length of the entire run 1,440 feet.

The Iron Mountain Ski Jump is the highest in the world.

The slide was built as a WPA or Works Progress Administration project in 1938. The first tournament was held the next year. Since then, there have been constant improvements. Longer jumps were made possible when the landing hill was dug out in 1948. The scaffold and knoll at the top of the hill were improved in 1956. After a 1977 fire burned out the top of the slide, reconstruction expanded the number of starting positions from six to thirty. When skiiers take off from the end of the scaffold, they are traveling at fifty-five to sixty miles per hour.

* * * *

For a look back in time, there's the House of Yesteryear, located just outside Iron Mountain. Thirty vintage cars, dating from 1904 to 1949, are among the exhibits. Other fascinating items include a dog-powered washing machine, a hand-powered vacuum, and a foot-operated dentist drill. There are farm implements that go back 150 years, including a self-raking McCormick Reaper, and guns that are as much as 400 years old.

* * * *

Those furry little creatures known as bats have found a friendly home in Iron Mountain.

The Millie Mine Bat Cave overlooks the city. It is 350 feet deep and stays at a constant year-round temperature of forty degrees.

Seven species of bats come here from around the United States and Canada to hibernate in the winter. They can only be seen when they leave the mine in spring and return in September. And, if you don't like bats, remember that during the summer they're out dining on those huge Michigan mosquitoes!

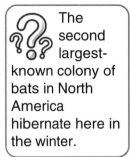

The second largest-known colony of bats in North America hibernate here in the winter.

Place Name

John Bell discovered the Quinnesec Mine in 1871. After successful developing of the mine, he platted the village which took the Native American name meaning smokey waters; referring to the mist hanging over the nearby Menominee River.

Historical Significance

In 1846 Wm. A. Burt, the discoverer of the Marquette Iron Range, noted signs of iron ore in the Crystal Falls area. In 1849, federal geologist J. W. Foster found ore near Lake Antoine and two years later he and J. D. Whitney confirmed Burt's report on the Crystal Falls district.

The first mining activity began in 1872 at the Breen Mine where ore had been discovered in the '60s by the Breen brothers, timber cruisers from Menominee. Development of the range was delayed until a railroad could be built from Escanaba. The Breen and Vulcan mine shipped 10,405 tons of ore in 1877 when the railroad was built as far as Quinnesec.

By 1880 it reached Iron Mountain and Florence, and in 1882 tracks were laid to Crystal Falls and Iron River. Twenty-two mines made shipments of ore that year.

A few crumbling ruins are all that remain of most of them, but in subsequent decades more mines were developed which have produced vast amounts of ore for America's iron and steel mills.

(Historical marker located on US 2)

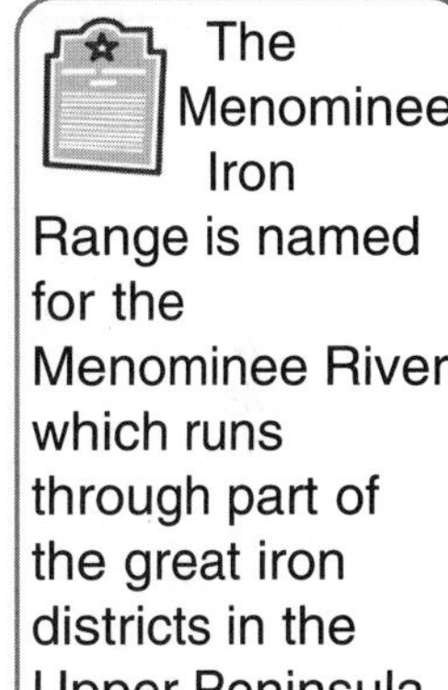

The Menominee Iron Range is named for the Menominee River which runs through part of the great iron districts in the Upper Peninsula.

Place Name

This small town was born (and named) with the sinking of the first test pit of the Norway Mine in 1877. It was sunk, of course, by a Norwegian. His name was Anyton Odell and he was also the man who platted the town in 1879.

Local Landmark

Just two miles southwest of Norway, off Highway 8, is the Piers Gorge Nature Trail. The trail winds along the Menominee River to Piers Gorge. The Menominee is a fast-moving river and it has cut deeply into the bedrock walls to create the Gorge. It forms a magnificent boundary between Michigan and Wisconsin. Nature lovers, shutter bugs and rock hounds all enjoy coming to Piers Gorge for their own particular reasons. During the spring and summer, water cascades over a ten-foot-high waterfall and drops into souse holes large enough to sink a bus (but not a motorcoach!). Piers Gorge is especially magnificent in the fall when the leaves turn color.

Place Name

This village was developed by Lewis Whitehead in 1877 and named for the Greek god for metal-working. The city built up around the famous Vulcan Mine.

Local Landmark

Iron Mountain Iron Mine and Museum winds through 2,600 feet of underground drift and tunnels. A lighted cavern gives a close-up view of odd geologic formations. Visitors ride on underground trains to see today's miners operating modern machinery. The excellent gift shop claims to have the largest rock selection in the U.P., as well as minerals, antique ironware and general souvenirs.

Place Name

Waucedah, a Native American word for over there, began as an iron mining settlement when a mine was discovered by Thomas and Bently Breen in 1866.

Place Name

Wisconsin lumberland Charles Meyer purchased land in the area where he built a mill and the town was established. Named for his younger son, Herman, the town became the headquarters of the Wisconsin Land & Lumber Company which he started.

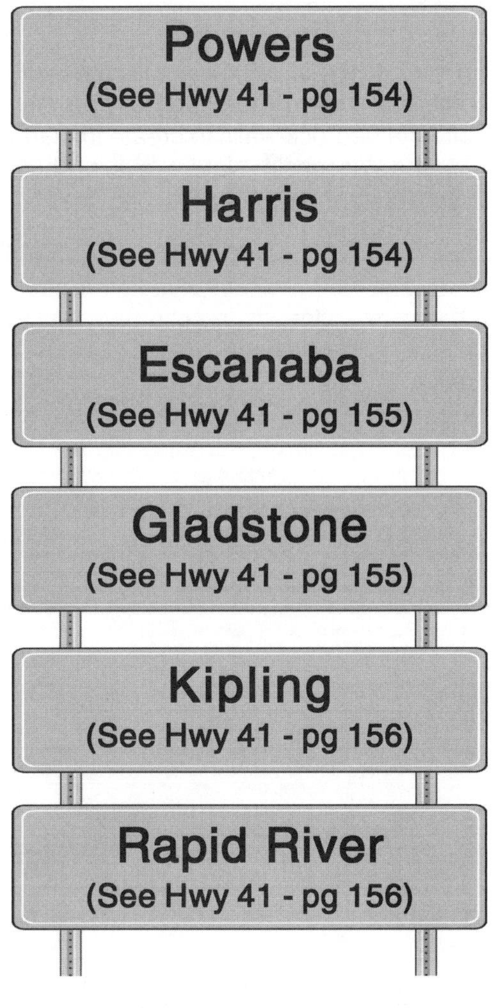

Nahma Junction

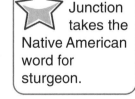

Nahma Junction takes the Native American word for sturgeon.

General Trivia

Henry Longfellow's Hiawatha "saw" the sturgeon, Nahma, leaping, scattering drops like beads of wampum."

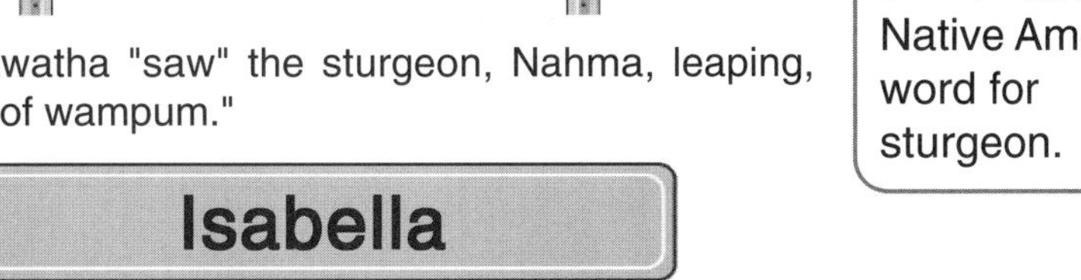

Isabella

Place Name

The town was named in memory of the little daughter of Peter Mallman, a pioneer logger and kiln operator in the area.

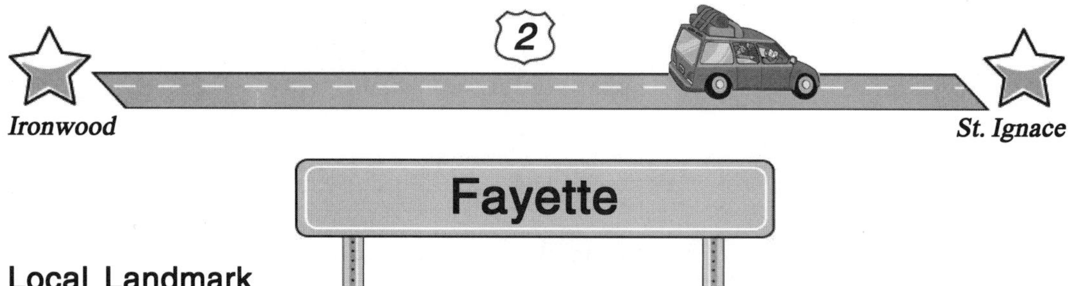

Local Landmark

Fayette Township was deeded to the state of Michigan in 1958 and is now a state park. Fayette was an iron smelting town from 1867 to 1891. It was operated by the Jackson Iron Company.

> The town had been platted by Fayette Brown, the Jackson Iron Company manager in 1866.

The peninsula was chosen because of its natural resources and location. There was lots of wood to make charcoal and limestone to use for the furnaces. It was also close to the company's ore mines and had a natural harbor for shipping. Over 14,000 tons of high-quality pig iron were produced here annually.

Fayette was a company town. The homes, hotel, opera house, boarding house, doctor's office, stores, and jail -- all were built and owned by Jackson Iron. Workers with families lived in small frame homes or log cabins. Single men lived in the hotel and boarding house.

Today visitors can stop at twenty-six interpretive stations in fifteen surviving buildings. The opera hall has been restored and lime kilns and iron furnaces can be seen. The costs of the restoration and cleanup of the site has been paid in part by the second owner of Fayette, Cleveland Cliffs Iron Company.

Place Name

This town was named for E.L. Thompson, from Detroit. Thompson was president of the Delta Lumber Company which had a mill here on Lake Michigan.

> Kichi-it-kipi is associated with the legends of Hiawatha.

Local Landmark

Palms Book State Park, 12 miles north of Thompson features one of the Upper Peninsula's major natural attractions.

Kitch-iti-kipi or "The Big Spring" is two hundred feet across and forty feet deep. Over 10,000 gallons a minute gush from many fissures in underlying limestone, the flow continuing throughout the year at a constant 45 degree temperature.

By means of a self-operated observation raft, you are guided to vantage points overlooking fascinating underwater features and fantasies. Ancient tree trunks, lime-encrusted branches and fat trout appear suspended in nothingness as they slip through crystal waters far below. Clouds of sand kept in constant motion by gushing waters create ever-changing shapes and forms, a challenge to the imagination of young and old alike.

Place Name

Michigan's famed historian and naturalist Henry Schoolcraft formed the village of Manistique in 1871. The name he gave it comes from the Ojibwa Indian word for vermilion and refers to the color of the water here.

The Indian word was actually "monistique". However, the spelling was altered when the name was registered with the state and the town became Manistique.

Local Landmark

Needing water to run its mill, the Manistique Pulp and Paper Company built a 3,300 foot concrete flume and dam. It was constructed between 1918 and 1920 on the Manistique River. It supplies 8,000 cubic feet of water a minute to the plant.

When U.S. 2 was routed through Manistique, its path crossed the river and upper flume. The solution to the problem was so unique it made "Ripley's Believe It or Not". A "Siphon Bridge" was built to float on the flume water, which is forced under it by atmospheric pressure. The roadway of the bridge is four feet below the flume water level and adjacent to an historic water tower.

The tower was built in 1922 for $62,450. It is a wonderful example of Roman Revival-style utilitarian architecture. The 200-foot-high octagonal brick structure can hold 200,000 gallons of water. It has been designated of outstanding historical and architectural significance to the United States.

* * * *

Over one million trout, 500,000 salmon and sixteen million walleye are produced each year at a nearby state fish hatchery. This is where the coho salmon was introduced into Michigan waters. The original hatchery on the site was built in 1929. The current facility opened in 1978. Most of the fish which are produced by the hatchery remain in the waters of the U.P.

Place Name

This lumber settlement began as a station on the Minneapolis, St. Paul & Sault Ste. Marie railroad. It was named Corinne to avoid confusion with Corunna a town near Flint.

Place Name

The first railroad agent in the area was Sam Peterson. A native of Switzerland, he had the named changed from Kennedy Sidings its original name, to Engadine, after a Swiss valley.

Place Name

The Native American name of this lumbering town means place of echoes.

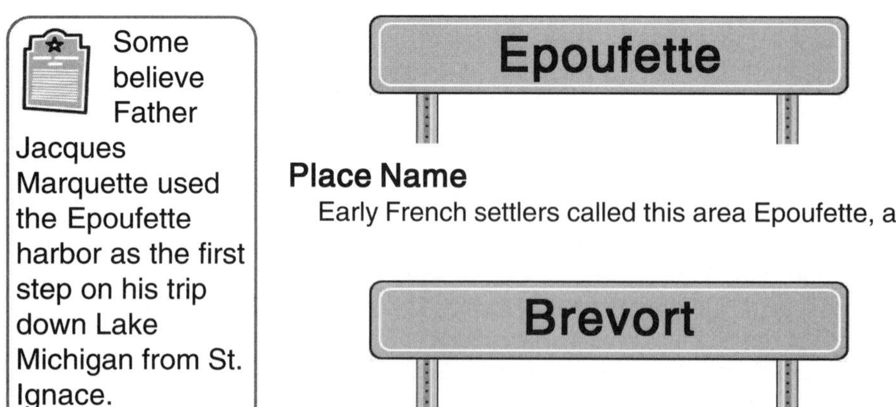

Some believe Father Jacques Marquette used the Epoufette harbor as the first step on his trip down Lake Michigan from St. Ignace.

Place Name

Early French settlers called this area Epoufette, a place of rest.

Place Name

Surveyor Henry Brevort was assigned to subdividing the area and subsequently the settlers named a lake, river and village after him.

Place Name

The township takes the French name for big cape, referring to its location on land jutting into the Staits of Mackinaw.

Index

Note: Since some cities are located on more than one route (highway and/or interstate), and because trip trivia information is included on only one, see the **bolded** listing for more detailed information

.

Muttonville	62	I-94
Nahma Junction	243	Hwy 2
Napoleon	134	Hwy 127
Naubinway	246	Hwy 2
Negaunee	158	Hwy 41
	192	**Hwy 28**
Nestoria	158	Hwy 41
	190	**Hwy 28**
New Buffalo	25	I-94
Newaygo State Park	123	Hwy 131
Newberry	200	Hwy 28
Newport	68	I-75
Niles	35	I-94
Nirvana	228	Hwy 10
Norway	241	Hwy 2
Norwood	182	Hwy 31
Novi	20	I-96
Nunica	29	I-96
Ocqueoc	221	Hwy 23
Oden	186	Hwy 31
Olivet	99	I-69
Omer	216	Hwy 23
Onekama	175	Hwy 31
Onota	195	Hwy 28
Osceola	162	Hwy 41
Oscoda	217	Hwy 23
Oshtemo	41	I-94
Ossineke	218	Hwy 23
Otsego	119	Hwy 131
Oversiel	113	I-196
Owosso	101	I-69
Oxford	74	I-75
Paradise	201	Hwy 28
Parchment	119	Hwy 131
Paris	124	Hwy 131
Parkville	118	Hwy 131
Parshallville	215	Hwy 23
Paw Paw	41	I-94
Pelston	186	Hwy 31
Pentwater	171	Hwy 31
Perry	101	I-69
Petoskey	**128**	**Hwy 131**
	184	Hwy 31
Pierport	175	Hwy 31
Pigeon	206	Hwy 25
Pinconning	84	I-75
Pinnebog	206	Hwy 25
Plymouth	19	I-96
Pointe Aux Barques	207	Hwy 25
Pompeii	138	Hwy 127
Pontiac	72	I-75
Port Austin	206	Hwy 25
Port Hope	207	Hwy 25
Port Huron	**63**	**I-94**
	104	I-69
	209	Hwy 25
Portage	119	Hwy 131
Portland	23	I-96
Posen	220	Hwy 23
Powers	**154**	**Hwy 41**
	243	Hwy 2
Presque Isle	220	Hwy 23
Prudenville	141	Hwy 127
Pullman	108	I-196
Quanicassee	205	Hwy 25
Quinnesec	241	Hwy 2
Ramsey	236	Hwy 2
Rapid River	**158**	**Hwy 41**
	243	Hwy 2
Rattle Run	63	I-94
Redford	17	I-96
Reed City	**124**	**Hwy 131**
	229	Hwy 10
Richville	148	Hwy 46
Riga	213	Hwy 23
Riley Center	104	I-69
Rochester	73	I-75
Rockford	121	Hwy 131
Rogers City	220	Hwy 23
Romulus	58	I-94
Roscommon	85	I-75
Rosebush	140	Hwy 127
Roseville	60	I-94
Rothbury	169	Hwy 31
Royal Oak	71	I-75
Rudyard	90	I-75
Saginaw	**79**	**I-75**
	147	Hwy 46
Saint Ignace	**90**	**I-75**
	246	Hwy 2
Saint Johns	137	Hwy 127
Saint Joseph	38	I-94
Saint Louis	**139**	**Hwy 127**
	146	Hwy 46
Saline	214	Hwy 23
Samaria	213	Hwy 23

Saugatuck	109	I-196
Sault Ste. Marie	92	I-75
Schoolcraft	119	Hwy 131
Scottville	**173**	**Hwy 31**
	227	Hwy 10
Sears	229	Hwy 10
Sebewaing	206	Hwy 25
Seney	199	Hwy 28
Shelby	170	Hwy 31
Shingleton	198	Hwy 28
Shoreham	37	I-94
Sidnaw	190	Hwy 28
Skandia	157	Hwy 41
Snover	149	Hwy 46
Somerset	134	Hwy 127
Soo Junction	200	Hwy 28
South Boardman	126	Hwy 131
South Haven	126	Hwy 131
Southfield	**17**	**I-96**
	70	I-75
St. Clair Shores	60	I-94
Stambaugh	238	Hwy 2
Standish	84	I-75
Stanwood	123	Hwy 131
Stephenson	153	Hwy 41
Sterling	84	I-75
Stevensville	37	I-94
Stonach	174	Hwy 31
Strongs	201	Hwy 28
Swartz Creek	102	I-69
Tallman	227	Hwy 10
Tawas City	217	Hwy 23
Tekonsha	98	I-69
Temperance	**67**	**I-75**
	213	Hwy 23
Thompson	244	Hwy 2
Three Rivers	117	Hwy 131
Tompkins Center	135	Hwy 127
Topaz	189	Hwy 28
Topinabee	87	I-75
Torch Lake	182	Hwy 31
Traunik	156	Hwy 41
Traverse City	180	Hwy 31
Trenary	156	Hwy 41
Troy	72	I-75
Tula	189	Hwy 28
Tustin	125	Hwy 131
Union Pier	35	I-94
Van	186	Hwy 31
Vanderbilt	86	I-75
Vassar	148	Hwy 46
Vestaburg	146	Hwy 46
Vriesland	113	I-196
Vulcan	242	Hwy 2
Wacousta	23	I-96
Wakefield	**189**	**Hwy 28**
	236	Hwy 2
Waldron	133	Hwy 127
Walhalla	227	Hwy 10
Washington	74	I-75
Waterloo	52	I-94
Watersmeet	237	Hwy 2
Watervliet	41	I-94
Waucedah	242	Hwy 2
Wayland	120	Hwy 131
West Branch	84	I-75
Wetmore	197	Hwy 28
Wetzel	126	Hwy 131
White Pigeon	117	Hwy 131
White Rock	207	Hwy 25
Wisner	205	Hwy 25
Wolverine	86	I-75
Wyandotte	69	I-75
Yalmar	157	Hwy 41
Ypsilanti	**56**	**I-94**
	214	Hwy 23
Zeeland	113	I-196
Zilwaukee	81	I-75